LOOKING AT MEDIEVAL BOOKS

EXETER MEDIEVAL TEXTS AND STUDIES

Series Editors: Vincent Gillespie and Richard Dance

Founded by M.J. Swanton and later co-edited by Marion Glasscoe

Looking at Medieval Books

Learning to See

RALPH HANNA

LIVERPOOL UNIVERSITY PRESS

First published in 2023 by
Liverpool University Press
4 Cambridge Street
Liverpool
L69 7ZU

This paperback edition published 2025

Copyright © 2025 Ralph Hanna

Ralph Hanna has asserted the right to be identified as the author of this book in accordance with the Copyright, Designs and Patents Act 1988.

All rights reserved. No part of this book may be reproduced, stored in a retrieval system, or transmitted, in any form or by any means, electronic, mechanical, photocopying, recording, or otherwise, without the prior written permission of the publisher.

British Library Cataloguing-in-Publication data
A British Library CIP record is available

ISBN 978-1-80207-857-2 (hardback)
ISBN 978-1-83624-343-4 (paperback)

Typeset by Carnegie Book Production, Lancaster

In memory of John, Jeanne, and Jeremy Griffiths,
patrons of Oxford palaeography

Contents

Abbreviations	ix
A memorial (and polemical) preface	1
What's in front of you? What's its shape?	12
How big is it?	15
The closed book: what do you see first?	20
Opening the book: what's it made of?	33
Membrane	33
Paper	38
Where's the first leaf?	43
What does the first leaf look like?	46
How come it looks so neat?	58
How does the scribe write?	63
What texts does it contain?	79
How has it been put together?	89
Are there other discontinuities?	99
Where's it been all this time?	113
Looking at Cambridge, Queens' College, MS 10	133
The raw file of notes	133
A basic organised report	136
Some preliminary analysis	141

Indexes 151
  Medieval authors and texts prominently mentioned 151
  Medieval institutional owners 152
  Medieval private owners and patrons 153
  Medieval persons engaged in book production and trade 153
  Modern owners and collectors 154
  Manuscripts cited 154
  Scholars cited 158
  General topical index 161

Abbreviations

BH	Richard Beadle and Ralph Hanna, 'Describing and Cataloguing Medieval English Manuscripts: A Checklist', *The Cambridge Companion to Medieval British Manuscripts*, ed. Elaine Treharne and Orietta da Rold (Cambridge, 2020), 13–38
BL	The British Library, London
BodL	The Bodleian Library, Oxford
BRUO	A. B. Emden, *A Biographical Register of the University of Oxford to A.D. 1500*, 3 vols (Oxford, 1957–59)
ChCh	Christ Church, Oxford[1]
Corpus	The Corpus of British Medieval Manuscript Catalogues, currently nearing completion, 16 vols in 19 (London, 1990–)
CUL	Cambridge University Library
ECBH	M. B. Parkes, *English Cursive Book Hands, 1250–1500* (Oxford, 1969; London, 1979)
EETS	Early English Text Society
GP	Jeremy Griffiths and Derek Pearsall, eds, *Book Production and Publishing in Britain 1375–1475* (Cambridge, 1989)
HEH	The Henry E. Huntington Library, San Marino CA
HM	The central collection in HEH

[1] Much dependent on the published catalogue, Hanna and David Rundle, using materials collected by Jeremy J. Griffiths, *A Descriptive Catalogue of the Western Manuscripts, to c. 1600, in Christ Church, Oxford*, Oxford Bibliographical Society Special Series: Manuscript Catalogues 2 (Oxford, 2017); a catalogue for Magd, with Rundle, is forthcoming; and SJ appeared as *A Descriptive Catalogue of the Western Medieval Manuscripts of St John's College, Oxford* (Oxford, 2002).

Ker coll	N. R. Ker, ed. Andrew G. Watson, *Books, Collectors and Libraries: Studies in the Medieval Heritage* (London, [1985])
Magd	Magdalen College, Oxford
MLGB	N. R. Ker, *Medieval Libraries of Great Britain: A List of Surviving Books*, 2nd edn, Royal Historical Society Guides and Handbooks 3 (London, 1964); and Andrew G. Watson, *MLGB: Supplement*, Royal Historical Society Guides and Handbooks 15 (London, 1987); now integrated, with Corpus, into Richard Sharpe, James Willoughby *et al.*, mlgb3.bodleian.ox.ac.uk
MMBL	N. R. Ker (volume 4 with A. J. Piper), *Medieval Manuscripts in British Libraries*, 4 vols (Oxford, 1969–92)
Parkes coll	M. B. Parkes, *Scribes, Scripts, and Readers: Studies in the Communication, Presentation and Dissemination of Medieval Texts* (London, 1991)
PH	*Pursuing History: Middle English Manuscripts and Their Texts*, Figurae: Reading Medieval Culture (Stanford CA, 1996)
s.	saeculo, i.e. 'during the century', followed by a roman numeral (see p. 67)
SC	R. W. Hunt *et al.*, *A Summary Catalogue of Western Manuscripts in The Bodleian Library at Oxford*, 7 vols in 8 (Oxford, 1895–1953)
Sharpe	Richard Sharpe, *A Handlist of the Latin Writers of Great Britain and Ireland before 1540*, Publications of the Journal of Medieval Latin 1 (Turnhout, 1997)
SJ	St John's College, Oxford
UL	University Library
Watson coll	Andrew G. Watson, *Medieval Books in Post-Medieval England* (Aldershot, 2004)

A memorial (and polemical) preface

It's probably true that senility is a second childhood. That's about the only excuse (other than epidemic lockdowns) for deciding to produce the book I wish I had had when I was growing up. I come from a generation when 'new English studies' in American graduate schools had effectively given up instruction in bibliography. As a result, everything I know about this subject is experiential, initially the product of examining two medium-sized corpora of materials (about 50 of the surviving manuscripts of *Piers Plowman*, all the insularly produced manuscripts and printed books to 1600 in the Huntington Library) and trying to see and to construct patterns of significance. I remain particularly grateful to the two people who were there and willing to answer questions, H. C. Schulz, then the Huntington's Curator of Manuscripts, and Richard Rouse; and, at a much later date, to fine points instilled by Malcolm Parkes and Andrew Watson.

The book has a precursor. Sometime around 1987, the late Jeremy Griffiths, one of my dedicatees, suggested to me that we should co-author a manual, mainly for students, about how to examine a manuscript book. We had, more or less, arrived at a division of labour and agreed on a manuscript to use as a guiding sample, with extensive illustration of points. (This was the rather decrepit remains of a book of hours now UCLA, MS Rouse 52.)[1]

Unfortunately (or otherwise), Jeremy was 'the great projector'. He never completed a spectacularly innovative dissertation that examined how the format of the underlying exemplars had influenced textual presentation in their surviving daughter manuscripts. (The script is among his extensive *relicta* in the English Faculty Library, St Cross, Oxford.) Besides being an astute student of medieval hands (his notes on repeated scribal stints, left as raw lists, form the core of the now ongoing 'Medieval Scribes' website at the University of York), he was an electric fountain of ideas for elaborate studies. (Only a strikingly mixed metaphor can communicate Jeremy's imagination and energy.)

---

[1] See Richard H. and Mary A. Rouse, *Medieval and Renaissance Manuscripts of the UCLA Library Special Collections. I, The Richard and Mary Rouse Collection*, MRTS 472 (Tempe AZ, 2017), 137–40.

He was so electric that another project would emerge before the last – like his thesis – came to fruition. Thirty years after the fact, Daniel Wakelin discovered among Jeremy's papers a completed project he had bruited – and which, like others, one assumed had lapsed in the wake of yet another brilliant idea. Jeremy had in fact done the research and gathered the materials for what has subsequently appeared as the independently conceived Mark Clarke, ed., *The Crafte of Lym[n]yng and The Maner of Steynyng: Middle English Recipes for Painters, Stainers, Scribes and Illuminators*, EETS 347 (Oxford, 2016), an anthology of all the medieval English recipes pertaining to book crafts. In the face of so mercurial a brilliance, our project lapsed.

One does need to see our plan as very much a project of its time and place, very much an 'eighties project. It came in the wake of Elizabeth Salter and Derek Pearsall's innovative effort at focussing the University of York's medieval English graduate programme around the study of manuscript books. After Salter's departure for the US and her untimely death, Derek convened the first 'York Manuscript Conference', largely an opportunity for a generation of brilliant graduates to show the fruits of Middle English manuscript study. Derek gathered and edited the resulting papers as *Manuscripts and Readers in Fifteenth-Century England: The Literary Implications of Manuscript Study* (Cambridge, 1983). Its keynote, a discussion in accord with coeval Pearsall publications, is probably struck by the title of Kate Harris's contribution, 'John Gower's *Confessio Amantis*: The Virtues of Bad Texts' (26–40).[2] This gathering inspired, and was succeeded by, Jeremy and Derek's collection on fifteenth-century English book culture, so frequently cited here that it gets its own abbreviation 'GP'. This remains the only responsible global guide to later medieval English book production.[3]

---

[2] Cf. such Pearsall contributions as 'Texts, Textual Criticism, and Fifteenth-Century Manuscript Production', *Fifteenth-Century Studies: Recent Essays*, ed. Robert F. Yeager (Hamden CT, 1984), 121–36; 'Editing Medieval Texts: Some Developments and Some Problems', *Textual Criticism and Literary Interpretation*, ed. Jerome J. McGann (Chicago IL, 1985), 92–105; 'Variants v Variance', *Probable Truth: Editing Medieval Texts from Britain in the Twenty-First Century*, ed. Vincent Gillespie and Anne Hudson (Turnhout, 2013), 197–205. See further his 'The Value/s of Manuscript Study: A Personal Retrospect', *Journal of the Early Book Society* 3 (2000), 167–81.

[3] It is scarcely rivalled by a later imitation volume, Alexandra Gillespie and Daniel Wakelin, eds, *The Production of Books in England 1350–1500* (Cambridge, 2011). See further n.7.

As Harris's title indicates, the interest sparked by York researchers, with the grand Ian Doyle as guru and advisor, was a reaction to contemporary practice.[4] At this time, medieval books were largely, in Middle English literary study, the province of editors. For them, The Book was valuable only as inky squiggles presenting a text, and otherwise inert. Moreover, as Harris's title also indicates, if the text provided wasn't, in the editor's mind, very compelling, the book was essentially valueless. The great exemplar of such procedures was George Kane, in his revolutionary and single-minded pursuit of the authorial text of *Piers Plowman* (with collaborators, 3 vols [London, 1960–97]). I vividly recall George saying to me once, when I pointed out to him that two *Piers* manuscripts had been in the same hands, and connected with others, all known to John Bale, of whom more anon, 'So what does it change in the text?'[5]

In the print world, Kane's analogue was the work of Fredson Bowers. Bowers's *Principles of Bibliographical Description* (Princeton, 1949), a guide to printed books, elaborated to the last jot and tittle, runs just over 500 pages. Yet Bowers found the subject of primary value only with regard to the light it could cast on the value to be accorded the text. However, the interests displayed in the York conference were contemporary with a more searching view of the book as a site of interactions not so author- and text-centred as Kane or Bowers would have wished, the interventions mounted by Jerome J. McGann, *A Critique of Modern Textual Criticism* (Chicago IL, 1985; Charlottesville

---

[4] With all who have an interest in these matters, I much lament both Derek's and Ian's recent passing. The pair's centrality to the discipline is indicated by a common monument: in my knowledge, they remain the only people ever to have had three Festschriften each in their honour (each iteration, obviously, chocked with informative work by their students and friends). In addition to materials cited below (n.64), Doyle has been honoured in A. J. Minnis, ed., *Late-Medieval Religious Texts and Their Transmission: Essays in Honour of A. I. Doyle* (Woodbridge, 1994) and in Corinne Saunders *et al.*, eds, *Middle English Manuscripts and Their Legacies: A Volume in Honour of Ian Doyle* (Leiden, 2022); and Pearsall (in addition to Kerby-Fulton, cited p. 74) in Minnis, ed. *Middle English Poetry: Texts and Traditions: Essays in Honour of Derek Pearsall* (York, 2001) and David Aers, ed., *Medieval Literature and Historical Inquiry: Essays in Honour of Derek Pearsall* (Woodbridge, 2000).

[5] Avowedly, it didn't change much, although all these individuals had the same scribal form of the text, from which Bale derived his cited incipit – and all had been Bale's informants, as he sought to uncover the insular literary tradition.

VA, 1992) and D. F. McKenzie, *Bibliography and the Sociology of Texts* (1986; Cambridge, 1999).

These authors broadened the action considerably, because, for them both, studying the book could not be just an ancillary discipline. Although the text remained important (and its editorial status potentially revealing), the McGann–McKenzie move highlighted one fact forgotten in the Kane–Bowers model, that the text was not a timeless artefact, a 'verbal icon', as then-current New Critical conversation would have it. It had not been written for the convenience imposed by modern scholarly edition. It had been intended to communicate – and pretty instantly so, given that, until nearly the coming of print, all books were originally 'bespoke', the product of what we would call 'special orders'.[6] As a result, the audience – and not just that immediately proximate one (although that has much primacy), but the audience down the centuries – could not be excluded from the study of the book. There are, as Kate Harris had it, a lot more 'bad texts' out there than good ones, but they are not, from this perspective, to be rejected on that account; they are still engaged in communication, and they potentially have much to say about audiences and book production.

Those interests Salter and Pearsall inspired were largely vernacular-centred, as they still remain, in spite of the fact that such books represent a small minority of the archive, well under 20 per cent, even in s. xv, among persistent copying of Latin.[7] This emphasis must be seen as an

---

[6] One salient lesson of a classic, and irrefutable, essay, Graham Pollard, 'The Company of Stationers before 1557', *The Library* 4th ser. 18 (1937), 1–38. As one example of the distance between pre-1980s 'literary history' and examination of the manuscript record, consider William Langland's *Piers Plowman*. Critical practice had long enshrined *Piers B* as the canonical version, but manuscript circulation would suggest that the poet's final version (C) had been an instant hit on its release in the early 1390s and was a staple of the London trade well into s. xv. Significantly, Salter and Pearsall early produced a volume of selections from C for their graduates, and Pearsall's expansions and reprintings of this preliminary version remain today the only widely available form of the poem for teaching.

[7] Gillespie and Wakelin's collection mentions Latin books only once in 400 pages and, on that occasion, the language is clearly so unfamiliar that the author mistranscribes it – and then 'translates' their erroneous and ungrammatical transcription. About all I can say of behaviour like this is that, if you think Geoffrey Chaucer is a figure comparable in intellectual value and medieval influence with, say, Gregory the Great or Bede, you need a reality check; my breadth of reference here is designed to intimate some of the riches closed off to the *illiteratus*.

anti-historical imposition upon the medieval evidence; only retrospectively was writing in English of any central intellectual importance. The interests exhibited in these vernacular studies were largely created by monolingual and, often, strenuously Protestant/alienated efforts from the 1580s.

However, such Pearsall-inspired efforts implicitly interfaced with longstanding Oxford projects a great deal more globally conceived. From the 1930s, the great triumvirate of Neil Ker, Richard Hunt, and Roger Mynors had been working steadily with manuscripts. Among their most notable achievements was the formalisation of a descriptive rota, a step beyond the grand Cambridge contributions of Montague R. James, one first revealed in Mynors's wonderful catalogue of the manuscripts of his college, Balliol.[8] All three were intensely interested in uncovering and cataloguing the monastic heritage (less so the academic one, which seemed to them, all members of colleges with extensive medieval collections, a soluble question), both its surviving books and its surviving catalogues. They were equally interested – Hunt, the Bodleian's Curator of Manuscripts, in particular – in more recent library history, the processes by which manuscripts had been gathered into their surviving collections. Their contributions were carried forward by their students, notably Andrew Watson and Malcolm Parkes, and further generations of inheritors: the late Richard Sharpe and, now, James Willoughby.

This Oxford stream, to which Salter and Pearsall's innovation joined (perhaps half-heartedly with regard to language), should be seen as perpetuating what has always been the Anglophonic tradition of manuscript studies. This has always focussed upon the individual instance, the 'central manuscript', as it were, linked through repeated

[8] James produced a 'descriptive catalogue' of virtually every Cambridge library (including unpublished notes on most of CUL's central collection, MSS Dd-Oo), as well as a number of libraries elsewhere, e.g. Aberdeen UL and Lambeth Palace. See further Richard W. Pfaff's meticulous biography, *Montague Rhodes James* (London, 1980) and Lynda Dennison, ed., *The Legacy of M. R. James: Papers from the 1995 Cambridge Symposium* (Donnington, 2001). Roger Mynors's contribution here – he was a distinguished classicist, for example, editor of the still standard edition of Virgil's poetry – is *Catalogue of the Manuscripts of Balliol College, Oxford* (Oxford, 1963). Along with the triumvirate I have identified, one should also mention C. R. Cheney, Oxford's Reader in Diplomatic, as his title indicates, a great deal more engaged with legal record than with MSS *per se*. His monument, with F. M. Powicke, is *Councils and Synods, with Other Documents Relating to the English Church. II, A.D. 1205–1313*, 2 vols (Oxford, 1964).

observations and induction with others, in order to construct some form of historical narrative. Richard Gameson, in a comprehensive account of the last century's contributions, aptly summarises: 'a fundamental consistency of approach: detailed, empirical examination of the material was ... a cornerstone'. Or, as Willoughby has recently characterised the work of Ker and Sharpe, they were 'miniaturist[s] who could step back and see an entire landscape'.[9] At least one goal of my study is to facilitate 'miniaturism' and suggest the 'landscape' in which it is situated.

Ker, Hunt, Mynors, et al. were following what had been defined as the appropriate local form of inquiry a century and a half before Mabillon (see pp. 63–64). Our founding fathers, in the early and mid-sixteenth century, were John Leland and John Bale. The latter had a particularly stormy career, beginning as a flack in Thomas Cromwell's household. Thus, as a young man, Bale had been complicit in the initial cycle, but, as he aged, he fretted over the sudden destruction, which had extended over about four decades, of medieval England. This had not occurred entirely for sectarian reasons, but by deliberate acts of learned men who, as they boasted, 'set Duns in Boccardo' and cleared their library shelves of medieval books. Bale's engagement represented an effort at reconstructing a tradition now being destroyed, to restore communicative power to surviving books, to reveal ourselves to ourselves through historical attentiveness. In particular, his interests, and those of another century's worth of researchers, were in seeking evidence for a national church independent of Rome, as well as for the protection of personal (and parliamentary) liberties. This background underlies Ker and Co.'s contribution, an intensely pragmatic pursuit, a monument to the Anglo-Scottish empirical tradition. These scholars would never, for example, assign a book to a religious house or describe it as dated without explicit written evidence in the book itself (but see p. 63).

Thus, I should make one thing clear from the off. As a (foster-)child of these giants,[10] I have long been extremely sceptical of the value

---

[9] Richard Gameson, 'History of the Book', *A Century of British Medieval Studies*, ed. Alan Deyermond (Oxford, 2007), 701–35, the citation at 719 (although I would distance myself from a number of Gameson's qualifications); and Willoughby, in the forthcoming Sharpe, *Libraries and Books in Medieval England. The Role of Libraries in a Changing Book Economy* (Oxford, 2023).

[10] As well as, through a fortuitous College association, others: the intensely welcoming Malcolm Parkes, who, in the first month, took me round the curtilage,

of various continental procedures. These, to my distaste, attempt to categorise or systematise the book, as a few prominent titles will indicate: G. I. Lieftinck *et al.*, *Nomenclature des écritures livresques du IXe au XVIe siècle* (Paris, [1954]); Denis Muzerelle, *Vocabulaire codicologique* (Paris, 1985); or Marilena Maniaci, *Archeologia del manoscritto* (Rome, 2002). My scepticism may have a good deal to do with biography, an upbringing that has fostered in me a deep respect for local community and for the creative (and, let it be said, destructive) power of its mores.

My distaste, while its interests may truly be insular, seems widely shared among a British community of manuscript scholars. I am reminded of a conference Ian Doyle convened in 2004 as a step toward offering an English Muzerelle. (That was itself a parochial endeavour, since 'English' usage does not necessarily correspond to North American.) Such a study should have provided an analogue to the Spanish Muzerelle, Pilar Ostos Salcedo *et al.*, *Vocabularia de Codicologia* (Madrid, 1997). Doyle assigned the crowd he had convened specific sections of Muzerelle's *Vocabulaire* and asked all the participants to bring along lists of suggested English equivalents for the French terms. Without exception, each of these London panels ended up arguing over the efficacy of being here at all. Like these exasperated panellists, I am here trying to produce a book about practicalities, observations, not about platonic reasoning.

While it's probably constructive to share a vocabulary, so that we ensure that we are discussing the same thing, it is maladept, an historical obtuseness, to impose typologies on pre-mechanical processes. There is also a basic logical confusion here, shared with certain interventions about discontinuous manuscript production to be discussed below (pp. 99ff.): nomenclature, prominent in these continental accounts, has no ontological status; it represents only an agreement to convention. Moreover, it thoroughly ignores, in a jejune pursuit of uniformities, the individuality of the instance and the basic purpose of making handwritten books in the first place: to communicate within some specifically designated space. While I cite profuse examples below

---

instilling local history with the same fervour that older men showed when they banged boys' heads on the parish bounding stones every Rogationtide; the great book-engaged predecessors on whom I tried to model myself: Noël Denholm-Young, Alan Bishop, and Alan Piper; and the former history tutor A. G. Dickens, who more than forty years ago introduced me, with a bit too much Protestant derision, to 'the last medieval Englishman', Robert Parkyn, and refuelled my passion for the culture of the North.

that might be seen as illustrating 'the type', I equally attend to the aberrant, the extreme (one does tend to remember those), for they equally exemplify the individualistic nature of the pursuit and, for the neophyte, will suggest that you should never be surprised.

By convention, the discipline of 'looking at manuscripts' has gone under the title palaeography, the study of 'old writing' (and not to be confused with palaeontology).[11] That term indicates the roots of our discipline in the study of script, and over the last half-century has come to be considered unduly restrictive. (All of us just penmanship engineers who will readily date anything.) A more recent and more fitting name, 'codicology', draws attention to broader interests always inherent in the study of anything related to 'old books', codices (see p. 12). I tend to think of the study more broadly still, following our roots in Leland and Bale, as 'book history'. Manuscripts represent the basic medieval form of communication, the convocation of diverse literary communities, the primary historical evidence for understanding the past – and its descent to, and continuing effect upon, the present.

What follows is not a handbook, although it may serve as such, but, just as I began my studies, an experiential exercise, a guide to seeing. I was moved to read Francis Pryor, *Home: A Time Traveller's Tales from Britain's Prehistory* (London, 2014), 110, where Pryor describes his adeptness in recognising various species of trees: 'This skill, if that's what it is, is a product of interest and experience; it didn't just happen. Put another way, you can only identify pattern if you have something to go on, such as experiences, memories, faded pictures in old books.' The closest thing to a manual I'm apt to do has appeared as 'Describing and Cataloguing Medieval English Manuscripts: A Checklist' (henceforth BH), and I often refer (or defer?) to its discussions and a good deal of its very basic bibliography. However, it is worth recalling that, in the *Cambridge Companion* in which it appeared, this essay required supplementation by the immediately following contribution, Donald Scragg's 'Reading a Manuscript Description' (39–48), an effort to connect one formal account with the observed detail of the book it describes.

For it is the case that in that essay Richard Beadle and I described a finished formal product, a report about a book within a rhetorical structure capable of general publication and, one hopes, communication. However, that presentation minimises the fact that there are at

---

[11] Fortunately, a good deal less frequent than the confusion of 'etymology' with 'entomology'.

least two other possible orders of presentation, in this case temporal ones, obscured in the process of reportage. On the one hand, there is what one would describe as the order of production, those stages by which the book was initially produced. For this chronology, stretching from preparing the materials to finishing the book with a binding, there are some outstanding basic guides:

G. S. Ivy, 'The Bibliography of the Manuscript Book', *The English Library before 1700: Studies in its History*, ed. Francis Wormald and Cyril E. Wright (London, 1958), 32–65

Christopher de Hamel, *Scribes and Illuminators*, Medieval Craftsmen series (London, 1992); rev. edn, *Making Medieval Manuscripts* (Oxford, 2018)

Barbara A. Shailor, *The Medieval Book. Illustrated from the Beinecke Rare Book and Manuscript Library*, MARTS 28 (Toronto, 1991)

Jean Vezin, 'La Réalization matérielle des manuscrits latins pendant le haut moyen âge', *Codicologica* 2 (1978), 15–51

Although now somewhat dated, there is also an excellent guide to basic studies in Leonard Boyle, *Medieval Latin Palaeography: A Bibliographical Introduction*, Toronto Medieval Bibliographies 8 (Toronto, 1984). Although dated, one should not assume that, because a study is old, it is to be ignored and that it may be assumed to have been superseded. After all, no one's done better with the London book trade than Graham Pollard, 80-odd years ago (n.6). Along with your investigation of MSS, you should read – and remember. There is a wide range of discussions, and they always include something relevant, even if doesn't answer your primary interest of the moment; you recognise by Pryor's 'skill', experience, and recall, and grouping experiences (which include your reading) by the rule of analogy. As Willoughby put it, you must be an observant 'miniaturist' before you can inductively offer a 'landscape'.

More importantly, and the most basic way in which one learns about any manuscript, is the order by which one examines (and re-examines) a book, which is very different from anything formal that might emerge. This book strives to address that third, yet most basic ordering: it is a study structured on what you can see. Observation, looking this way, tells one a lot about the making of books that escapes both the formalised descriptive presentation and the descriptions of 'the usual process'. Yet even attempting this reconstruction of examination will prove disruptive: individual features are frequently linked, not independent items of observation, and, in examining a book, you see them simultaneously. While I've tried to arrange this book in a developing order of observation/examination that presumes only minimal knowledge of the subject, I feel I have often been defeated. Hence, I have employed a number of cross-references and more detailed indexes than may be usual, including one mainly given over to book-production terms that stands in lieu of a glossary.

As a further way of obviating this difficulty, I have provided an appendix, a double account of a single moderately complicated book, Cambridge, Queens' College, MS 10. I have found word-processing an immense boon in looking at books. One creates a file dedicated to the single manuscript before one, and one dumps into it, higgledy piggledy, all one's observations as one goes through a book, examining it page by page. That simultaneous attention is enshrined in the file I have found from my first encounter, of several, often in textual detail, with the Queens' MS. Most of the time, my initial files do not survive, since I re-arrange the detail (a task made much simpler by word-processing) into the kind of shaped description that BH describes. This file, with a number of included errors and missteps, has managed to avoid that obliteration, and can be placed next to – on the following pages – a streamlined formalised account of what it is that I thought I saw, and a rather brief discussion of what it all might mean.

A couple of final notes: Malcolm Parkes, generally amid detailed conversations about something else, was fond of delivering maxims gnomic yet salutary, as if throwaways. One I recall most indelibly is the suggestion/command, 'When you come back from the library, always read your notes before you go to sleep.' The urge to completion is strong in all of us, but fundamentally leads to sloppiness, both about detail and conclusions. Be patient. There is always something you forgot, failed to describe or omitted to note down. You should always plan on more than one run at a book, always start from scratch on each occasion, and always recheck everything in detail.

In a rather random fashion, I attempt to instantiate my account of looking at a book with both manuscript examples and some basic bibliography. Since what follows is an experiential record, I have, in the main, drawn on a narrow, yet reasonably extensive, range of examples. These, in accord with my experiential bent, are taken primarily from the collections I have examined most thoroughly: in addition to batches in other libraries, whole collections at SJ, ChCh, Magd (where my account remains unpublished), HEH, Nottingham UL, Gray's Inn, Shrewsbury School, Jesus College (Cambridge); and many smaller Bodleian collections. My references to these collections are directive: don't just read secondary reports; go and look. It doesn't matter that you feel currently uninterested in what you are going to find; no experience is inherently valueless, and simple exposure will, like Pryor's observation of trees, shape memory and construct patterns you might never have been aware of. Most of the things I have ended up writing about have been accidents, a chance pattern that imposed itself on me while I thought I was engaged in looking for something else. Because, for detail, I can draw only on personal experience, there are also a large number of references to various interim reports on investigations I offered along the way.

Instrumental in assembling the materials here has been my profession as a teacher. Underlying the book are 15 years of lectures I stumbled through with fledgling Oxford manuscript scholars. The experience was alleged to prepare them for serious manuscript study and was examined by a transcription exercise and a written study of some relevant topic. I'm particularly grateful to this cadre, particularly for their inquiries urging me to clarify what I had presented with considerable murk.

I give James the final word: '*See* manuscripts for yourself. Do not trust that the cataloguer has told you everything' (my double emphasis).[12]

---

[12] *The Wanderings and Homes of Manuscripts*, Helps for Students of History 17 (London, 1919), 35, a reference I owe to Matthew C. Salisbury. Cf. Parkes's pointed title, *Their Hands Before our Eyes: A Closer Look at Scribes: The Lyell Lectures Delivered in the University of Oxford 1999* (Aldershot, 2008).

What's in front of you? What's its shape?

Is it a stack of pages that looks like a modern printed book, or something else? For this discussion and the next, see Pamela Robinson, 'The format of books: books, booklets, and rolls', *The Cambridge History of the Book in Britain: Volume II 1100–1400*, ed. Nigel Morgan and Rodney M. Thomson (Cambridge, 2008), 41–54.

If the first, you are looking at what is generically called a codex (plural 'codices'), a byform of Latin *caudex* 'a tree trunk'. This designation perhaps alludes to a feature typical of the genre, a wooden covering. Books in this form were probably inspired by a writing device attested since late classical times and used throughout the Middle Ages, the tablet or table. This was a (or a succession of) small wooden framed plates filled with wax, for taking notes or drafting a text with a stylus. The most prominent surviving examples are probably the tablets found in the Roman fortress at Vindolanda on Hadrian's Wall. Some of the texts from these can be legibly reconstructed by imaging, because the stylus that scratched the wax, now long lost, also left scratched traces on the surviving wooden plates.[13]

Although codices will provide the near totality of my focus, a book in this form was a late historical innovation, one in origin strongly associated with the propagation of Christian scripture; see Colin H. Roberts and T. C. Skeat, *The Birth of the Codex* (London and New York, 1983). Further, the codex never entirely displaced an earlier form of book, the roll or scroll. Today, Jewish book culture provides the most available example of a book in this form: the great scroll of The Law, Torah. Modern examples are comprised of around 100 feet of skin, individual members sewn side by side, and bearing, on one side of the leaf only, the text of the first five biblical books in Hebrew. Scripture describes Moses writing the original (Exodus 24:4–8) – by ritual law, the source of every other copy; and Ezra reading from a version of Moses's scroll, imaginatively reconstructed, before the people (Ezra 7, events placed in 457 BCE). However, the earliest extant examples are the

---

[13] See Alan K. Bowman and J. David Thomas, *The Vindolanda Writing Tablets* (Newcastle, 1974); the scholarly version, with J. N. Adams, *The Vindolanda Writing-Tablets*, 3 vols (London, 1983–2003); more generally, Richard H. Rouse and Mary A. Rouse, 'The Vocabulary of Wax Tablets', *Vocabulaire du livre et de l'écriture au moyen âge*, ed. Olga Weijers (Turnhout, 1989), 220-30.

famous 'Dead Sea Scrolls' from Qumran. These are not limited to Torah and, indeed, traditional Judaism to the present day displays a persistent attachment to the textual scroll.[14]

The most prominent example of a book in this form is, however, the papyrus roll, the only form of book known in the classical Mediterranean world and surviving in thousands of examples, virtually all fragments. The most famous and extensive of these remains – much still unpublished, even after 80-odd volumes – come from materials discarded in a garbage dump on the site of the ancient Egyptian city Oxyrhynchus. These were excavated in the late nineteenth century and removed to Oxford.[15] Exceptionally, because of the disaster that befell Herculaneum in the eruption of Vesuvius (79 CE), a number of full ancient scrolls survive; they are obviously extremely delicate, because of their submergence in hot ash, but efforts at both unrolling and deciphering them through X-ray imagery are ongoing.

Papyrus gives us the modern word 'paper', but this form of book was written on fibres extracted from a reed grown only in Egypt: two layers of this pounded together and joined side to side into long strips. Unlike Torah, papyrus rolls were limited in dimension and typically included only a portion of a text. The extent of the usual papyrus roll is probably responsible for book-divisions in classical texts such as Virgil's *Aeneid*, promulgated as multiple rolls, each limited to a single book.

The triumph of the codex as a book form obviously reduced writers' recourse to rolls. In English culture, their great home is in legal affairs. The official version of the Statutes of the Realm was the roll of the

---

[14] Other commonplace Jewish examples include the texts in *mezuzoth* and *tefillin*, as well as, traditionally, the liturgical *megilloth* (a plural; the singular *megillah* 'scroll'), five biblical books associated with various festivals. Because sacred objects, all these save the last are subject to elaborate regulations governing material, copying, and form; see further 'Masseketh Soferim: Tractate for Scribes', tr. Israel W. Slotki, *The Minor Tractates of the Talmud*, ed. A. Cohen, 2 vols (London, 1965), 1:211–55; and Rambam, ed. tr. Eliyahu Touger, *Misneh Torah: Hilchot Tefillin UMezuzah V'Sefer Torah; Hilchot Tzitzit* (Jerusalem, 1990) (Hebrew text with facing-page English translation).

[15] For general discussion, see William A. Johnson, *Book Rolls and Scribes in Oxyrhynchus* (Toronto, 2004); for a prominent literary text transmitted in this medium, Maria C. Scappaticcio, *Papyri Vergilianae; l'apporto della papyrologia alla storia della tradizione Virgiliana (I–VI D.C.)* (Liège, 2013); and for popular accounts of Oxyrhynchus, Peter Parsons, *The City of the Sharp-Nosed Fish: Greek Lives in Roman Egypt* (London, 2007); and the play, Tony Harrison, *The Trackers of Oxyrhynchus*, rev. edn (London, 1991).

Statutes, now with sheets joined end to end. Any variety of local records, such as decisions in manorial courts, survive on rolls, in this case individual sheets sewn at the top to make a joined set of (rolled up) 'pages' loose at the foot. Equally, rolls are commonplace with certain textual genres: genealogical materials, most typically the biblical history 'Considerans', often extended into a roll showing the descent of the kings of England, but there are also rolls associated with The Great Cause of Scottish independence, or the Percy family's imitative pretensions to royalty;[16] and the *schedula*, small rolls associated with private devotion, the 'arma Christi', the instruments of the passion.

'Schedula' is the generic name for a small parchment roll or fragment, usually associated with notes or prompts for oral delivery. These are obviously for personal use and only infrequently survive. The great bishop of Lincoln, Robert Grosseteste (d. 1253), devised an elaborate system of signs for identifying theological discussions; some of these he wrote marginally into his books, but others, like modern note-cards, according to early reports, were written on *schedula* preserved at Oxford Greyfriars.[17] A famous *schedula*, s. xiv in., removed from an unidentified binding and now BodL, MS Rawlinson D.913, fol. 1, apparently records fragments of a minstrel's repertoire. A fourteenth-century rent roll, now UCLA Library, MS Rouse Doc/XIV/ANG/1, measuring 370 mm × 125 mm, is a small *schedula*, probably rough notes awaiting some more permanent record.[18]

---

[16] Respectively BodL, MS Bodley Rolls 3 and Alnwick Castle (Nhb.), MS 79 and Bodley Rolls 5. See W. H. Monroe, 'Two Medieval Genealogical Roll-Chronicles in the Bodleian Library', *Bodleian Library Record* 10 (1981), 215–21; and M. L. Holford, 'Family, Lineage, and Society: Medieval Pedigrees of the Percy Family', *Nottingham Medieval Studies* 52 (2008), 165–90. On genealogical rolls and their various forms of preservation, see A. C. de la Mare's extensive discussion *Catalogue of the Collection of Medieval Manuscripts bequeathed to the Bodleian Library Oxford by James P. R. Lyell* (Oxford, 1971), 82–85; and, for the (translated) text of one example, J. E. T. Brown (introduction by G. L. Harriss), 'The Scroll *Considerans* (Magdalen MS 248) Giving the Descent from Adam to Henry VI', Magdalen College Occasional Paper 5 (Oxford, 1999).

[17] See R. W. Hunt, 'Manuscripts Containing the Indexing Symbols of Robert Grosseteste', *Bodleian Library Record* 4.5 (1953), 241–55; and 'The Library of Robert Grosseteste', *Robert Grosseteste Scholar and Bishop: Essays in Commemoration of the Seventh Centenary of his Death*, ed. D. A. Callus (Oxford, 1955), 121–45.

[18] See, respectively, J. A. Burrow, 'Poems without Contexts', *Essays in Criticism* 29 (1979), 6–32; and the Rouses, *Medieval and Renaissance Manuscripts*, 418 (see further p. 3/8).

How big is it?

You're next aware of how big the thing you're holding is, and you should record an accurate account of these dimensions. The sizes of books are reported in millimetres (mm), and it is conventional to record first the book's height and then its width, such as 300 mm × 175 mm. It may not be immediately obvious how to measure a leaf. R. B. Haselden, who wrote one of the great predecessors to this book, *Scientific Aids for the Study of Manuscripts*, Supplement to the Bibliographical Society's Transactions 10 (Oxford, 1935), 1–17, with a flow-chart for examining a manuscript, counselled measuring 'from the top edge to the bottom edge and, with the book closed, from the fore-edge to the outside of the headband of the binding'. You have to be careful, since customarily bindings do not present the edges of the closed book's pages evenly; make sure you are measuring across the upper or lower edge of the volume from the fore-edge of the leaves (not of the binding) to the immediately opposite headband.

That will give you overall dimensions, but you must also record the size of the writing area. This is a measurement equally inobvious, but the width should be from left edge of the writing (customarily at a vertical bounding line) to wherever the scribe stops writing; if the right edge is ragged, as it often is with verse texts, you take an average. The height of the writing area extends, as Neil Ker says in another basic guide to manuscript description (*MMBL* 1:ix), 'from the top of minims in the first line to the bottom of minims in the last line'.[19] (In other words, ascenders and descenders are outside your measurements; for these terms, see p. 65.) Since it's most convenient in this context, you should also count and record the number of lines per page and notice how many columns of writing there are, or whether the book is written 'in long lines'.

Scribes aren't machines, and these measurements may vary quite a bit within any individual book. For this reason, rather than an absolute number, you might think of rounding your measurements to the nearest five millimetres – for example, 290 mm, rather than the

---

[19] For a third such guide to description, by the greatest (and most prodigious) cataloguer of the early twentieth century, see Richard W. Pfaff, 'M. R. James on the Cataloguing of Manuscripts: A Draft Essay of 1906', *Scriptorium* 31 (1977), 103–18.

288 mm you may have measured. To further accommodate possible minor variation (or, as you may discover in the process, substantial such), you should initially examine several pages dispersed through the book, each time measuring the written space and counting the number of lines on a leaf. Most efficiently, you should do this once each at the head, middle, and late in the book. That, along with your subsequent leaf by leaf inspection, should reveal any marked variations in format. If the format does change radically, the distribution of your three samples provides you with markers to guide you as you proceed, and, if you can't wait for leaf by leaf examination, try dividing the affected increments into halves, halves again, etc., until you find the boundaries between differing formats. You should record these as well.

Any survey of a large book population will indicate that book sizes are not arbitrary. The surviving examples tend to cluster into groups, and these indicate books prepared for certain types of use. The clustering is predictable, quite simply because book producers had a natural limitation on their procedures: the size of sheets available to receive writing. Without trying to prejudge the issue of materials (see pp. 33ff.), one is guided by Pollard's classic essay, 'Notes on the Size of the Sheet', *The Library* 4th ser. 22 (1941), 105–37. At 110, Pollard points to the constraints imposed by the size of a typical English sheepskin; this he estimates at 1200 mm × 900 mm. This may, improvements in agriculture and animal husbandry having occurred, be somewhat larger than what was available in the Middle Ages.[20]

Size matters. The very largest surviving books cannot have been portable and must always have been used on lecterns. In this extreme case, the books were designed for some variety of public performance. The two largest Middle English manuscripts, 'The Vernon MS' (BodL, MS Eng. poet. a.1, which weighs in at a full four stone) and 'The Simeon MS' (BL, MS Additional 22283), must have been constructed as single-volume libraries for the spiritual edification of a religious community, presumably to have been read aloud in refectory or chapter-house. These companion volumes measure 545 mm × 395 mm and 585 mm × 395 mm, respectively. Probably their nearest rival was commissioned by Sir Thomas Chaworth of Wiverton (Notts.), a connoisseur of out-sized volumes who d. 1439: his copy of Lydgate's *Troy Book*, now BL, MS Cotton Augustus A.iv, measures 540 mm × 355 mm.

[20] See 'The Sizes of Middle English Books, c. 1390–1430', *Journal of the Early Book Society* 18 (2015), 181–91, a study that assumes that books were produced by folding single skins, a topic to which I return at p. 77.

Books associated with liturgical performance are similarly supersubstantial. Chaworth again commissioned the largest surviving insular manuscript before 1500, a book to be used by one side of a chapel choir, 'The Wollaton Antiphonal', now Nottingham UL, MS 250. At the fullest, its leaves measure 590 mm × 410 mm; however, the book offers plentiful evidence of being a limit case, since most of the leaves are narrower and many have been 'sized up' by pasting on additional strips at the tops. Although the book is opulently decorated, there were clearly problems with getting skins of an appropriate size. Other service books are similarly substantial – such as a missal, ChCh 87, at 420 mm × 285 mm – and there are a great many large 'lectern Bibles', such as Oxford, Queen's College, MS 52 (425 mm × 305 mm) or SJ 1 (400 mm × 260 mm). The notion that Wycliffism might have been a universally persecuted sect is belied by comparable Middle English Bibles such as BL, MSS Egerton 617+618 (two volumes of a three-volume set, 440 mm × 290 mm); Oxford, Queen's College, MS 388 (430 mm × 305 mm); or ChCh 145 (385 mm × 265 mm). And CUL, MS Dd.1.17, a very substantial historical miscellany, certainly from a monastic library, although also including *Piers Plowman* and *Mandeville's Travels*, comes in at 440 mm × 305 mm.

However, the most usual surviving medieval bibles represent the opposite end of the size spectrum – undersized books. These, frequently called 'Parisian' or 'pocket Bibles', were produced on an industrial scale across northern France and England c. 1230–90. A pair of French examples, both about 140–45 mm × 90 mm, are reproduced at actual size at Scott McKendrick and Kathleen Doyle, *Bible Manuscripts: 1400 Years of Scribes and Scripture* (London, 2007), 110–11 (plates 97–98). They are pretty much identical in size to Magd lat. 1 or Oxford, Queen's College, MS 358 (and Magd lat. 2 is only a little larger). Similarly, BodL, MS Lyell 26, with Wycliffite gospels, measures only 120 mm × 85 mm. One might notice that, although very small, the extensive contents of a Bible require that books in this format be very thick. Thus, the examples I cite above contain, respectively, 496, 770, 579, and 349 leaves. (See further p. 36.)

There is a usual narrative to explain this form of the book. These Bibles appeared as and when they did to accommodate a new user-group, university- (or at least convent-) trained itinerant preachers, many from the new orders of the mendicants. They were to be carried on the person (hence 'pocket') as ready consultation volumes while these individuals went about their work of conversion. Moreover, persons like these didn't carry just Bibles, but equally ancillary texts relevant to their profession. For example, BodL, MS Tanner 335 (145 mm × 100 mm, 208 folios) is a portable copy of Raymond de Penyaforte's standard *Summa de penitentia*, s. xiii ex.

But this narrative also serves to explain a variety of genres equally prevalent as small portable volumes. Just like the wandering friars, seeking souls to bring to penance, these represent various sorts of practitioner volumes, designed to be readily available for consultation. Lawyers, for example, appear to have been persistently given to on-the-trot statute checking. I once, in a half-hour search, found 14 copies of the Statutes of the Realm in volumes smaller than 120 mm × 70 mm. Typical, and rivalling Parisian Bibles in the number of folios one can gather in small compass is BodL, MS Tanner 450, 110 mm × 70 mm, 382 folios, with not just the Statutes but the more useful forms for instituting civil actions provided by a *Registrum brevium* 'register of writs'. MS Tanner 337, 130 mm × 95 mm, 313 folios, is a comparable volume on the religious side, something one imagines carried by a rural dean or an archdeacon, responsible for diocesan discipline. It's a pocket book of locally applicable canon law, mostly devoted to William Lyndwood's commentary on the two great English provincial canons, with added examples.[21] Similarly, although formal medical texts are often extensive, books for on-site practice, typically recipe collections, are often quite small: for example, Magd lat. 221, 110 mm × 75 mm and 224 folios.

Another large trove of small personal books can be found in materials for private devotion. The most frequently surviving medieval books, books for private prayer, *Horae beate virginis Marie* 'the hours of the blessed Virgin', very frequently assume on-the-person portability: for example, the northern French ChCh 100, 120 mm × 80 mm and 259 folios. These personal accoutrements, not necessarily a Catholic 'book of hours' but a personal prayerbook, appear frequently in manuscript painting and later in early modern portraits of noble women. There the books are depicted as inside a binding hanging from the subject's belt, a 'girdle-book', an alternative means of personal carriage to the notion 'pocket'.[22]

---

[21] These are the *Constitutiones Ottonis* and *Constitutiones Ottoboni*, named for the papal legates who promulgated them in the thirteenth century, ed. Powicke and Cheney 1:245–59, 2:747–92 (full reference at n.8).

[22] For an introduction to the expected, and generally standardised, contents, see Roger S. Wieck *et al.*, *Time Sanctified: The Book of Hours in Medieval Art and Life* (New York, 1988, 2001), 149–67. There's also an at least interesting, if unduly

However, dwelling on the extremes does not address the normal case. I composed this book on sheets of the British paper-stock called 'A4'. Comparable to the normal North American so-called '8½ × 11', this measures 297 mm × 210 mm. It is a common sheet-size because it reflects the dimensions of a folio routinely used in producing late medieval reading texts, a size of book familiar to readers of popular works such as *Piers Plowman*, Nicholas Love's *Mirror*, and Richard Rolle's *English Psalter*. Such moderately sized books were a regular staple.

This in-between book includes one particularly strange example, the 'holster book' or 'agenda format', typically a narrow volume, but approaching a height three times its width. Books associated with the antiquarian William Worcestre exemplify both the format and its origins. Worcestre's earliest appearance in manuscript is his 1436 book of manorial accounts for his master Sir John Fastolf, BL, MS Additional 28208, in this format. But, beyond its origins in accounts culture, it was also the format Worcestre used in the three volumes that collect the oddments published as his *Itineraries*; one of these, Cambridge, Corpus Christi College, MS 210, measures 295 mm × 135 mm. Similarly, one of the most (in)famous manuscripts of Middle English, 'The *Orrmulum*' (BodL, MS Junius 1) measures 500 mm × 200 mm (see further p. 36). As a literary vehicle, the format is perhaps most widely attested among early modern amateur 'local' poets, although their behaviour is forecast by an earlier example of this format, BodL, MS Ashmole 61. This is a book for pre-electronic household entertainment, compiled by a Leicester burgess, s. xv ex.; it measures 420 mm × 140 mm.[23]

---

sentimentalised and pietistic, introduction to these books and their use, Eamon Duffy, *Marking the Hours: The English People and Their Prayers, 1240–1570* (New Haven CT, 2006).

[23] See K. B. McFarlane, 'William Worcester: A Preliminary Survey', *England in the Fifteenth Century: Collected Essays*, ed. G. L. Harriss (London, 1981), 199–224, at 221 n.129; Lynne S. Blanchfield, 'The Romances in MS Ashmole 61: An Idiosyncratic Scribe', *Romance in Medieval England*, ed. Maldwyn Mills et al. (Cambridge, 1991), 65–87; and George Shuffelton, ed., *Codex Ashmole 61: A Compilation of Popular Middle English Verse*, TEAMS (Kalamazoo MI, 2008).

The closed book: what do you see first?

Your initial sight of the book is from the outside, the binding. Rather than the book's most prominent feature, this is the most exiguous. Binding always went on apart from the actual production of the book. Because it required extra craftsmen and extra expense, it was always totally optional and, over the life of any single book, owners have routinely discarded received bindings and substituted their own. Both costing and optionality are recorded in the accounts written on the rear pastedown of HM 132: 'In leddur bongre ij d, in whyte threde ij d, ij new bordes i d, ij skynys of perchement viij d, a skyn of red lather ij d, in blac sylke and greyne i d obolus, in glw obolus, ij claspys ij d, summa totalis xix d'. The book includes the partially autograph copy of Ranulf Higden's *Polychronicon*; the author died in 1364, but the binding note (and there is no evidence that the book had any binding other than that still in place) is in a hand a century later.

As a result, numerous medieval references to books describe them simply as 'in quaternis': that is, preserved either as loose leaves or simply in a wrapper of heavy parchment. For example, SJ 39 presents glossed gospels, s. xiii[1]. At the rear, as if flyleaves, are three leaves, two joined and one single, with Jerome's commentary on Isaiah. These are from a much larger manuscript than MS 39 itself, and a little older, s. xii ex.; they formed the book's enveloping wrapper and one of its pastedowns, probably imposed by the book's likely medieval owners, the Cluniacs of Northampton. This formed the book's only protection – as a tab with a new shelfmark affixed to one of these leaves shows, it still formed the cover when St John's reshelved their books in the mid-eighteenth century – until an archaising rebinding, probably Victorian, which preserved these leaves more or less *in situ*.

Similarly, in early print culture, booksellers provided not books but only the printed sheets; it was up to the purchaser to impose a binding, if they wished, and full-edition standardised binding of a newly published book is usual from only c. 1800. (As late as the 1960s, I bought a 'new' copy of *Sir Gawain and the Green Knight* – the book had been published in 1940, but there was still plenty of stock about; it was in a loosely sewn paper cover, with uncut pages and wildly uneven edges, up to ¾ inch wider in places. I was expected, this being a publication of the Early English Text Society, an organisation originally for learned gentlemen, to take it to my binder, who'd fix it up in my full-library binding so that it would not look amiss on the shelves in my stately home.)[24]

The point of binding, obviously enough, is to protect the book, most particularly to ensure that all the leaves remain intact and in order; secondarily, to shield the book-block from soil. The accidents to which books are subject are manifold: readers inadvertently spilling fluids, or someone deciding a wooden cover might be a useful place to prop up a hot spit (both which accidents befell 'The Exeter Book' of Old English poems, Exeter Cathedral, MS 3501).[25] Equally, covers should, but frequently don't, protect against vermin; University of London Library, MS S. L. V.88 ('The Ilchester *Piers Plowman*') has at some point been rat-infested, and Cambridge, Pembroke College, MSS 36 and 142 left open to provide an avian latrine.

Deliberate human predation of earlier bindings is even more widespread. At least two Oxford Colleges, Merton and Magdalen, undertook extensive rebinding programmes, s. xvii in., and we have no idea what the books may originally have looked like. The practice was particularly rife throughout the Victorian era, when manuscripts were 'sanitised' by restoring the primacy of the central text-block and usually discarding everything else as extraneous. Much of the historical collection of the BL (e.g. Cotton, Royal, and Harley MSS) was subjected to such 'conservation', and the Library, when called upon to examine the books of Shrewsbury School in 1897, declared them in need of such treatment and stripped nearly all the books and rebound them. Thus, it is relatively rare to find any manuscript in what's certainly its original binding, and much of the information many bindings offer is valuable only in discussing a book's provenance.[26]

Moreover, even the most well-intentioned conservation of intact bindings inflicts damage. In 1630 a group of students recatalogued

---

[24] Similarly, Oxford, Merton College still has a large stock of a classic study, surely an inspiration to the youthful Ker, Mynors, and Hunt: F. M. Powicke, *The Medieval Books of Merton College* (Oxford, 1931). These copies are entirely of the sheets as they came from Clarendon Press, folded but uncut, and held in a bundle by a glued paper strip.

[25] Not to mention, it would appear, the sacred *Beowulf* MS, BL, MS Cotton Vitellius A.xv, where a page damaged by spillage and subsequently re-inked has produced some fantastic theories about the poem and its transmission. See further the example discussed at p. 110.

[26] Although see the privately owned Edinburgh MS in my discussion, p. 34, and, on provenance, see pp. 113ff.

Binding: A plain binding, s. xii², of whittawed leather over boards, with strap and pin. Just visible, a feature of bindings of this era, are leather tabs at each end of the spine to protect the rolls securing the sewing. The book, the prophet Ezekiel glossed, includes the *ex-libris* of the great Cistercian house Fountains Abbey (NRY), and belonged for at least three centuries to the Ingilby family of Ripley, devoted local collectors of abbey remnants. Another book with a common provenance, BodL, MS Lyell 8, in a binding of s. xiv in., still retains both bosses and the abbey's label under horn, illustrated de la Mare (see n.16), plate xxxv (a, b). (BL, MS Davis 80, the cover, reproduced at 45%).

Magd's manuscripts, in the process assigning them new shelfmarks. Unfortunately, they wrote these on the covers in black ink, ignoring the fact that these covers were in suedey 'reversed calf', not a very stable medium. In s. xx, Magdalen equipped all the manuscripts with boxes prepared by Bodleian conservators, a useful step – except that several decades of readers' sliding the books in and out of the boxes has abraded away most of the cataloguers' work.[27]

There is a Bible of medieval bookbinding, a book that explains the procedures involved in great detail and with useful explanatory drawings and images: J. A. Szirmai, *The Archaeology of Medieval Bookbinding* (1999; Abingdon and New York, 2017).[28] As Szirmai describes the process, the fundamental action is sewing the leaves to bands, usually heavy strings or leather thongs. One decides how many bands are necessary to a secure structure (typically taller books require more bands), and one anchors the book's individual constituents, its quires (see pp. 90–91), to these. This involves both sewing vertically down the centre of the quires and anchoring this stitching to the horizontal bands themselves. The bands are secured by drawing them through channels in the covers, usually oak slabs – hence the usual term 'boards', rather than 'covers'; they are typically fixed there by knotted ends held in place by small dowels. Finally, the boards are covered with skin pasted over both the boards and the sewn bands (medieval bindings are 'flat-backed', unlike those usual in early twentieth-century trade printed books). In the Middle Ages, this covering was usually of alum-tawed ('whittawed') skin.

The binding of a book entails things other than the sewing and covers. It is quite customary to add additional leaves around the text block. First of all, the skin covering is held in place only by paste over the spine and boards, unless it is folded over and fixed by further

---

[27] Here I am particularly aware of the difference between what Neil Ker could read in 1942ff., before the collection was 'conserved', and what I could, 2000ff. Fortunately, these rearrangers of the library left a record of their efforts, now Magd MS 776.

[28] Much less extensive, but offering tastes of the basics, are Graham Pollard's three articles: 'The Construction of English Twelfth-Century Bindings', *The Library* 5th ser. 17 (1962), 1–22; 'The Names of Some English 15th-Century Binders', *The Library* 5th ser. 25 (1970), 193–218; and 'Describing Medieval Book Bindings', *Medieval Learning and Literature: Essays Presented to Richard William Hunt*, ed. J. J. G. Alexander and Margaret T. Gibson (Oxford, 1976), 50–65. G. D. Hobson, *English Binding before 1500* (Cambridge, 1929) is still useful.

pasting to the inside of the boards. (These leather bits inside the cover are called 'turn-ins' and, because not exposed to the same wear as the covers, often show that they had been stained, usually with red dye.) To strengthen this structure, binders frequently paste over the turn-ins a further piece of skin, a 'pastedown'. Most typically, these are from substandard 'waste' skin, but very frequently come from books now deemed 'waste' (even medieval institutions recycled old books in this way), and may present fragments of interesting texts.[29]

The most extensive discussion of this subject is Ker, *Fragments of Medieval Manuscripts Used as Pastedowns in Oxford Bindings: with a Survey of Oxford Binding c. 1515–1620*, 2nd edn, ed. David Rundle and Scott Mandelbrote, Oxford Bibliographical Society 3 ser. 4 (Oxford, 2004 for 2000). This is an important guide, but one should understand that it's a carefully delimited one. Ker surveyed only books bound in Oxford, and only from a single century; he was interested in books predictably from college libraries dispersed in the mid-sixteenth century, much of which had been sold by the cartful to binders for this purpose. Other studies take a broader view, such as Robert G. Babcock, *Reconstructing a Medieval Library: Fragments from Lambach* (New Haven CT, 1993); Kerstin Abukhanfusa, *Mutilated Books: Wondrous Leaves from Swedish Bibliographical History* (Stockholm, 2004); Ana Suárez Gonzales, *Fragmentos de Libros, Bibliotecas de Fragmentos* (Zamora, 2003); or Andreas Lehnhardt and Judith Olszowy-Schlanger, eds, *Books within Books: New Discoveries in Old Bookbindings* (Leiden, 2014).[30]

Many such 'waste leaves' remain *in situ* in their bindings, and you should not be surprised to find materials clearly from another book there (and to be forced into describing them and identifying their contents). For example, John Felton, vicar of St Mary Magdalen, Oxford, a famous (and widely disseminated) preacher who d. 1434, is ascribed an alphabetical index/*distinctio*-collection formed of extracts

---

[29] Cf. SJ 39, mentioned above, and a wad of covers formed from two discarded old Psalters (probably not library books, but from the Cathedral proper) mentioned by Roger Mynors, *Durham Cathedral Manuscripts to the End of the Twelfth Century* (London, 1939), 70.n.

[30] This 'waste' extends well beyond copies of manuscript material. Early modern binders routinely used non-selling print books in the same way. See Strickland Gibson, 'Fragments from Bindings at The Queen's College, Oxford', *The Library* 4th ser. 12 (1932), 429–33. In a substantial number of the books he rebound for Magd in the 1610s, Robert Way used leaves from a single copy of the canon law collection *Sext*, printed at Paris, 1510, for pastedowns.

from Robert Grosseteste's *De oculo, corde, lingua* … . This text survives in but a single copy, CUL, MS Ii.1.30. However, there's a paste-covered and often illegible pair of leaves from the head of another copy in Coventry History Centre, where it was originally used as a pastedown in MS BA/A/1/2/3, one of the sixteenth-century Corporation record books. Similarly, Geoffrey of Burton's life of St Modwenna, now surviving in only two full copies, also appears as a pair of leaves used to bind a printed report of parliamentary acts, 3–4 Edward VI (1550), now BL, MS Additional 63642.[31]

Pastedowns are fine, but not altogether helpful. They are not part of the binding structure, only pasted bits. More effective are a pair of leaves, or larger units (four-six leaves); these not only protect the text-block from abrasion from the covers, but, as small units, can be sewn into the full binding. They thus they provide a much more stable structure than does a pastedown. The most usual minimal device is a bifolium, a pair of leaves, in which one leaf serves as pastedown, the join with its partner leaf sewn into the full binding structure, and the second leaf left loose, as a 'flyleaf'. But more complicated structures appear with some frequency. Again, these are most frequently 'waste' skin. For example, 'The Ellesmere Chaucer' (HEH, EL 27 C 9) has four flyleaves at each end; these had been prepared along with the rest of the book to receive text – as insurance, lest some disaster befall during production. However, once copying was completed, they were simply 'waste', and incorporated in the binding. As we will see shortly, binding leaves complicate a good deal the notion 'what is the book?'

Moreover, although these are not part of the integral volume, pastedowns and flyleaves are magnetic text-catchers. Users and owners may respect and leave uninscribed the textual portions of a book, but they feel no such compunction when it comes to the blank spaces at its ends. Very often, these leaves are covered with various odd jottings: pen-trials, trial alphabets, short verses in English and Latin, recipes, brief prayers, theological notes. They are also often the place where owners record that fact. See further Julian Luxford's provocative 'Additaments from Peterborough Abbey and the Problem of the "Busy Flyleaf"', *Journal of the Early Book Society* 23 (2020), 213–25. Very frequently, these user additions have been subject to erasure (for example, new owners want clear title and eliminate their predecessors). When looking at a binding, you should always run these associated leaves under an

---

[31] For Felton and Geoffrey, see Sharpe's indispensable 'new Bale', 243–45 and 122, respectively.

ultraviolet lamp; that special lighting will frequently reveal textual material illegible to the naked eye and of interest in assessing a book's ownership and use (see pp. 114, 119).

At least two odd forms of binding deserve at least passing notice. In a 'chemise binding', the book is enveloped by covering materials on all sides, including the edges, like a sleeve enclosing both the boards and the leaves. Many books given this ornamental treatment are ostentatious volumes, often with expensive cloth over the whole structure, like ChCh 92 or 339. But even rather humble books are preserved in chemises, such as BodL, MS Rawlinson C.285, or a dilapidated example that escaped the BL's 1897 predations, Shrewsbury School, MS 1.[32]

In the early modern period one often finds cloth coverings, sometimes on new books, sometimes rebindings, typically in velvet, sometimes with embroidery. SJ 64 has such a binding in red velvet, and the ostentatious ChCh 339 (again) in tawny velvet. In a famous bravura display of her childhood skills, Elizabeth Tudor, having already translated the text from French and transcribed it in her best humanistic hand, embroidered the cloth covers of BodL, MS Cherry 36.

Elizabeth decorated her binding. Much more frequently, for a century or so from the late fifteenth century, decoration was provided by professional binders to leather coverings. This, a sophisticated version of your childhood fun with a wood-burner set, involved applying heated metal tools directly to the leather ('in blind'). Typical decoration of this sort includes images left by small stamps or punches, bands of decoration produced by heated cylindrical rolls run along the surface, and, occasionally, panels (large-scale pictorial material). The comprehensive catalogue of these imprints on the surface is J. Basil Oldham, *English Blind-stamped Bindings* (Cambridge, 1952). Oldham offers a rational system for classifying these ornaments, as well as grouping examples as the work of single individuals (often known by such evocative names as 'The Bat Binder'). In many cases, these individuals can be named and because, at this point, binders were dealing with both manuscripts and printed books, a number of their activities are datable.

Oldham's catalogue is exhaustively illustrated by 'rubbings': images of the decoration. To identify your example – potentially important for dating the binding and for locating where it was imposed (London?

---

[32] See the only extensive study, Jan Storm van Leeuwen, 'The Well-Shirted Bookbinding: On Chemise Bindings and Hülleneinbände', *Theatrum Orbis Librorum: Liber Amicorum Presented to Nico Israel on the Occasion of his Seventieth Birthday*, ed. T. Croiset van Uchelen *et al.* (Utrecht, 1989), 277–305.

Oxford? Cambridge?), perhaps a clue to early ownership[33] – you must repeat his procedures. Just as the imposition of stamps and rolls may recall childhood hobbies, this, 'rubbing a binding', will as well. It's your childhood tracing all over again: put a sheet, tracing paper best, over the board, rub on it with the side of your pencil, watch (magic!) the image appear. You can then compare it with Oldham's images.

Alas, alas. As I've indicated above, bindings are susceptible to abrasion and wear. As a result, many libraries, including the Bodleian, no longer allow you to rub a binding. You'll have to do the job by eye (or with an image from your handy iPad). Any good research library has a copy of Oldham, and you'll need to hold this copy by the MS as you search for images. A poor third option is trying to reproduce what you see as a freehand sketch and then going to compare your doodle with Oldham's more accurate rubbing.

However, bindings come scarred far more frequently than they do decorated. This reflects the imposition (and frequent removal) of what is generically considered 'furniture'. First of all, medieval books appear to have been sewn relatively tightly across the spine (a good way to ensure the integrity of the textual content). But, as a result, they frequently survive not in the rectilinear forms to which we are accustomed but with a pronounced trapezoidal splay along the leading edge. To counteract this splay (and to protect the text pages from spills, dust, and other accidents), bindings frequently include devices to hold the books closed, the 'claspys' mentioned in the Higden account I have quoted above. These generally involve either 'straps and clasps' or 'straps and pins'.

In both techniques, in an English book (but not a continental one, where the procedure is reversed; cf. SJ 64), the upper/front board has

---

[33] For example, three books at Cambridge, Jesus College, all in bindings of s. xv ex.: MS Q.D.3 (James 45) is stamped with the 'old standard' tools used on Oxford books in the 1480s; see Strickland Gibson, *Early Oxford Bindings*, Bibliographical Society Illustrated Monographs 10 (Oxford, 1903), stamps 12–15, illustrated plate xxxiii. Since it is a Durham Cathedral book, it probably reflects work done for the priory's Oxford college (the site now Trinity College). In contrast, MS Q.G.7 (James 55) uses three tools, two not in Oldham, one of these a slightly elongated fleur de lis, most like, but not identical to, Oldham no. 314 (plate xxv), which Oldham associates with 'the Half-stamp Binder'. However, this tool also appears, with a second stamp not in Oldham, on the binding of MS Q.G.28 (James 75). Both these books have secure medieval owners, the abbeys at Easby (NRY, OPraem) and Kirkstall (WRY, OCist), and one should infer that one is looking at provincial work, probably done in York.

one or more grooves to hold leather strips, the straps, anchored under the skin cover and in the board by nails. These strips run to some form of anchorage on the lower/back board; to achieve this, the leather straps have at their ends metal fixtures, often embossed or otherwise decorated.[34] In a strap and clasp binding, the straps generally run only the length of the text-block, since they are anchored on staple-like metal fittings, the clasps, along the edge of the lower/back board. A strap and pin binding has a longer leather strip, since its anchorage is a pin that protrudes from somewhere near the middle of the lower board. Unlike the strap and clasp, where the upper board fixture is largely external, lower board pins have been driven through the wooden board and frequently sit within a decorative metal plate.

As I have said, books are persistently subject to rebindings. A number of these are undertaken to facilitate book storage in ways not originally envisioned (principally to accommodate the volumes to the case and shelf systems that have been normal in libraries since the seventeenth century). In these circumstances, old 'furniture' is frequently viewed as deleterious (and expendable). Thus, a great many medieval bindings survive without their straps; and pins, which are positively harmful to adjacent volumes in modern shelving, have almost invariably been cut off. But these features leave traces, scars, on the bindings that one should notice. At least in early modern rebindings, their function has been served by less destructive means, paired cloth ties, now again frequently pared (although you will often see the holes in the boards where they were anchored, and the nubs of the excised materials).

You will frequently in early bindings see the grooves cut into the upper board for straps, as in SJ 2 and 58, sometimes with later repairs, as in SJ 114; or surviving clasps but no straps, as in SJ 17. Examples of removed pins occur in SJ 167, ChCh 87 and 88 (stubs of nails or holes in the lower board), the surviving seating of the pin in ChCh 341. At least seven books at Cambridge, Jesus College have at least scarring from pins (and three of them still intact bits of the pins); the outstanding example is MS Q.A.14 (James 14), in a twelfth-century binding, with an intact lower board pin, a stub of one in the upper board, and scars from a strap and clasp imposed later. Sometimes, although no trace remains, you will be able to intuit the prior presence of these fittings from verdigris stains from the metal or holes from the chafing of the affixing nails on the opening folios, as in SJ 75 and 123.

---

[34] For example, in ChCh 339 these brass buckles are ornamented with floral designs and inscriptions ('ihs' on the upper strap, 'maria' on the lower).

'Furniture' is not limited to such utilitarian items. Particularly early in the Middle Ages, sumptuous books were equipped with 'treasure bindings'. These included such rich items as jewels, gold, and, usually in a container carved into the upper board, saints' relics.[35] Other decorative features are a bit more mundane – and thus, more common. Many bindings have or had decorative metal corner- and centrepieces. More frequently, particularly with stamped bindings, they have bosses, vaguely hemispherical raised metal pieces in similar positions.

While treasure-bindings have often survived intact because of their beauty and richness, bosses, like pins, impede modern storage techniques and have been removed, leaving only their scars, round impressions at the corners and centre, as in SJ 17 or ChCh 88. Gray's Inn, MS 8 has a full set of corner bosses on both boards (and ChCh 339, the college statutes, has Tudor rose ornament on similar fixtures). Corner- and centrepieces, in imitation of medieval examples, were an Oxford fad of s. xvii in.; they appeared on the 'Register of Benefactors' (aka 'Donors' Book') established by Sir Thomas Bodley to record gifts to his library (used, but not closely described, SC 1, 76–77), and were subsequently imitated in mirroring volumes in college libraries by, for example, President William Laud at St John's.

Much more frequent scarring (and very occasional preservation) speaks to historical preservation in one or another library, an area where your investigation of any single book will slide over into book history. Medieval libraries (and many in Oxford and Cambridge down to the end of the eighteenth century) customarily had divided book collections: some volumes freely circulated, while others, typically works of basic reference, thus of predictably frequent consultation, were secured – not just non-circulating, but chained to the library furniture. Although there have been local studies, the only general overview remains Burnett H. Streeter, *The Chained Library: A Survey of Four Centuries in the Evolution of the English Library* (London, 1931).

A couple of such collections are still extant: a substantial number of printed books, chained in imitation of Oxford practice (and by

---

[35] Prominent examples include 'The gospels of Henry the Lion', s. xii ex., when last sold, the most expensive manuscript ever at auction, now Wolfenbüttel, Herzog-August Bibliothek, MS Guelf. 105 Noviss. 2°, or 'The cathach of St Columba', covering a Psalter, s. vi ex., now Dublin, Royal Irish Academy, MS 12 R, on display in the national archaeological museum. In both cases, the extravagant bindings were imposed centuries after the books were produced.

Oxford joiners), s. xvii in., at Hereford Cathedral Library; and a small purpose-made parish library of s. xvii med. in a book chest at Manchester, Chetham's Library. Virtually all the manuscripts at Gray's Inn still have their chain-staples, the looped metal seatings that held the chains (and in one case, a bit of the chain), fixed to the lower leading edge of the upper board; these were affixed s. xvii med. to counteract an alleged wave of book theft.[36] The shelving, including the rail that took the chains that secured collections, survives more frequently, as at Trinity Hall and Jesus College, Cambridge, and a good many libraries, such as the Bodleian's Duke Humfrey, or the Old Library at Oxford, St John's College, still preserve and show tourists sample chained volumes *in situ*.

There is a variety of ways to chain a book, and individual libraries followed local practices. All require affixing either a metal loop or plate (the 'staple') to one of the wooden boards. Books with loops presumably were secured as a group by a single chain run through the loops; in those with plates, the chain was affixed to the plate on the book and ended in a metal loop that could be slid along a locking bar or rail. You should not be surprised to find more than one sign of scarring, usually in different positions along the binding, indicating that a book has passed through more than one institutional collection.[37]

In Oxford, from s. xvi ex., books were chained by a small brass plate along the upper leading edge of the upper board, and their library storage followed the second option I have described. In the library furniture served by this system, the books were shelved, as they are still at Hereford and Chetham's, with the 'fore-edges' outward. This allowed them to be pulled off their shelves and opened easily on a flat lectern below the shelving.[38]

---

[36] Images on the library website, https://www.graysinn.org.uk/library/medieval-manuscripts; see particularly those of MSS 1, 5, 7, 8, and 22.

[37] The options are customarily reported following the system ('position X') developed by Andrew Watson, *A Descriptive Catalogue of the Medieval Manuscripts at All Souls College, Oxford* (Oxford, 1997), xxii. Thus, Gray's Inn was universally chained in Watson's position 4, and 'usual Oxford chaining' is in position 6.

[38] In contrast, 18 surviving books at Magd (MSS lat. 4, 18, 32, etc.) have marks from chaining by a very large staple in position 4, affixed by a deep recess cut into the board, so that the staple would sit within the board itself, lifted away from the leaves of the book, to prevent damaging them. This recess severely weakens the board, and several such bindings have broken upper boards.

This raises a point related to binding that one is apt to ignore. If the spine of a book (where we nowadays look for a 'title-label') is not visible, but positioned against the frame of the chest, the book will be readily identifiable only by some variety of 'fore-edge' mark, a notation inked across the leading edges of the leaves. This is most usually the book's shelfmark, the equivalent of a modern library 'call number'. Such black-ink marking, a product of library reorganisation, s. xviii, appears on many SJ books, as well as on ChCh 98.

However, decorated fore-edges are not rare, and you should always check (just as you should to see whether later library use has gilded or reddened the book's edges or red-spotted them). For example, Magd lat. 100 (a psalter + office of the dead, s. xiii^1) has painted edges; Mirjam M. Foot, *Studies in the History of Bookbinding* (Aldershot, 1993), 442, describes the work as 'a simple linear pattern of crossed and parallel lines with triangles, in red', and thinks it perhaps represents crossed arrows or spears. There is another example on the edges of a book famous for its 'Fenland' illumination, s. xiv in., 'The Barlow Psalter', BodL, MS Barlow 22, in this case a form of the English royal arms.

The fore-edge title, as I point out, isn't medieval. Instead chained books in early libraries, here presumably with a large looped staple and single chain, lay flat on a book-press, with their upper boards downward. They were identified by labels, usually under transparent horn, secured by a metal rectangular frame and nails near the top of the lower board. There are intact examples on Magd lat. 81 and 214 (as well as on a printed book of 1478, apparently donated in 1494/5, Arch. B.III.3.2). More frequently, one encounters only scars or marks left by these fixtures, as on Magd lat. 24,[39] 35, 138, 211, and 225; ChCh 88, or Gray's Inn, MSS 1 and 5. Another label, with nailholes from the original horn covering, is attached to fol. ii, a flyleaf, in a rebound book, BL, MS Royal 6 E.iii, originally part of the same donation to Magd as its current lat. 24 and 81. Similarly, in Shrewsbury School, MS 13, a medieval label that, before the BL-enforced rebinding, should have been displayed

---

[39] Where it is visible from marks on the front flyleaf, fol. i, in a book rebound s. xvii in. Frequently, extant binding materials are retained in a new binding, but removed from their original position (recall SJ 39). Here, inferentially, the old flyleaves have been reversed, so that leaves originally at the rear (under the horn-covered label) are now at the front. Occasionally, the old boards have been retained but reversed, as in Cambridge, Jesus College, MS Q.G.26 (James 73) (here only the lower board, with a scar from an earlier pin).

under horn on the lower board now appears pasted to the rear flyleaf intruded in 1897.

While binding generally represents an effort at protecting a book, one should understand that it is commonly destructive, as well. This occurs because one of the binder's tasks is to ensure that all the leaves are of the same dimensions by 'planing' the book's edges. In medieval bindings, this procedure usually results in the pages being reduced to the dimensions of the boards; in modern rebindings, the boards are usually slightly larger than the pages. As a result of the process, achieved with a small draw-knife, anything very near the page-edges will be lost.

Especially among binders engaged in full-library rebinding in the early modern period there was a commonplace indifference to what might, in this process, be destroyed. It is fairly routine to find cut-off or cut-into running titles at the tops of pages, nearly universal at Merton College, where adjectives such as 'savage' are commonplace in describing this binder's behaviour. An overzealous s. xviii rebinding reduced the great London MS of romances 'The Auchinleck MS' (Edinburgh, National Library of Scotland, MS Advocates' 19.2.1) from a customarily oblong medieval book to one approaching square. Early modern marginalia fell to the binder's plane as well. (In this instance, we have some notion of the original dimensions from leaves pillaged from the book before this disaster, now preserved at St Andrews UL.)[40]

One product of decimated edges may always have been planned, or at least expected. A considerable amount of the detail that shows the scribe's production of his book (and his preparation of it for binding) takes place around the page-edges. These marks and notations may have appeared at the edges precisely with the expectation that they would be eliminated by the binder (leaving behind a pristinely continuous product). See further the discussions of pricking, catchwords, and signatures, pp. 60–61, 89–93. Because of the binder's activity, you should not feel alarmed to find none, or only a selection, of these features in any book.

---

[40] For a few further examples of binders' various indifference to text and decoration, see SJ 128 and 256, ChCh Allestree M.1.10, ChCh 98 and 103.

Opening the book: what's it made of?

Medieval books, almost universally, are written on one of two materials: membrane or skin (treated animal hides), or paper.

Membrane

Most classical books, as I have indicated, appear on papyrus rolls. However, another form of support was developed at Pergamon, in western Turkey. Allegedly as the result of an Egyptian trade embargo, the inhabitants of this city were forced to improvise for book materials and developed the use of prepared animal skins as a writing support. Pergamon had a major livestock market, and the raw materials were universally available as the otherwise waste offal from butchers. This 'invention' has given the material its universal name, Latin *pergamen(t)um*, 'the stuff from Pergamon'.

In general, it is probably best to refer to this material as 'membrane' or 'skin'. 'Parchment' and 'vellum' commonly appear in discussions and descriptions, but the latter properly refers only to calf-skin (cf. 'veal'), and the fastidious believe that 'parchment' should thus only refer to material derived from sheep. However, matters are not quite so simple; any prepared skin will do,[41] and the only very certain mode of identifying the source of the membrane you are looking at depends upon scientific analysis. One flamboyant recent demonstration of the available techniques involved a manuscript in private hands (William Zachs, Edinburgh), Luke glossed, c. 1120, from St Augustine's Abbey, Canterbury (OSB). For the results and discussion, see Anne Gibbons, 'The Biology of the Book', *Science* 357, issue 6349 (28 July 2017), 346–49, with a diagram at 349; and Bruce Barker-Benfield *et al.*, *The Glossed Luke with the Letter A: A Manuscript from St Augustine's Abbey Canterbury* (Edinburgh, 2020), 11.

The results of the non-invasive scientific analysis revealed on this occasion were striking. One's expectations with an insular MS are that it

---

[41] Malcolm Parkes used to joke (or so I hope) that 'the Hereford mappa mundi', a world-map on a very large single skin, displayed at Hereford Cathedral, had been derived from the carcass of the elephant recorded as kept in Henry III's menagerie. See his 'The Hereford Map: The Handwriting and the Copying of the Text', *Pages from the Past: Medieval Writing Skills and Manuscript Books*, ed. P. R. Robinson and Rivkah Zim (Farnham, 2012), I.

will be on sheepskin; England's agricultural wealth, after all, depended upon the wool trade, and there should have been plenty of this raw material about. And, indeed, more than half the book – the researchers estimated that these portions had involved ten full skins (plus another half-skin for the flyleaves) – had been written on sheepskin.

However, although a substantial continuous chunk of the volume (fols 123–54) was ovine, in most cases this material was mixed with membrane from other sources – indeed, if one will pardon the inaccurate expression, routinely sat cheek by jowl with it. For most of the book, the scribes alternated leaves from sheep with those from calves, who provided a total of eight and a half further skins. At one point (fols 107–14), half a goat skin was pressed into service. Moreover, the book's (here original) binding had involved non-domesticated species: the covering of whittawed leather had come from a roe deer, but the straps that closed the book from a red deer or from a non-native species imported by the Normans for their sport, a fallow deer. This study shows there's clearly a lot to learn about 'raw materials' here.

'Raw materials' is an apt locution, because membrane is a prepared product. It requires the parchmener, a profession that once featured on a BBC programme entitled 'Britain's Worst Jobs'. Pollard, in a survey of Oxford's medieval book-trade community in Catte Street, found that parchmeners were concentrated at an end of the street proximate to a gate in the city wall, so that they could practise their trade outside, away from residential areas.[42] (My first paying job was a city block west of a related, but distinct leather-craft profession, a tannery; one always hoped the wind was coming from the west.)

Medieval recipes for the process, which begins with raw skins, survive (e.g. Ivy, p. 35 [full reference at p. 9]). The skins must steep for about ten days in a lye bath (the truly stinky part of the procedure). Removed, they are scraped by the parchmener with a half-moon-shaped blade to remove the now-loosened hair and flesh. The stripped skins are then stretched on a frame, and stretched and scraped further until they are supple and have a relatively smooth surface. A final step involves 'pouncing', rubbing the skins with chalk; this fills in the pores, so that ink will not just 'bleed' on the writing surface.

That surface, even in the most finished examples, is not uniform. The sides of the skin vary in both colour and surface, depending on whether they they bore the animal's hair or were next to its flesh.

---

[42] 'Notes for a Directory of Cat Street, Oxford before A.D. 1500', BodL, MS Pollard 168, passim.

With the customary inventiveness of palaeographers, these are known as the 'hair-side' and the 'flesh-side' of a sheet or leaf. The first is darker and often feels a bit sandy to the touch; the second brighter and smoother. Customarily in manuscripts this variation is muted; carefully produced books follow what is known, after its discoverer, as 'Gregory's rule'.[43] For copying, the sheets are arranged so that a hair-side always faces another hair-side, and vice versa; thus the reader is always looking at homogeneous openings and is not shocked by some alternation between dark and bright supports. Some copying centres are recognisable in arranging this alternation so that one of the sides is always on the outside of a textual unit; to aid in their identification, scrupulous cataloguers frequently identify their membrane as 'FSOS' (the flesh-side always on the outside of textual units) or the reverse 'HSOS' (the hair-side always outside).

Like everything else about manuscript production, parchment-making is a handicraft, and its products variable in quality. In part, this reflects the natural material and its imperfections. The skin may have blemishes – in essence, places where the animal was scarred.[44] In many MSS, the skin is marred by small holes (possibly from its stretching, not a mishap to the living beast). In many instances, the scribe writes around this gap; in others, it has been crudely sewn up before writing. And failures of the production process show through; on sloppily produced material, you'll have no trouble recognising a hair-side, because the membrane has been inadequately scraped, usually only near the edges, so that the hair follicles are immediately visible.

Two further notes on membrane. Preparation of this material is subject to local customs of production, often with distinctive effects. Continental scholars frequently express their distaste for insular membrane, often with good reason. Perhaps their kindest descriptor is 'suedey', and, certainly, the product contrasts sharply with often very slick and shiny Italian membrane. The distinctive quality of the insular product is of ancient standing; on its peculiarities, see T. Julian Brown, 'The Distribution and Significance of Membrane Prepared in

---

[43] From Gaspar R. Gregory, 'Les cahiers des manuscrits grecs', *Comptes rendus de l'Academie des inscriptions et belles-lettres* 29 (1885), 261–68.

[44] Cf. the discussion at *PH* 144–45, where a blemish on a constituent skin shows that an oddly disruptive bit of 'The Hengwrt *Canterbury Tales*' (Aberystwyth, National Library of Wales, MS Peniarth 392D [Hengwrt 154]) was produced by extracting leaves from elsewhere in the book.

the Insular Manner', *A Palaeographer's View: The Selected Writings* ... , ed. Janet Bately *et al.* (London, 1993), 125–39.

I have mentioned above some very thick small MSS of the whole Bible. This compact format was achieved by a very small script written on extremely thin membrane sheets. This support is often referred to as 'uterine vellum', on the assumption that there was a steady supply of aborted calves awaiting transformation into Holy Scripture. This is not the case; in addition to turning out normal full skins, parchmeners knew how to split skins into two layers to produce thinner sheets.[45]

A good deal of membrane is decidedly substandard, material never meant for formal use, but pressed into service for making a book anyway. Before going into a book, skins are customarily cut down to eliminate unserviceable portions, particularly those around the beast's limbs and belly. This is usually considered waste material, but, as Erik Kwakkel points out, was not infrequently used to produce formal volumes (a classic case is 'The *Orrmulum*'); see 'Discarded Parchment as Writing Support in English Manuscript Culture', *English Manuscript Studies* 17 (2012), 238–61; 'Classics on Scraps: Classical Manuscripts Made from Parchment Waste', *Manuscripts of the Latin Classics, 800–1200*, ed. Kwakkel (Leiden, 2015), 106–29.

Again, some membrane was apparently produced for everyday use, to make up informal legal rolls or documents (written on one side only) or for packaging. It's unduly thin, translucent, rather than opaque; as a result, writing on one side shows through on the other. However, one well-known scribe apparently collected such material, indeed even excised blank folios of it to save for later use; it appears frequently in his mixed version copy of *Piers Plowman*, Oxford, Corpus Christi College, MS 201. Similarly, a scribe apparently at Winchester Cathedral used a large stock of inferior stuff to complete the insertion of a copy of *The Prick of Conscience* into an already mostly completed MS on better material at BL, MS Sloane 2275, fols 169–83.

Far from all membrane is new. We tend to associate book destruction with the coming of print and the Reformation (and the later destruction of monastic culture). However, at various points libraries, which are never fixed entities, have recycled their contents and found some old books valuable only as support for new ones, washed the old text off the leaves, and imposed on them a new text. (You'll recall another example of such efforts at collection management from the discarded book used

---

[45] See the discussion at Elizabeth Solopova, ed., *The Wycliffite Bible: Origin, History and Interpretation* (Leiden, 2017), 248–49.

to make the wrapper of SJ 39, p. 20.) The result is a book with two layers of script, called a palimpsest (and the original, now lower, layer of writing is said to have been 'palimpsested').

A classical example brought this phenomenon to attention. In his effort to present himself as the Roman Plato, Cicero had written a *Republic*, *De re publica*. A portion of the book, but only a small portion, Cicero's riff on the climactic 'dream of Er', was a well-known medieval text, the subject of Macrobius's commentary (and a routine source of information about dreams). The remainder of the text, like much classical literature, was pronounced 'lost'. So matters remained until 1819, when the prefect of the Vatican Library, Angelo Mai, found large portions of *De re publica*, copied s. iv, in MS Vaticanus latinus 5757. It was under a text of Augustine's *Enarrationes in Psalmos*, imposed at Bobbio, a monastery outside Milan, s. vii/viii.[46]

Palimpsesting was especially prominent in the Greek world, where Byzantine scribes recycled classical texts as support for Christian ones. For a recently prominent example, involving the recovery of important scientific texts and Athenian orations (as well as the considerable scientific expertise required to decipher the lower text), see Reviel Netz and William Noel, *The Archimedes Codex: Revealing the Secrets of the World's Greatest Palimpsest* (London, 2007) (the popular version), as well as an edition, with a facsimile, under special lighting conditions, ed. Netz, 2 vols (Cambridge, 2011). Similarly, an important early MS of Virgil, Verona, Biblioteca capitolare, XL (*olim* 38), s. v ex., with extremely interesting annotations, was palimpsested at Luxueil in Burgundy, s. vii/viii, the upper text here Gregory the Great's *Moralia in Iob*.[47] For general accounts of the phenomenon see E. A. Lowe, 'Codices Rescripti. A list of the oldest Latin palimpsests with stray observations on their origin', *Palaeographical Papers, 1907–1965*, 2 vols (Oxford, 1972), 2:480–519; and Georges Declercq, ed., *Early Medieval Palimpsests* (Turnhout, 2007).

However, palimpsesting is scarcely foreign to English MS culture. Neil Ker discusses an outstanding early example at 'A Palimpsest in the National Library of Scotland … ', coll 121–30; and Cambridge, Jesus College, has two examples from Durham Cathedral Priory. MS Q.A.15 (James 15), Peter Lombard, *Sententiae*, s. xiv, is partly over

---

[46] For an image, see Ehrle–Liebaert, plate 4, and the discussion at xv–xvi (full reference at p. 70).

[47] The 'scholia Veronensia' are partially ed. Aldo Lunelli, 'Scholiorum in Vergilium Veronensium reliquiae: notizie degli scavi, edizione provvisoria … ', *Maia* 53 (2001), 63–131; 55 (2003), 5–83.

leaves from Ælfric's *Catholic Homilies*, s. xi. The book is described by Ker, *A Catalogue of Manuscripts Containing Anglo-Saxon* (Oxford, 1957, 1990), 123–24, and there is a facsimile, *Anglo-Saxon Manuscripts in Microfiche Facsimile: Volume 16 Manuscripts Relating to Dunstan, Ælfric, and Wulfstan* ... , ed. Peter J. Lucas and Jonathan Wilcox, MRTS 343 (Tempe AZ, 2008), 5–13, with images. MS Q.B.12 (James 29), the canon law collection *Clementinae*, s. xv in., is on washed leaves of a book twice the size, folded across their centre and rewritten across the original long dimensions of the leaf over (apparently) theology, s. xiii ex., in a very small academic script suggestive of Durham College, Oxford provenance.[48] In addition, another Durham book, MS Q.A.14 (James 15), uses washed leaves from a slightly earlier Bede MS, s. xii, as flyleaves.

Paper

Paper, like nearly everything else, was invented by the Chinese; it appears in Europe, the end of the Silk Road trade route, only at the end of the thirteenth century. It becomes a widespread form of manuscript support during the fifteenth. The best brief introduction, although in a book about print culture, is Philip Gaskell, 'Paper', *A New Introduction to Bibliography* (Oxford, 1972, 1974), 57–77.[49] Gaskell is particularly valuable for his descriptions of producing traditional 'rag paper' from cloth waste dissolved in water, of the mould that takes up this soup as sheets, of the impressions the mould leaves on the sheets produced (most particularly watermarks), of the sizes of sheet produced, and of the ways in which these are customarily folded to produce books. There you'll find, for example, that, like membrane, paper has sides, conventionally called Z (zugewandt)/'mould-side' and A (abgewandt)/'felt-side', depending on which side of the sheet was immediately in contact with the paper mould.

---

[48] A few additional examples: the very early Virgil commentary of Aemilius Asper, Paris, Bibliothèque nationale, MS lat. 12161, appears as four folios palimpsest, s. v?, from Italy or southern France; the upper text, Jerome and Gennadius's bibliographies, was imposed at Corbie (near Amiens), s. vii/viii. A later Italian example, in this case a religious text subordinated to a secular one, appears at Magd lat. 51, fols 128–29 (Constantine the African, *Pantegny*, s. xii med.), apparently over an earlier s. xii liturgical manuscript.

[49] See further Alan H. Stevenson's classic essays, 'Watermarks are Twins', *Studies in Bibliography* 4 (1951–52), 57–91; and 'Paper as Bibliographical Evidence', *The Library* 5th ser. 17 (1962), 197–212.

In looking at a book produced on paper, your most important task is finding the trademarks or advertising that individual paper-mills built into their products through a metal emblem attached to the mould, the watermark. You have to do two things: as you go through the book, first identify all those leaves with watermarks and record their foliation. These marks will appear, if present (some paper lacks watermark), if you shine a light through the leaf from behind; they typically show up as bright lines that stand out from a relatively brownish background. In addition to the mark, you will see other bright lines imposed by the paper-mould during manufacture: heavy lines, called 'chain lines', and fine ones, like window screening, called 'wire lines'. To keep track of things, as a preliminary, I usually assign each distinct mark I see a letter, 'A, B, C, etc.'.

You must then trace or sketch each mark carefully. In sketching the mark, it is important that you indicate its relationship to the heavy chain lines (is it between them? affixed to one of them?). This sketching will present difficulties: books in large format typically are made by folding a sheet of paper once ('folded in folio'); in this situation, the chain lines will run vertically and the watermark will appear on half the leaves, at the centre of the page. However, in smaller books, you will probably never see the complete watermark. If the sheet of paper has been folded twice ('quarto fold'), the chain lines will run horizontally, and the watermark will be in the gutter, the inner margin by the book's spine. Again, half the folios will be marked, but each marked folio will have only half the mark, with a certain amount buried in the binding. You'll thus have to exercise your jigsaw puzzle skills to figure out how to join the two 'partial halves' you have sketched. A third fold ('octavo') providentially occurs much less frequently than the others; in it, chain lines again appear vertically, but the watermarks will appear, again on half the sheets, as one quarter of the full mark, typically at either the head or foot of the gutter. See Gaskell's unusually helpful illustrations: figures 46–47 and 50 (pp. 88–89, 92).

You must then try to identify the mark you are looking at, a two-stage procedure. Here your guides are the two great catalogues of early watermarks:

Briquet = C.-M. Briquet, *Les filigranes: dictionnaire historique des marques du papier dès leur apparition vers 1282 jusqu'en 1600*, rev. edn, ed. Allan Stevenson, 4 vols (Amsterdam, 1968). The collection is now online at https://briquet-online.at.

Piccard = Gerhard Piccard, a sequence of volumes, all the titles beginning *Wasserzeichen* ... , with a general series title *Der Wasserzeichenkartei Piccard im Hauptstaatsarchiv Stuttgart: Findbuch*, 17 vols in 25 (Stuttgart, 1961–97). At this point print publication ceased and the collection, a good deal more extensive than what was available in print, was put online; see Peter Rückert et al., *Piccard-Online: digitale Präsentionen von Wasserzeichen und ihre Nutzung* (Stuttgart, 2007), and https://piccard-online.de.

On the whole, one should prefer Piccard, who examined a substantially larger sample of more carefully identified examples; however, Briquet remains useful, particularly for marks Piccard did not survey. Both are regularly cited by the number assigned a watermark in their respective catalogues. You may also wish to consult Edward Heawood, 'Sources of Early English Paper Supply', *The Library* 4th ser. 10 (1929–30), 282–307, 427–54; and, much more generally, R. J. Lyall, 'Materials: the paper revolution', GP 11–29. All these collections share a similar debility: like the tracings or sketches you are making, they are handmade representations only, and subject to all the vicissitudes one might expect. The only certain way of identifying a watermark exactly is by comparison of photographic images, an expensive (and thus not widely used) technique called beta-radiography.

In both catalogues watermarks are presented in a classified order. This follows conventional names given to each image, as if they were pictures, and the names vary by the language of the researcher. It may require some imagination to discover where either Piccard (in German) or Briquet (in French) has placed the relevant images. I recall once asking Jean-Pierre Maillon, the ruler of Bodley's Duke Humfrey's Library, what he would call in French an image (a bunch of berries) I had traced from a MS.

You then need to do the best you can, comparing your tracing(s) with those in the catalogues of examples. Once you believe you have identified a matching image, you must then find Briquet or Piccard's discussion of it. In both catalogues, the images appear separately from these discussions: in a separate volume of Briquet; at the head of the individual fascicle in Piccard. The discussions rely upon the fact that paper had many uses besides making manuscripts. Most helpfully for your purposes, it was increasingly the customary support for archival materials. Thus, individual paperstocks are routinely datable and localisable on the basis of the legal documents written on them. In addition, Piccard, in particular, often offers suggestions as to the location of the mill where the product was produced. However, you should be warned: identifying the mark and finding the images often produces only information vague or conflicting, because many commonplace stocks prove to be undatable. Types such as Mountains/ Monts/Dreiberg, Bull's head/Tête de beouf/Ochsenkopf, Scales/ Balance/Waage, among many others, were used, in similar forms, by a great many paper manufacturers and over many decades.

However, in a reasonable number of cases watermarks may very accurately identify the age of the book you are examining. A number of scribes date their work of copying a book, usually its completion. When they are copying on paper, their subscriptions often show a close correlation with what one might guess from identifying the material on which they wrote. Consider four examples:

SJ 40, written in Italy, is dated 25 May 1500; the paper, part certainly from north-east Italy, is from 1496×99 (catalogue 58–59);

SJ 64, written in the Netherlands, is dated 9 October 1414; the paper, two distinctive stocks, is recorded only in the Netherlands 1408×14 (85–86);[50]

SJ 80, a student notebook probably from Paris, at one point is dated 27 May 1507; the paper is French and perhaps specifically Parisian, dated 1504×14 (107–9); and

SJ 97: an index from Durham, dated 29 November 1532; the paper is Norman, datable 1524×26 (133–34).

One should notice that all these books are relatively late and three of them continental. English scribes are generally reluctant to date anything, even in s. xv (and it had not been normal in legal documents, where one might have thought it significant, until the mid-thirteenth century).

Catalogues of dated manuscripts, of which more below (pp. 68–70), are categorised by pragmatic literalism. They rely upon

---

[50] Rather than '9 October', the MS itself reads 'in festo dyonisii et sociorum eius martirum sanctorum'. You should be aware of a standard guide for deciphering little riddles like these: C. R. Cheney, rev. Michael Jones, *A Handbook of Dates for Students of British History*, Royal Historical Society Guides and Handbooks 4 (Cambridge, 2000), here at 70.

explicit statement or a narrowly inferred account of date. The one thing they do *not* rely upon is paper information. But, as Jean Irigoin, 'La datation par les filigranes du papier', *Codicologica* 5 (1980), 9–36, points out, many manuscripts on paper with no explicit dating information may be dated just as or more narrowly than 'datable manuscripts'. To do so depends on a conjunction of several factors: your ability to identify a precise watermark, significantly aided in the case of distinctive marks (as with SJ 64 above); and the scribe's use of multiple paperstocks. Because multiple, these will predictably reflect different dates of recorded use, and the manuscript should logically fall within a time-span in which these overlap. On that basis, undated manuscripts where paperstocks would indicate a narrow window of copying include:

SJ 54, fols 1–48: 1410×12 (catalogue 72); SJ 56: early 1450s (74); SJ 69: late 1430s (92); SJ 141: early 1430s (204); and SJ 147: later 1450s or 1460s (208–09).

SJ 266 is a particularly pregnant case: the paper can be dated 1475×82 (catalogue 329), and the manuscript appears always to have been bound with printed books, works produced by William Caxton, England's first printer, in 1483. As we'll see below (pp. 97–99), dating does not exhaust the usefulness of paper.

I have described membrane and paper as if they were antithetical. However, particularly in s. xv, they appear together in books, in examples of what one might call 'mixed support'. This probably occurs as a result of paper's relative fragility – the fact that, unlike membrane, it tears easily – and the consequent difficulty of ensuring that paper leaves will remain intact in a binding. (Generally descriptions ignore a more peripheral but easier mixture that achieves the same goal, strengthening the sewing imposed on paper leaves with strips of membrane.)[51] Although other combinations occur with some frequency, there is what one may call a 'normal fold' in these 'mixed support' books. This uses

---

[51] Nonetheless, when you see these, you should always open them out. Most of the time, they come from discarded legal texts, deeds, inventories, accounts, etc. (not entirely a waste, potentially useful for provenance, discussed pp. 113ff.). However, HEH, EL 26 A 13, a John Shirley book, has one such strip with an entry from an itinerary paralleled in Wynkyn de Worde's *Information for pilgrims to the holy land* (printed c. 1500), and would direct you to a large literature on the Jerusalem tourist trade.

membrane sheets as a kind of 'mini-binding'; they form the centre and outside surround of a group of paper leaves.

Where's the first leaf?

Now that you're ready to open the book, you'll turn immediately to see if you can find the first text leaf. Hopefully, everything you see preceding it can be explained as extraneous, a leaf that can be associated with that final supererogatory act, binding the book. However, for example, at the head of ChCh Allestree L.4.1, there's a blank leaf that's actually not from the binder, but a covering protector for the opening text leaf, and thus integral with the following text. But, generally, the first leaf with formal text will be the first leaf of the book proper, and aberrant examples will be clearly evident to you at a later stage (see pp. 90–91.).

The first thing you must do is to ensure that this leaf is numbered fol. 1 (most typically in pencil in the upper right corner). Check the other side of the leaf as well: ensure that this is not the beginning of a pagination, numbered by the side. If it isn't, the MS has been 'foliated', numbered only on the 'recto', the right-hand sheet when the book is opened; to identify the reverse/back of the leaf, use 'verso' (literally 'turned over', Latin *versus*). (In references, they are abbreviated as fol. 1r and 1v, the 'r' and 'v' often in superscript, and, like many authors, I use the unqualified 'fol. 1' to mean the recto and specifically mark only versos.) This foliation has usually been imposed by the library where the book now resides, and there may be older cancelled foliations, which you should notice, particularly if they appear medieval. However, the library's current foliation is the guide you must follow in all your references, and you must never change it in the book (because doing so will render all past references confusingly inaccurate).

Following received manuscript foliation does involve problems, because, from a medieval book perspective, this numeration is nearly always incorrect. Received foliations are usually wrong for two reasons: (a) library conventions; and (b) numbering leaves is a boring business and one people don't always do with care – they skip leaves, repeat or skip numbers. So far as the first is concerned, individual libraries have followed differing conventions for foliation. Merely a rough guide: BL assigns a number to every leaf with writing, regardless of origin and date, thus regularly including front binding leaves in the count;[52] BodL (and Oxford libraries generally) regularly ignores front binding leaves, or assigns them roman foliation, never numbers a blank leaf, but also numbers every leaf to the end of the book, thus regularly including rear binding leaves in the count; CUL assigns foliation to leaves now lost but presumed to have been once present.

A particularly egregious example: Magd lat. 162 is foliated in a modern hand ii (as usual, these are the leaves associated with binding) + 1–246 (and on to fol. 252, to accommodate the rear binding leaves, as is this library's usual Oxford practice). However, in gross, its text portions (not fols i–ii + 247–52), foliated as 246 leaves, actually total 258. The book, a collection of tracts on university logic, was put together by a team of scribes, s. xv med., and is a loose conjunction of six separate units (a topic that will occupy us at some length below, pp. 102–04). At the end of each of these, the scribe, having finished that portion (apparently one assigned him by the team), simply left the rest of his leaves blank. Following Oxford convention, these are unnumbered and have to be indicated by appended asterisks. Thus, there are both fols 19 and 19*, 76 and 76*–76******* (i.e. a succession of eight [!] blank leaves), 165 and 165*–165***, 182 and 182*. Just to add to the potential confusion, the person who foliated the book skipped '21' and jumped in their numeration from fol. 20 to fol. 22.

These unfoliated examples are the concluding leaves of their segments. This indicates that, just as you must separate out at the head of the book leaves associated with binding, you must equally attend to the foliation imposed by the library at the manuscript's end. Persistently, the foliation of SJ manuscripts simply ignores blank leaves in this position; it thus implicitly treats portions of the book proper as if they represented binding materials, flyleaves; for examples, see SJ 53, 66B, 87, etc.

As you run through the book, you must keep track of foliation. Generally, you should expect to check every eight leaves (for the reason, see pp. 89–91). Ensure your total corresponds to the current imposed

---

[52] In Cotton MSS, quite routinely, his librarian, Richard James's notation of the contents on a flyleaf, e.g. MS Cleopatra C.ix, where the leaf is assigned fol. 1. MS Vespasian E.iii has three vellum flyleaves, assigned fols 1–3, with a table of contents for the whole volume, in James's hand (fol. 2), and at the top of fol. 1, rendering this a leaf requiring foliation in the BL system, Cotton's instructions to his binder, 'Bind this book very hansomly vp and cut it as litle on the head as you cane and bottome; sett the last part shorte at the head, then the rest; lett it be strong bound vp'.

folio number: so, for example, if the last time you checked was eight leaves ago, you should be looking at that folio number plus eight.

The current library foliation may not be the only one you spot on offer. These earlier foliations have been rejected by the library, and you shouldn't follow them in referring to the book. But you should note them; especially important are any original or early ones, since they may indicate that the contents of the book have changed or been reordered at some point in its history.[53] One particular system you might look out for: a number of Oxford manuscripts (and manuscripts of Oxford scholars who have returned to their monastic houses) include an unusual system. They number the columns (occasionally the leaves or pages) of the manuscript in arabic and provide arabic line-numeration, usually every five lines. This system was first identified by Franz Pelster, 'Das Leben und die Schriften des Oxford Dominikaners Richard Fishacre (+ 1248)', *Zeitschrift für katholische Theologie* 54 (1930), 518–53 (note especially 522 n.2), but there are many more examples.

Having found the first text leaf, you should also remember to turn over and record the first words at the head of the second leaf. In manuscript catalogues, this is routinely referred to as the '2° fo', '[the opening to] the second leaf'. Its medieval title was 'dicta probatoria' (the words that give evidence [of ownership]). Medieval librarians considered that one could distinguish even copies of the same text by how much material a scribe had managed to include on the first leaf; they thus identified volumes as 'theirs' by noting in their collection catalogues the opening words of the second text leaf. Cf. SJ 1, where the second-folio opening 'ista omnia' corresponds to no. 13 in a Reading Abbey booklist of s. xiv ex.[54] For further discussion, see James Willoughby, 'The *Secundo Folio* and its Uses, Medieval and Modern', *The Library* 7th ser. 12 (2011), 237–58.

---

[53] For example, medieval roman foliation appears on rectos in SJ 18, 61, 197, 265; arabic foliation in SJ 29 (several sequences), 36, 45, 65, and two sets in 97. SJ 203 has foliations and paginations in both arabic and roman, showing that constituent fragments of the book have been re-ordered. Frequently, medieval 'foliation' appears on versos and covers 'the opening' (i.e. the verso and its facing recto); examples appear in SJ 11; Cambridge, Sidney Sussex College, MS 85; and in 'The Vernon MS' (where they are all roman).

[54] This catalogue also appears in a book at SJ, MS 11, fol. 3 = the booklist designated B74 in the Corpus, printed in the fourth in that series, Richard Sharpe et al., eds, *English Benedictine Libraries: The Shorter Catalogues* (London, 1996), 451–53.

What does the first leaf look like?

Patience is a palaeographic virtue. Rather than follow your immediate first impulse and begin to read, look at the format of the first page, its 'ordinatio'. Attention to this combination of features, the layout or the mise-en-page of a book, is due to Parkes's seminal essay, 'The Influence of the Concepts of Ordinatio and Compilatio on the Development of the Book', coll 35–70. Whatever qualifications one might wish to introduce,[55] Parkes identified an important watershed in book production. His emphasis upon the divided and directive, consultable page corresponds, as we will see repeatedly, to a major shift in production – the movement, from the last third of the twelfth century, of active and prominent book production out of monasteries, where it had been before, and into commercial, and particularly (Parkes's major interest) university, environments.

The first page of a manuscript is customarily the most ornately decorated, but it is also the visual template that's going to guide you in your examination of the book. Your initial hope is that the presentation of the text(s) is going to be more or less consistent throughout; thus, as you are examining the book leaf by leaf, you will achieve a rhythm of inspection – the awareness that this opening is essentially repetitive, that it includes those elements that you recognise from all the preceding openings you have examined. You will then be attuned to visual shocks and difference, and will notice these, identify and record them, and think further about them.

In what follows, you will have to excuse one, perhaps unfortunate, part of my upbringing. While I never made the full jump to iconoclast, I was certainly raised an iconophobe, someone who believes that The Word matters a great deal more than an image, because intellectually, rather than just decoratively, engaging. At times, and maybe even here, I've overcompensated, worried a great deal more about incidental textual marking than many colleagues (who have occasionally remarked negatively on this attentiveness).

Unlike most printed books (where it is avoided, because it requires multiple impressions of the same sheet), manuscripts, even the most informal, are typically polychrome, marked by colour. However, a great many books were prepared for such treatment where it was never

---

[55] See the Rouses, reference at BH 37 n.20.

completed. One can watch the process in two manuscripts handled by the scribe, translator, and book-owner Michel of Northgate (d. shortly after 1340). In CUL, MS Ii.1.15, fols 20^v–39, a MS he inherited or purchased, although chapters were divided from one another, they had not been given headings or titles. These headings Michel supplied, in an informal hand at the feet of the leaves, an example of what are called 'guides' – i.e. instructions for filling in an absent element. However, in Oxford, Corpus Christi College, MS 221, fols 1–68, Michel copied the full text – except for the chapter headings, which again he noted, in the same ink as the text, here in the margins. He then apparently went back through his copy and copied the marginalia in red ink in the appropriate blank spaces he had left for them, following his guides.

This example shows that print-book reluctance to engage in double-inking/-impression of a page accords with MS practice. Because it is potentially a considerable mess to switch inks (and probably pens as well), the polychrome process is separate from the copying. It thus is frequently referred to as 'finishing', an extraneous operation that need never be completed. Michel's example certainly shows that a practised scribe could provide much of the basics in these situations, but more frequently blank spaces with 'guides' have been left by the scribe for someone else, a specialist. Such a person may never have appeared to 'finish' the book, for the operation requires extra expenditure (and a book with marked 'guides' is perfectly legible).[56]

Evidence for such second- or other-hand specialist ministrations occurs with some frequency. It appears as counts for payment – supplying decorative initials at text breaks at one costing, supplying coloured punctuation at a different one – at intervals (or as a single *summa totalis*) in surviving books. Reasonably full sets, often placed low on the verso of a leaf, and thus often cut into or away by a binder, survive in SJ 31 and 202, and there is a summary set of such notes at Cambridge, Pembroke College, MS 121, fol. 215^v; at Magd lat. 35, fol. 236; and two such in ChCh MS 340 (pp. 116, 348). A note in HEH, MS HU 1051, fol. 48, s. xv ex., indicates not only grading of decoration but that, the bigger your order, the better your wholesale rate ('c' and 'm^1', of course, represent the roman '100' and '1000'):

---

[56] Examples are utterly ubiquitous, e.g. blanks for headings in SJ 102, 139, and 158; blank headings but surviving guides in SJ 26, 59, and 153, ChCh 99; guide letters for unfilled initials in SJ 132 and 154. In ChCh 92, a MS with elaborate heraldic illumination, guides for the illuminators were washed out after the work was completed.

S[m]all lettris blew and rede: the c at i d., a m¹ vi d.

Small lettris blew and rede florisshid: precium c ij d., a m¹ × d.

Small lettris gold and blew florishid: þe c iiij d., a m¹ xij d.

Just as these accounts for directive decoration, 'guides', customarily provided in greyish lead, show gradation. Instructions for headings necessarily are provided in full; spaces for large initials, used to mark off chapters or other segments, while blank, often include (or include in a nearby margin) a notation of the letter to be provided. Finally, punctuational marking, typically the sign '⁋' (a 'paragraphus' or 'paraph'), is signalled by a double solidus, '//'.[57]

Parkes's study of *ordinatio* draws attention to the increasingly segmented presentation of texts by means of, for example, narrower divisions into books and chapters. These divisions are routinely signalled, as Dan Michel did, by headings, frequently presented in red ink, and thus often called 'rubrics' (Latin *ruber* 'red'). Such headings are frequently set off not just by colour but by script. Because they should attract the eye searching for a reference, rubrics frequently follow a rule called 'hierarchy of script': that some forms of writing are, as it were, 'nobler' than others and should be reserved for special use. And, even where the script does not differ in type from that of the text, rubrics often show a more formal version of the text-hand.

One example will illustrate both 'hierarchy of script' and the great divide signalled in Parkes's study. When insular scribes came to write, the Irish in s. vi, the English from s. vii in., they fashioned their normal writing hand from the available Roman models in imported books. Their distinctive script was a formalised version of a Roman document script with clubbed or spatulate ascenders.[58] But even as

---

[57] On punctuation, see p. 75. As Parkes points out, the sign '⁋' is derived from the reversed letter 'K', an abbreviation for 'kapitulum', used in Roman manuscripts to mark the beginning of a 'colon', an extended clause.

[58] This is an example of the Parkesian maxim, actually a citation from E. A. Lowe, 'Scripts are always recruited from below', i.e. new scripts are predicated on hands originally informal and subsequently 'upgraded' into more presentable forms for MS use. The first image I saw of the 'inscribed strip' from the Staffordshire Hoard, although inscribed, rather than penned, was immediately identifiable on the basis of its ascenders as a very early example, s. vii (Stoke-on-Trent, Potteries Museum and Art Gallery, K550).

they adopted this relatively informal hand for book use, early scribes were apparently fascinated by the range of now extinct scripts they saw in Roman manuscripts. These they adopted as decorative features, particularly for rubrics. One such styling, in the Roman script called 'rustic capitals', survived well into s. xii – but no longer. At St John's, with a large population of s. xii books, many explicitly monastic products, you can see these as the normal script of headings in MSS 17, 28 (s. x^2), 38, 63, 89, etc.

Another, rather more flamboyant example of such marking is what is known as 'the diminuendo opening'. If you put 'cathach of St Columba' (mentioned in n.35) into your internet browser, you can go immediately to an image displaying the technique. At the head of Psalm 90 there appears a sequence of letters in variously alien scripts, steadily diminishing from a large initial down to an example roughly the size of the text hand. While pure diminuendo openings don't survive s. ix, similarly decorative openings have a long history in insular MSS. (See further p. 52.)

Along with rubrics, textual segments are customarily introduced by inked or painted initials, in varying colours and sizes. These constitute perhaps the most ubiquitous decoration in manuscripts, even in amateurish productions. There often awkward examples appear in the hand of the scribe (not a hired-in professional) in red ink or, more crudely, simply the ink of the text. A good example would be the rather slapdash, and perhaps amateur, rendition of the Wycliffite Pauline epistles in BodL, MS Dugdale 46.[59]

Initials represent another area in which s. xii/xiii marks a great divide. Before that date, the most usual palette for MS decoration is green and red; the large initials marking textual segments often alternate between initials in these colours, as in SJ 183, Magd lat. 19 and lat. 40. Moreover, the initials themselves are curvy allusions to vines or leaves, shapes generally described as 'arabesque initials', an allusion to their origins in Islamic decoration.[60] One can see examples in SJ 17, 38, 46, and

---

[59] See Elizabeth Solopova, *Manuscripts of the Wycliffite Bible in the Bodleian and Oxford College Libraries* (Liverpool, 2016), 131–34 and Plate 9, following 76.

[60] 'Arabesque' should remind you that cultural interchanges over what seem to us improbable distances were reasonably commonplace from a very early date. The 'Faddan More Psalter', in the National Museum of Ireland, includes Egyptian papyrus in its binding and, similarly, the nearest analogues to some border decoration in the famous 'Book of Kells' (Dublin, Trinity College, MS 58) can be found in Coptic MSS.

51.⁶¹ In ChCh 341, a very late example (1196–97), the colours persist, but the initials themselves follow the style that will become prominent in s. xiii and later. Conversely, the contemporary Magd lat. 8 and 22, the first possibly French, retain arabesque forms, but in the palette I will describe as characteristic of s. xiii. Although red and green tend to dominate in these books, their palette is frequently much broader than in later centuries: arabesque initials in a wide range of colours – not just red and/or green, but also gold, slaty blue, or violet; such diversely coloured examples appear in SJ 95, 96, and 128, or ChCh 88.

From around 1200, decoration of this sort becomes much less artistic, flamboyant, and various. From that date, the palette is reduced, and red and blue, together or in alternation, are almost universal. And the sweeps and swirls of arabesque initials are replaced by a much blockier form, usually called a 'lombard' or 'lombardic initial'. The most ubiquitous example of such formatting occurs in the widely distributed 'pocket Bibles' I have mentioned above (p. 17). While these MSS often have painted initials at the heads of books, elsewhere colour is standardised: three-line-high blue lombards at the openings of chapters, generally with some red decoration ('flourishing'; see the next paragraph); roman chapter numbers, either marginally or set into the text, in small alternating red and blue lombards; the same alternating lombards in the running titles across each opening (identifying the biblical book and enabling the user to find their place quickly).

What does not change at this divide are the basic principles at issue. Directive colouring is always, as the account I have cited from HU 1051 suggests, graded, first by size (how many text-lines high is the initial?), second by degree of elaboration. The first indicates the prominence of the division signalled: larger at the head of major units like books, decreasing in size for chapters or subordinate units. The latter concerns a feature highlighted in HU 1051, added 'flourishing', the provision of penwork allusions to leaves, vines, or flowers that surround the lombards or coloured paraphs, usually in a contrasting colour.⁶²

---

⁶¹ And Richard Gameson, *The Earliest Books of Canterbury Cathedral: Manuscripts and Fragments to c. 1200* (London, 2008), 150–51 (Cathedral, MS Add. 172, s. xi^{4/4}).

⁶² Flourishing and its elaboration are clearly important, but have yet to attract much scholarly attention; see, however, Sonia Scott-Fleming, *The Analysis of Pen-Flourishing in Thirteenth-Century Manuscripts* (Leiden, 1989); A. I. Doyle, 'Penwork Flourishing of Initials in England from c. 1380', *Tributes to Kathleen L. Scott: English Medieval Manuscripts: Readers, Makers and Illuminators*, ed.

At the bottom end of the scale, one finds red lombards, potentially provided by the scribe, since he will have had this ink for his rubrics. But most usually lombards are in blue ink, occasionally particoloured, half the initial in red and half in blue; on many occasions, this colouring is reserved for larger initials at major divisions. Quite routinely, the single-coloured lombards appear in alternation (as red and green had done in s. xii arabesques), one division in blue, the next in red, and so on. While these indicate divisions, they are not particularly decorative. That function is provided by the penwork flourishing for which HU 1051 would charge extra. This is almost universally contrasting with the colour of the initial; in the most routine examples, blue lombards have red flourishing and red ones have blue flourishing (or, occasionally, a practice thought to be 'northern', red lombards with violet flourishing). The large or particoloured examples at openings may be further set off by multicoloured flourishing, both red and blue, sometimes even a splash of violet.

This same grading and colour-scheme appears within the text. There is a routine effort at breaking textual expanses into variously consumable units, not necessarily equivalent to modern sentences but rhetorical *cola*, clauses. In more down-market productions, these divisions are marked by 'slashed initials' at the heads of units, the text-hand capital highlighted by a drop of coloured ink, most conventionally red, as in many Bibles, but in s. xv, often 'ochre' (a rather disgusting yellowish brown pigment). Much more frequent are coloured paraphs, in less formal examples all red, in the more normative case the same red–blue alternation one sees in the lombards used to divide textual units. In many books with formal pretensions, these, just as the lombards, are flourished. Most usually, these echo the flourishing of lombards, the paraph in one colour, the flourishing in another. But often they are a good deal more elegant: red examples flourished in purple, or the blue with red flourishing alternating, as HU 1051 indicates, with gold-leaf paraphs flourished in navy ink.[63]

Marleen V. Hennessy (London, 2009), 65–72; and, on an important English book, Timothy A. Shonk, 'Paraphs, Piecework, and Presentation: The Production Methods of Auchinleck Revisited', *The Auchinleck Manuscript: New Perspectives*, ed. Susanna Fein (Woodbridge, 2016), 176–94.

[63] As in Yale UL, MS Osborn fa.54 ('The Heneage MS'), a particularly ornate presentation of its texts, here Latin works of Richard Rolle, the cover illustration of Publications of the Journal of Medieval Latin 13. Comparable examples appear in ChCh 87 and 94.

I mentioned above diminuendo openings and their persistence in English MS culture. Very often, particularly early on, it is not simply rubrics or initials that show analogous decorative patterns, but textual openings. At the opening of SJ 128 (an image as catalogue, Plate I, s. xii in.), there's a shockingly bright alternation of differently coloured lines of rustic capitals. And such openings, in a variety of script styles, persist: similar decoration in alternate coloured arabesques at SJ 34, ChCh 115, Magd lat. 17 and 105; in the ancient script called 'uncial' at SJ 149 (s. xii ex.), ChCh 95 (s. xii in.), Magd lat. 207 (s. xii^2); even the originally monumental/epigraphic 'Roman square capitals', at Canterbury Cathedral, MS Lit. A.8 (s. xi/xii, illustrated Richard Gameson, *Earliest Books*, 185).

While lacking anything like such bold colouring, such decorative reliance for textual materials remains commonplace as late as s. xviii. Here its home is in legal materials. The origin of this styling is in the decorative opening lines of charters from s. xiii ex., a style used as headings in the collection of statutes and tracts of ChCh 103 (s. xiii/xiv). Cardinal Thomas Wolsey's flamboyant foundation charter for Cardinal College (1525), ChCh 339, has enlarged decorative openings in gothic bookhand (what's colloquially considered 'Old English script'). Nor are late MSS entirely immune from such styling; in Magd lat. 141 (written in a plain cursive, c. 1430), early portions have opening lines of chapters in a formalised display form of the text script.

As I have said, when you look at the first leaf of a manuscript, you will see its decoration at its best and most elaborate. Beyond the kind of textual styling I have been describing, this may well include painted work, 'illumination', usually some variety of border and perhaps not just an inked-in lombard but a fully painted initial. At the most elaborate this may include not simply a representation of the text's initial letter but figural material, an 'inhabited' or 'historiated' initial, or an associated image, a 'miniature'. A good deal of this may be only workmanlike, but frequently painted openings were the place top-line medieval painters showed their stuff, and it is thus the province of specialists, art historians. For general introductions, see Christopher de Hamel, *A History of Illuminated Manuscripts* (Oxford, 1986, 1994); J. J. G. Alexander, *Medieval Illuminators and Their Methods of Work* (New Haven CT and London, 1992); and Stella Panayotova, ed., *The Art and Science of Illuminated Manuscripts: A Handbook* (London, 2020).

English painted borders are typically focussed by a bar of painting surrounding the text, elaborated by flower and leaf forms. They often

What does the first leaf look like? 53

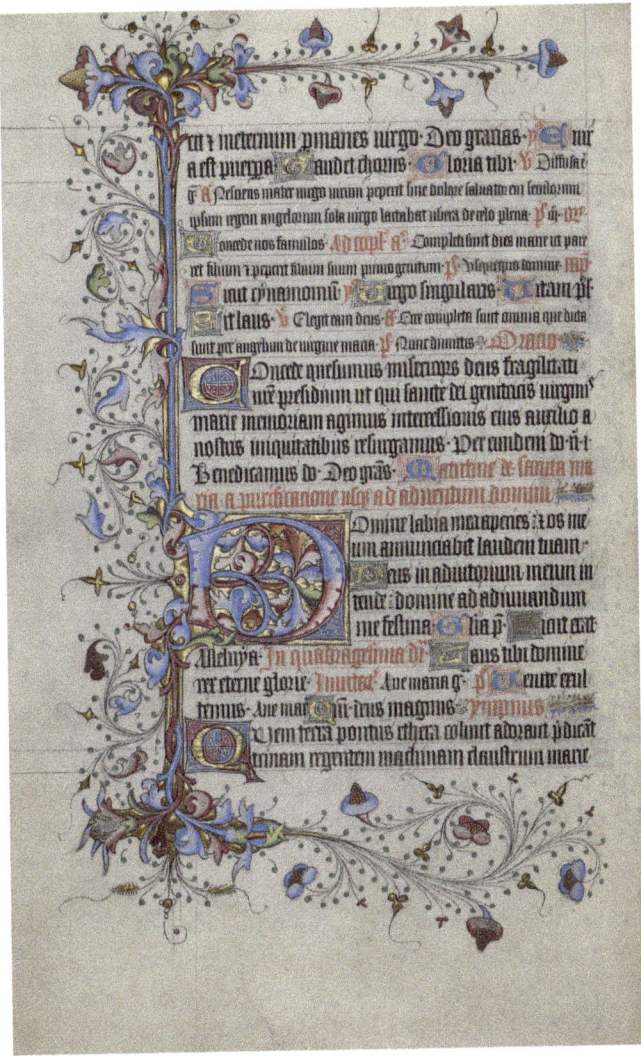

Decoration: This image comes from a psalter with liturgical offices, produced in London, s. xv in. The divine deserves the very best, and the page, with floral demivinet and a splash floral champ, does not disappoint. The page also demonstrates the customary decorative hierarchy: subsidiary larger divisions are marked by smaller, plainer champs – notice the reversed positions of painting and gold leaf – and divisions within the text by small lombards in alternate colours – blue and gold leaf – and with alternating flourishing – red and navy, respectively. This palette is repeated in the small blue and gold leaf line-fillers typical of psalters and books of hours, where no writing line is left incomplete. (Los Angeles, The Getty Museum, MS 17, fol. 100ᵛ, reproduced at 39%).

show elaborated knots at the corners and halfway along both the vertical and horizontal barlike shapes. Their palette is various, although, given the vegetative allusion, rather heavily green, but frequently including blue, gold leaf (see below), violet, and orange. Medieval illuminators called these borders 'vinets' and distinguished between examples that ran around all four borders, a 'vinet', and those that enclosed the text on only three sides (the leading edge blank and unpainted), a 'demivinet'. For a catalogue of examples, see Kathleen L. Scott, *Dated and Datable English Manuscript Borders, c. 1395–1499* (London, 2002).[64] Cheaper productions merely allude to the painted examples; most frequently, if they include borderwork at all, it is comprised of simple red and blue rectilinear segments.

Painted borders are regularly accompanied by painted initials, in the Middle Ages known as 'champs' ([painted] fields). These typically involve a combination of gold leaf with painting in magenta and blue, usually with further floral allusions and often a considerable amount of white highlighting. In this decoration, the gold leaf goes on the page first: a thin sheet is pasted on with a glue made from egg-white (called 'gleyre'). In perhaps the majority of examples, the initial itself is formed in the gold, and the magenta and blue, typically half the 'field' for each, provide a floral background. Frequently, however, the reverse is the case – the initial painted as a split field of magenta and blue, the gold leaf providing a background. You can get a pretty good idea of the options by scanning London, Lambeth Palace Library, MS 330, which contains 36 examples, no two of them identical.

Frequently, such initials at the openings of texts include, as I have said, figural representations. These often include self-referential images of the book itself: the author at work in composition, the scribe at work copying, or the author presenting his completed book to a patron. There's an example in SJ 78 (illustrated plate 16), and a pair of large presentation images, here Giles of Rome presenting his *De regimine principum* (the text is John Trevisa's English translation) to a king, in BodL, MS Digby 233.

Other illuminated initials are content-centred and highlight specific features of the text. Frequently, texts are not simply introduced by such

---

[64] And her discussion of the medieval terminology, 'Limning and Book-Producing Terms and Signs *in situ* in Late-Medieval English Manuscripts: A First Listing', *New Science out of Old Books: Studies in Manuscripts and Early Printed Books in Honour of A. I. Doyle*, ed. Richard Beadle and A. J. Piper (Aldershot, 1995), 142–88.

images, but present, at specified intervals, full illustrative cycles or programmes. Among common texts marked in this way is the psalter, where there is a reasonably fixed rota of illustrations at the divisions mandated by liturgical performance; you can see examples of the programme in SJ 293 (s. xv med.); or BodL, MS Bodley 953 (s. xiv/xv, a lectern-book, 380 mm × 260 mm, from the chapel at Berkeley Castle [Glos.]); or ChCh 98 (s. xiii ex., from St Omer, but in English hands very shortly after production).

A couple of grace notes, things to keep your eyes peeled for: in many cases, illumination is not thoroughly integral with the textual material it illustrates. 'Books of hours' conventionally have the illuminations at the opening of the 'Hours', the liturgical divisions, modelled on monastic practice, that make up a daily round of prayer. However, often these appear on inserted sheets, painted on one side, blank on the other, and intended to be inserted into the text block at appropriate points. In this instance, one probably is looking at mass-produced products, in which a basic text might be supplemented for buyers seeking devotional visual stimulation, for a fee. Similar insertions appear in the MS of *Sir Gawain and the Green Knight*, BL, MS Cotton Nero A.x, although here the illustrations were probably planned and the separation simply a question of the book's production in discrete chunks.

In a good many books illumination received special protection in the form of coverings to keep the painting pristine while the pages were turned. Such silk guards or curtains – or remnants of the sewing that held them in place on the leaf – appear, for example, in such glamorously illustrated MSS as Oxford, Keble College, MS 49 ('The Regensburg lectionary', s. xiii$^{3/4}$), or the extra-illustrated ChCh 92 (Walter Milemete's handbook for princes, 1327). Magd lat. 113 (Peter Lombard on the Psalter, Italian, s. xii ex.) still includes the curtain that protected an initial now excised at fol. 58vb. On the practice of silk guards generally, see Christine Sciacca, 'Raising the Curtain on the Use of Textiles in Manuscripts', *Weaving, Veiling, and Dressing: Cultural Approaches to Textiles and their Religious Functions in the Middle Ages*, ed. Kathryn M. Rudy and Barbara Baert, Medieval Church Studies 12 (Turnhout, 2007), 161–90.

You can get a good idea of the commoner illustrative options from the multi-volume survey, from s. vi to 1500, by various hands, general-edited by J. J. G. Alexander, *A Survey of Manuscripts Illuminated in the British Isles* (London, 1975–96). This series runs to 14 volumes in all, each of the seven eras surveyed presented in a paired set of detailed catalogue and numerous plates. Chronologically arranged, these will also highlight for you various picture-book crazes, such as illustrated Bestiaries, s. xiii in.; or illustrated Apocalypses, s. xiii² (and on into s. xiv); or sumptuous 'East Anglian' Psalters, s. xiv in.

More extensive materials appear in the indexes to painting in collections: the BL's annotated site for digitised manuscripts, https://www.bl.uk/catalogue/illuminatedmanuscripts/welcome.htm; Otto Pächt and J. J. G. Alexander, *Illuminated Manuscripts in the Bodleian Library, Oxford*, 3 vols (Oxford, 1966–73), with J. J. G. Alexander and Elźbieta Temple, *Illuminated Manuscripts in Oxford College Libraries, the University Archives and the Taylor Institution* (Oxford, 1985); Paul Binski and Stella Panayotova, *Western Illuminated Manuscripts: A Catalogue of the Collection in Cambridge University Library* (Cambridge, 2011); Nigel Morgan *et al.*, gen. eds, *Illuminated Manuscripts in Cambridge: A Catalogue of Western Book Illumination in the Fitzwilliam Museum and the Cambridge Colleges*, currently 8 vols (London, 2009–).

In this field, exhibition catalogues are often very useful. Examples include N. Thorp, *The Glory of the Page: Medieval and Renaissance Illuminated Manuscripts from Glasgow University Library* (London, 1987); François Avril and Patricia D. Stirnemann, *Manuscrits enluminés d'origine insulaire, V^e–XXe siècle* (Paris, 1987); Paul Binski and Stella Panayotova, *The Cambridge Illuminations: Ten Centuries of Book Production in the Medieval West* (Cambridge and London, 2005); Scott McKendrick *et al.*, *Royal Manuscripts: The Genius of Illumination* (London, 2011). Although scarcely limited to painting or, for that matter, to books, a great deal of information lurks in a sequence of catalogues exhibiting medieval English culture: Claire Breay and Joanna Story, eds, *Anglo-Saxon Kingdoms: Art, Word, War* (London, 2018); J. J. G. Alexander and Paul Binski, eds, *Age of Chivalry: Art in Plantagenet England, 1200–1400* (London, 1987); and Richard Marks *et al.*, eds, *Gothic: Art for England 1400–1547* (London, 2003).

Manuscripts also include a considerable variety of less formal illustrative material. Owners and users quite regularly leave drawings of variable quality and subject matter in the margins of books. The range runs from the elaborate memorials of the Norfolk Whetenhall family, among added flyleaf drawings and painting in BodL, MS Don. d.85 (Pächt and Alexander 3, no. 803 and plates 76–77), to what might charitably be described as 'doodles'. For example, ChCh Allestree F.1.1, a sober copy of Bernard of Clairvaux's sermons, acquired sketches of horses, human heads and faces, and flowers, s. xiii. A recent catalogue unusually treats all illustrative material as if equal, and thus chronicles a great deal of this informal illustration: Anne E. Nichols *et al.*, *An*

Index of Images in English Manuscripts ... c. 1380–c. 1509. Bodleian Library, Oxford, 3 vols (Turnhout, 2000–02).

A great deal of painted decoration now survives apart from its original surroundings. You cannot read an auction catalogue without finding a large section devoted to 'cuttings', illuminated materials, often of high quality indeed, that someone or another has removed from their constituent books. Culprits include such notable 'friends of the arts' as John Ruskin, who once described cutting materials from a decorated missal as 'hard work'. Illustrations on inserted leaves in books of hours are, of course, easy game, and a nefarious reader famously removed several from manuscripts at the Hunnold Library, Claremont CA, 50 years or so ago. The quality of this material varies, but some very fine books are now only loose fragments, such as the companion volume, for the other side of the choir, to the glorious 'Gorleston Psalter' (BL, MS Additional 49622), a partial page from which passed through a Sotheby auction on 25 April 1983 as part of lot 91.

The Gorleston fragment was, in a sense, 'ancient spolia'. Inscriptions and creases in the leaf show that it had been used, as early as the eighteenth century, as a cover for a small book. However, over the years, the great villains have been profit-hungry bookdealers. A nice, but run of the mill, manuscript frequently fetches better prices cut into single illuminated leaves (even just industrialised Flemish borderwork, these days, £500 and up) than left whole. For example, in the mid-nineteenth century James O. Halliwell, no mean book larcenist himself, saw whole a psalter, s. xiv, 'discovered in a farm-house in Leicestershire', from which he printed excerpts. The book, a good deal too nice for such a fate, was dismembered in the 1980s, allegedly in the Port Authority Bus Terminal in New York, by a bookseller here to remain anonymous, and bits of it went far and wide.[65]

However, those who were allegedly the books' custodians have been far from immune to criminality. Oxbridge college libraries have been persistently targeted by the Fellows themselves, and no one knows how many folios and miniatures from these books hang framed on the living-room walls of their posterity. Magd provides a series of

---

[65] See Thomas Wright and James O. Halliwell, *Reliquiae Antiquae: Scraps from Ancient Manuscripts ...* , 2 vols (London, 1845), 2:117; and D. A. Winstanley with Hunt, 'Halliwell Phillipps and the Trinity College Library', *The Library* 5th ser. 2 (1948), 250–82. Cf. Peter Kidd's presentation, https://mssprovenance.blogspot.com/2015/06/the-cotterell-throckmorton-hours.html.

particularly egregious examples of plunder. Perhaps the worst atrocities were committed on Magd lat. 100, a fine psalter from Worcester, s. xiii in., originally with pasted-in illumination. Of the ten original examples, only four remain *in situ*, and two of these show evidence of abandoned efforts at peeling them from the pages, like some of their now lost companions. (In two instances, the thieves lost patience and just excised whole leaves.) In the handsome lat. 134 (William of Paull's *Summa summarum*, s. xiv med.), such ill-treatment extends to the removal of rather minor decorative features, the small champs, admittedly very attractive ones, at the chapter divisions. But almost no book with painting escaped such unwelcome attentions; a few further examples include Magd lat. 114, 128, 156, 196, and 214. Even such a waif as SJ 235, fragment 56, a pastedown removed from a printed book, was not immune from spoiling, and SJ 61 has a Fellow's note, dated 1816, confessing to have removed leaves from the MS.[66]

How come it looks so neat?

Now, you will be saying, we can finally can get down to what everyone thinks books are for, texts. Apologies, but not just yet; first comes the scribe; obviously, one can't read a text without assessing his work.

First of all, however nice and neat the page appears and however professional the hand may look, a manuscript is not produced by unregulated freehand writing. Before the pen hits the support, there has been a prior decision as to format. As you look at the page, you may find that what you see does not resemble modern print, single lines of writing running from one justified margin to the opposite. Your book may approximate this form, and then is written 'in long lines'. But it is just as likely to have some other format. Double columns routinely present very large texts. (An aid to readers; it's very easy to lose your place when your eye must run across the full page, packed with material.) Multiple columns typically are reserved for texts one might describe as 'indexal', such as Stephen Langton's *Interpretationes nominum hebraicorum* (Sharpe 628), a routine component of Vulgate Bibles; or the *tabule* 'indexes' that accompany many texts.

---

[66] Cf. Richard Gameson's comments, *The Medieval Manuscripts of Trinity College, Oxford: A Descriptive Catalogue*, Oxford Bibliographical Society Publications Special Series: Manuscript Catalogues 3 (Oxford, 2018), 52.

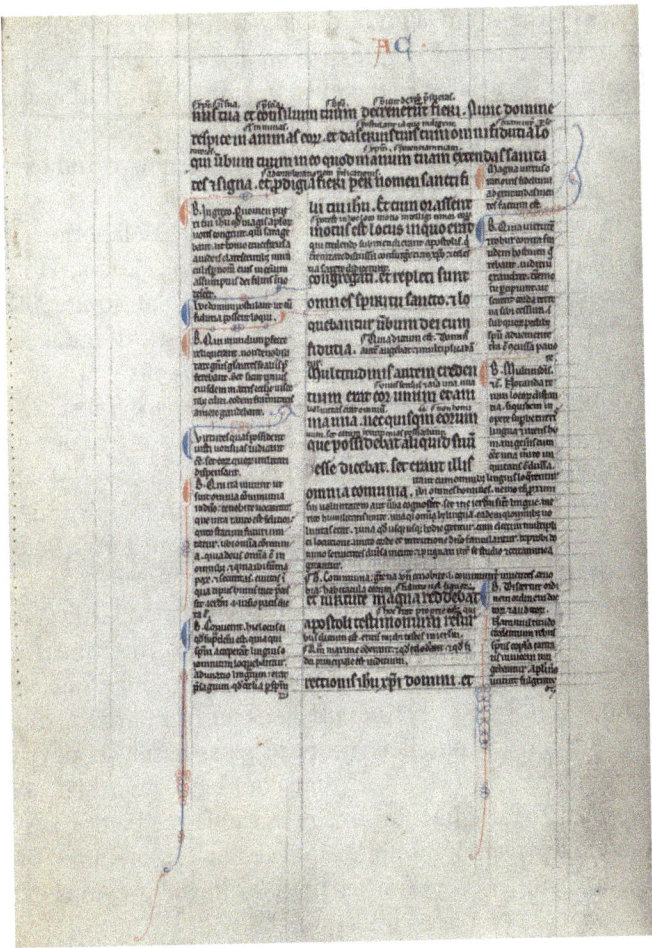

A glossed book: As Holtz points out, the earliest glossed books were awkward and wasteful. The text and explanatory gloss appeared in parallel columns and, depending upon how much information was provided, tended to use only a portion of the page. A step-change in these productions involved formatting each page individually, balancing the amount of text against the amount of explanatory material. This example, s. xiii med., presents Acts 4 with what is known as the 'ordinary gloss', produced at Laon a little over a century earlier. Besides its depicting the distinction between text and gloss hands, the image shows the complicated interweaving of the two segments. The text is spaced so that brief glosses can appear interlinearly. But, equally, the longer, marginal glosses, beyond engulfing it, also displace the text. It appears in the full width of the leaf only in the top three lines, and in the lower middle of the leaf the gloss is so extensive as to interrupt the text altogether. (Oxford, Queen's College, MS 313, fol. 14ᵛ, reproduced at 42%).

More variously, the many standard texts central to all levels of school curricula are commented or glossed books, involving an apparently erratic display of a variable central text surrounded by other materials. Henri-Jean Martin and Jean Vezin, eds, *Mise en page et mise en texte du livre manuscrit* (Paris, 1990) provide an informative and extensively illustrated global conspectus of page formats.

On the development of the sometimes elaborate formats for producing a text with commentaries, see Louis Holtz, 'Les Manuscrits latins à gloses et à commentaires de l'antiquité à l'époque carolingienne', *Atti del convegno internazionale 'Il libro e il testo'* ... , ed. Cesare Questa and Renato Raffaeli (Urbino, 1984), 141–67; and 'Le rôle des commentaires d'auteurs classiques dans l'émergence d'une mise en page associant texte et commentaire (Moyen Âge occidentale)', *Le commentaire entre tradition et innovation* ... , ed. Marie-Odile Goulet-Cazé et al. (Paris, 2000), 101–17 + plates; and C. F. R. de Hamel, *Glossed Books of the Bible and the Origins of the Paris Book Trade* (Woodbridge, 1984).

'Eadwine's psalter', Cambridge, Trinity College, MS R.17.1 (see p. 73), offers an elaborate page, with both marginal and interlinear glossing (much of the latter translation), and it well illustrates one universal of this genre. This is the distinction between the large formal hand of the text and and the smaller, informal gloss hand, its development described by Holtz. Eadwine's format could be described as transitional, as is also that in SJ 26 (an image as catalogue plate II). SJ 152 (an image as catalogue plate 17) is an example of a book prepared to receive glosses ad lib. from its users (rather than, as in the previous examples, a set commentary). Its spaced lineation and wide margins typify many school, perhaps especially grammatical, texts (here Priscian).[67]

This initial decision about page-format tells the scribe how he is to prepare his sheets. Virtually all manuscripts on membrane have been ruled horizontally for writing, and the scribe's neat hand has received an assist. This procedure typically has involved two steps: first, 'pricking' – making guiding holes for the edges of the writing area and for where the writing lines should go by piercing the sheet at intervals; and then 'ruling' – using a straight edge of some kind to make vertical (for the 'bounds' or 'frame', the edges of the writing area) and

---

[67] One printed book of my acquaintance reproduces the most simplified version of a glossed manuscript (lawyers are eminently practical); see Augustine Thompson and James Gordley, trs, *Gratian: The Treatise on Laws ... with the Ordinary Gloss* (Washington DC, 1993).

horizontal (for the actual writing lines themselves) impressions or thin lines on the sheet, following these guiding punctures.[68]

One can prick a sheet with any kind of sharp instrument. Awls leave small round holes (and thus seem a ready instrument of choice); a penknife, as in the book of hours Jeremy and I originally planned to describe, leaves slits. There is evidence, however, for variously 'mechanised' instruments for the job – small rolling spur-like devices, for example. And, particularly in Hebrew and Arabic manuscript culture, there is evidence for ruling-boards – wooden frames holding spaced strings – that would render pricking unnecessary.[69] Scribes in other cultures may have had other implements, such as frames with wires or rake-like tools. Very little has been written about the procedure since Leslie W. Jones, 'Where are the Prickings?', *Transactions and Proceedings of the American Philological Association* 75 (1944), 71–86; and 'Pricking Manuscripts: The Instruments and their Significance', *Speculum* 21 (1946), 389–403. For two classic articles on these preliminary procedures see Léon Gilissen, 'Un élement codologique trop peu exploité: la reglure', *Scriptorium* 23 (1969), 150–62; and 'La Composition des cahiers: le pliage du parchemin et l'imposition', *Scriptorium* 26 (1972), 3–33. One warning: because pricking for horizontal rules customarily appears at the edge of the leaf, it has often been lost in binding, when the pages have been planed.

Ruling materials display the same kind of 'great divide' I have noticed elsewhere. There is a rough historical succession of the materials used for the purpose. Down to about the 1160s, manuscripts are ruled unobtrusively, in what is called 'drypoint' (or 'ruling in blind'); the leaves are ruled simply by running a stylus, guided by a straight edge, over the support. While visually unobtrusive, this system does leave characteristic 'ridge and furrow' indentations one can feel by running a fingertip over the sheets. The furrow appears on the side of the sheet to which the stylus was applied, and the ridge on the other side, as in SJ 154 (Ælfric's grammar, s. xi in.).

Drypoint ruling was initially replaced by ruling in lead, s. xii$^{3/4}$. Many early examples appear simply as thin lines left by something

---

[68] Paper manuscripts are frequently less formal and often show only the bounding/frame ruling. Indeed, with sheets folded in folio (see p. 39), a very frequent book-size, the scribe need never rule. The wire-lines of his paper, which run horizontally in this folding, obviate other ruling, since they provide an automatic line for writing.

[69] See Malachi Beit-Arie, *Hebrew Codicology* ... (Jerusalem, 1981), 78–83 with images.

resembling a modern pencil. However, various forms of lead implement were available to and put to use by medieval scribes. Many of the guides for initials you will spot are not provided in the ink of the text, but in a smudgy grey lead, usually called 'plummet', also occasionally used for rules. Frequently, rules appear in a rather broad reddish-brown smear, another species of lead, usually called 'crayon'. There are persistent examples at SJ, in MSS 96, 101, 106, 127, 152, etc. This innovation was quickly succeeded, from s. xii/xiii, by ruling in ink, usually either black or brown, and the two forms for ruling continue until the end of the Middle Ages.

Early scribes, with their drypoint, may have sought to conceal that the page was ruled at all. In contrast, particularly s. xv, ruling can turn ostentatiously decorative through the use of brightly coloured inks. For an early example (s. xiii$^{3/4}$), relatively restrained, in blue ink, one could point to a French MS, ChCh 178. But considerably more flamboyant are books ruled in red and purple inks, such as SJ 102, 117, 131, and 197. Without exception, these books are continental. At least initially in England, coloured rules are mainly confined to liturgical books, almost universally red only, as seen in SJ 179 (quite unusually in violet ink), 187, 196, 208, and 293. However, from s. xv med., red rules begin to appear in non-liturgical contexts, such as SJ 182 and Magd lat. 30, and they become quite normal under the Tudors, where examples include a London-produced book (although for a French fraternity), ChCh 179; the Garter statutes of Magd lat. 227; or Wolsey's flamboyant foundation charters, ChCh 338 and 339 (mainly violet). It may be significant that all these late examples represent formal legal instruments.

Ruling systems, as Gilissen says, are 'Un élement ... trop peu exploité', and investigations have only just begun. The standard rota of conventional catalogues is only to note its presence ('framed/bounded and ruled ... ') or absence, and the material used ('in plummet').[70] The one can't-miss study of ruling, another example of 'the great divide', is Ker's 'From "Above top line" to "Below top line": A Change in Scribal Practice', coll 71–74 (and cf. de Hamel's *Glossed Books* for a likely source of this shift in practice). Following Ker, before c. 1240 scribes across Europe used the top ruled line as the first writing line on a page; after that date, the top line enclosed the writing, and the text began

---

[70] If Gameson's unusually precise descriptions in his Trinity College catalogue are indicative, the usual convention may shortly become a thing of the past; cf. his account of a ruling system as distinctive as the Vespasian MS I will describe, at 91.

on the second ruled line. One should add that frequently in s. xv this convention becomes more flexible, and scribes feel free to write on top of or above the first ruled line (see p. 106).

However, odd examples suggest there's potentially a good deal of useful mileage in the study of ruling systems. For example, when Ker examined BL, MS Cotton Vespasian E.iii, he identified 'art. 1' as being from the abbey of St Modwenna, Burton-upon-Trent (OSB) (*MLGB* 15). The identification was pretty easy, since it was based on the contents; the first item, fols 4–100^v, is an abbey chronicle, unlikely to have been produced anywhere else.

The ruling system used in the Vespasian MS tells a somewhat different story, however. All of fols 4–108, 117–78, 11 separate texts in all, share a comparable (although not absolutely consistent) ruling system. The materials used for bounds and rules are the same (mostly brown crayon), and the dimensions of the writing area are closely comparable (double columns, 165–70 mm x 110–15 mm, 37–40 lines to the column, more generous dimensions in the chronicle than elsewhere). More importantly, the horizontal rules show comparable extensions outside the frame-ruling to the edges of the surviving leaf. Extended ruling appears typically for the top and bottom lines of the column, which is fairly normal in many ruling systems. However, such extended rules also appear for the fourth lines from the top and from the bottom of the page, and for two lines at mid-page (generally in the chronicle, lines 22 and 23; elsewhere, fairly precisely at mid-page, lines 18 and 19). There are three hands involved, and fols 117–78 are substantially earlier than other items, but here one clearly is looking at some form of house-styling for the page, common to both the chronicle and other materials, and Ker's identification of a 'Burton book' is too restrictive.[71]

How does the scribe write?

Before the text comes the hand that writes or copies it. Identifying this, by script-style and date, is one of the most basic acts of investigating a manuscript. Such study returns you to the foundations of the discipline, in Jean Mabillon (almost always known as l'abbé M.; he was a Benedictine monk), *De re diplomatica* (1681). Palaeography actually began as an offshoot of a related manuscript discipline, 'diplomatic', the study of legal documents. Mabillon wished to write a history of

---

[71] For another distinctive example, cf. ChCh 107, a Bible.

Merovingian France, but the primary documents for the task were legal materials, charters donating land to monasteries, for example, and a substantial portion of these were undated. Since his goal was a conventional narrative history, that posed a major problem. His solution – and fundamentally that adopted by every palaeographer since – was a simple one: arrange all the dated items in a series, attempt to identify significant and variable script features in this group, and then compare his 'unknowns', the undated materials, and see where in the sequence their rendering of these same script features would fit best.

Mabillon was engaged in historical research, but dating the script of your manuscript is a fundamental responsibility (and, of course, presupposes your competence at recognising datable script features). At a certain level, our entire understanding of the past, and of its literature, is utterly dependent upon this skill. Our knowledge of the careers of authors and of the origin of texts, perhaps most particularly anonymous ones – rife in the Middle Ages – depends, in large measure, upon accurately dating and locating the manuscripts that communicate them. Dating also offers clues as to possible addressees, the community the text was composed to serve, and the text's transmission (later copies are apt to be derivative, although not necessarily so). For a classic demonstration of these issues see Parkes, 'On the Presumed Date and Possible Origin of the Manuscript of the *Orrmulum*: Oxford, Bodleian Library, MS Junius 1', coll 187–200.

Rather basically, a limited number of scripts are used in European MSS. These are characterised and differentiated by the variation in form of a limited number of features: the shapes of and the sequence of strokes that produce the letters a, d, f/s,[72] g, r, and (where it appears) w. To these, one can add a few minor but commonplace details: the form for *et/and*, the handling of minims and ascenders (see the following paragraphs), and the form of the 'common mark' – the superscript line that customarily instructs you to 'supply a nasal, "n" or "m", here'. Of these, the most revelatory are apt to be forms of 'g' and 'w', the most complicated letters to produce – the lower lobe of 'g' in a disciplined gothic bookhand, for example, involves five separate segments, produced by turning the pen).

For an immediately legible example of distinction between scripts, see T. A. M. Bishop, *English Caroline Minuscule* (Oxford, 1971), plate xx,

---

[72] At least in their usual formation, within the word, these are formed identically, except that 'f' has a cross-stroke and 's' does not. Equally, the final -*s* in a word has various distinctive forms, their succession datable.

an image of Cambridge, Corpus Christi College, MS 178 (II), s. xi in. In this image you can see, at the top of the page, the script called caroline minuscule; and, at the foot, that called insular square minuscule. (And, in accord with my earlier discussion, the separation between them is marked by a heading in rustic capitals.)

Discussions of script rely upon a few basic definitions. Generally speaking, all scripts look as if they form long bands of heavy stroking, usually reasonably spaced out, across an otherwise blank sheet. This is the purpose of the horizontal rules, to set one boundary for the rendition of individual letters. There is a fundamental distinction between majuscule scripts (like rustic capitals), which use most of the space between these rules, and minuscule scripts. The latter in effect divide that narrow space between the rules and use only a small part of it primarily, what is called 'x-height' or 'minim-height'. This is the space above the ruled line the height of the letter 'x' or of the smallest graphic unit, thus a minim (Latin *minimus* 'the least'), the stroke that forms the letter 'i'. (A minim is also a component part of 'm', three minims; and of 'n' and 'u', both two of them.) In minuscule scripts, that imaginary unruled line at the top of 'x' or 'i' is where the reader's eye is to be focussed, and it is there that letters that look similar are distinguished from one another. For example, this is where, in early hands, the flat bar of 't' is written, distinguishing that letter from 'c', which is curved at the top.

All minuscule scripts display a certain number of strokes outside this writing band. Palaeographers are not masters of invention, and their names for such things are predictable. Strokes that rise above the writing band and approach the rule above it are called 'ascenders'; those that extend below the rule at the foot of the writing band are 'descenders'. Typically, 'b', 'd', and 'h' are examples of the first; examples of the second, in most hands, when writing Latin, are limited to 'p' and 'q', but in two common English scripts, insular and anglicana, for example, 'r' has a descender (as also does 'f/s').

Bishop's plate xx records, as do all the transitions between major script types, a cultural interaction in script. The caroline was an import from the continent, introduced by Englishmen who had spent time abroad absorbing the practices of French monasteries; its earliest dated appearance in England occurs in 961, in a charter from the first fully Benedictine house, at Abingdon. However, the travellers imported the script as part of a massive effort to reform English monastic practice ('the Benedictine revival'). One of them, Æthelwold, eventually bishop of Winchester, as part of this reform, translated the Benedictine Rule, the foundation of continental monasticism, into the local language, Old English. That is the text illustrated in Bishop's plate xx. The original Latin is here recorded in the continental script, but the translation in the local one, which had been developed from earlier insular scripts in Winchester, c. 920–30. So the form in which the page is written records both importation and naturalisation, reform and its acceptance.

In England, as well as elsewhere in Europe, there is a conventional succession of these script types. Following from the two reproduced in Bishop's plate come protogothic bookhand (s. xii) and gothic bookhand (first identifiable c. 1180, and having a long life into s. xvi, particularly in biblical and liturgical contexts). Both of these scripts are formal bookhands, produced stroke by stroke, letter by letter. The latter is another example of Parkes's dictum, 'scripts recruited from below'; gothic bookhand is a development from the less formal, typically compacted scripts that in the preceding century had been the hand of the (secondary) gloss, not the text.[73]

However, many of the functions originally filled by gothic bookhand (often called 'textura' or 'textualis') were subsumed by less elegant scripts. These are cursives, 'running scripts' (Latin *cursus*, past participle of *currere*), where letters are joined by linking strokes. These represent prettied up versions of document hands, scripts originally developed for informal records, primarily those of business and the law – yet a further example of 'recruitment from below'.

The earlier of these is the distinctive local 'anglicana', in documents from c. 1240, first appearing as a formal script for manuscripts c. 1270. This script was identifiable as 'English' all over Europe, primarily because it is the only prominent script with a two-compartment a, conveniently enough displayed thrice in a*nglica*na). Around 1370, bureaucrats returning from the chancery that had administered English-occupied Gascony brought with them the local cursive script, in English known as 'secretary'. Although originally limited in use to the office of the Privy Seal, stocked with Gascon veterans, this rapidly became a common bookhand, in one form or another the dominant English script for two centuries from c. 1440. (Meanwhile, anglicana retreated to exclusively legal use, where highly formalised versions, called 'court hand', persisted as a documentary script until s. xvii ex.) Near the end of the Middle Ages, a Florentine invention of s. xiv ex.,

---

[73] In addition to images of Eadwine's psalter (see p. 73), Barker-Benfield *et al.*, *Glossed Luke* includes a number of salient images of the contrast.

'humanistica', begins to appear in English manuscripts, often produced by foreign scribes working in insular environments.[74]

Rather than lengthy prose descriptions, scripts are dated through a compact abbreviated system. As BH 15–16 indicates, this begins with 's.', for Latin *saeculo*, the dative of time, 'in/during the century'. From early in your career you should be able to offer such a dating by centuries, be able to distinguish a hand of s. xiii from one of s. xv. Further practice will enable you to make narrower distinctions. Using 's. xv' as an exemplary form, you'll learn to distinguish between books from the first and second half of the century, s. xv^1 and s. xv^2. In some cases, you will be able to make narrower distinctions still: by rough thirds of a century, s. xv in. (i.e. c. 1400–30), s. xv med. (i.e. c. 1430–70), s. xv ex. (i.e. c. 1470–1500). And, in some instances, you will be confident enough to offer a dating by quarter-centuries, such as s. $xv^{2/4}$, etc. In the absence of compelling external evidence, no responsible palaeographer offers a dating narrower than two or three decades; unlike scholars of illumination, where fashions change with alacrity, and datings to a five-year period are commonplace, script is conservative (and you must always remember that you may be looking at the hand of a very old man, trained decades previously).[75]

'Script' defines a generally imagined or visualised template which the scribe follows. What he produces is not 'script', the template, but 'hand', an individualised rendition of features he imagines or intuits from the model, that image he carries memorially. What distinguishes 'hand' is its 'ductus', its customary individual movements of the pen as the scribe seeks to reproduce his mental template. The force of 'ductus', the scribe's left-to-right movement across the page, means that his performance is always contextualised, both by what he has just copied and by what he anticipates. As a result, the single letter-form models

---

[74] On the coming of secretary, see *ECBH* xix–xxi and plate 9; *London Literature, 1300–1380* (Cambridge, 2005), 223–27; and on humanistica, David Rundle, *The Renaissance Reform of the Book and Britain: The English Quattrocento* (Cambridge, 2019), with extensive references.

[75] Michel of Northgate, whom I have mentioned above (p. 47), is a classic example, his (increasingly antiquated) formal script reasonably stable over more than three decades. Similarly, a person whom I would identify as William Wall, eventually a prebendary of Chester Cathedral, who indexed and/or annotated more than 20 local books, was probably trained to write in the 1480s or early 1490s, but may have been writing in this style as late as 1540, perhaps indeed to his death in 1574.

for 'a script' I have mentioned above are always subject to adjustments guided by the nature of the surrounding strokes.

As someone who examines MSS, you will develop a ready familiarity with 'script'. You need to examine lots of images of a script and try to develop, like the scribe, an inner visual image of a template version. Then you can recognise and match up features between the book in front of you and the inner image you see. Eventually you will create an inner image of a script, with some notion of its date, and things will become easier. Here, just to choose one distinctive, script-defining feature, in Bishop's plate xx, 'the common mark' in the caroline script at the top is a light stroke with an elegant upward curve at the right; in contrast, in the insular script below, the same mark of abbreviation is flat and rather like a barbell, with a slightly blobby terminus at both ends.

The best introductory survey of scripts remains Bernhard Bischoff, tr. Dáibhí O Cróinín and David Ganz, *Latin Palaeography: Antiquity and the Middle Ages* (Cambridge, 1990), heavily tilted toward Bischoff's speciality, older materials, and, depending on the edition you read, sloppily proofread.[76] For later materials, you could consult Albert Derolez, *The Palaeography of Gothic Manuscript Books* (Cambridge, 2003), in many respects a child of Lieftinck *et al.*, another continental exercise in nomenclature, and not particularly useful for books produced in England. For these, the bible is Parkes's *ECBH*. Notice that, although we inhabit the same island, Scotland and Wales, historically nations with individual cultural traditions, have their own distinctive local scripts; see Daniel Huws, *Medieval Welsh Manuscripts* (Cardiff, 2000) and G. G. Simpson, *Scottish Handwriting 1150–1650* (Aberdeen, 1986).

To familiarise yourself with scripts, there is volume upon volume of plates (and now of images on the web), most pertinently 'Dated and Datables' (known colloquially, following Parkes, as 'Damned and Damnables'). These volumes enable you to repeat Mabillon's experiment, to try to place an unknown hand within a range of ones with fixed dates. The English examples of this genre, all of them two volumes, one a catalogue, the second with a plate illustrating the hand in each book discussed, are:

---

[76] On this point, see Braxton Ross's review, *Speculum* 66 (1991), 121.

Watson, *Catalogue of Dated and Datable Manuscripts, c. 700–1600, in the Department of Manuscripts, The British Library*, 2 vols (London, 1979);

Watson, *Catalogue ... Manuscripts, c. 435–1600 in Oxford Libraries*, 2 vols (Oxford, 1984);

Robinson, *Catalogue ... Manuscripts, c. 737–1600 in Cambridge Libraries*, 2 vols (Cambridge, 1988); and

Robinson, *Catalogue ... Manuscripts, c. 888–1600 in London Libraries* (London, 2003).[77]

These are the local avatars of an international series, one subject to any variety of local options that render volumes variously useful. Many French catalogues restrict themselves to manuscripts in not just Latin script but language; many Italian ones are overrun with local books of s. xv (when Italian scribes routinely dated their writing) and of little help for anything else, while their plates frequently show only the dating subscriptions, not the text-script.

One should have thought that a manuscript with a date would put an end to the story. Such is not the case; see Jean Destrez and G. Fink-Emera, 'Des manuscrits apparemment datés', *Scriptorium* 12 (1958), 56–93. As a local example, consider BL, MS Royal 17 C.viii, in Watson's BL catalogue as no. 903 (1:156) and plate 351, ascribed the colophon date 1418 (although this is not in the text ink, appears over an erasure, and does not appear to be in the scribal hand).

Watson should here have been a bit more critical. The scribe routinely writes a reduced form of *w*, common through the later s. xv (and later in secretary scripts); however, the form appears in no plate of an English 'Dated and Datable' catalogue predating 1430.[78] Moreover, the paper, as

---

[77] You should notice that the images in these volumes are invariably black and white. All reproductions falsify, modern digital full-colour scanning more than most (a little too pretty and a little too sensitive, often apparently highlighting features invisible *in situ*). Colour distorts that feature most valuable to palaeographers, as Parkes repeatedly insists in *Their Hands*, the chiaroscuro rhythm of strokes. While the online images of a site like 'Parker on the Web' are useful and convenient for many purposes, for serious study you need to haul yourself over to Cambridge, Corpus Christi College and examine the beast itself.

[78] For the earliest examples of this letter form, see *Dated ... British Library*, plate 418 (1433); *Dated ... Cambridge*, plate 221 (1432); *Dated ... London*, plate 107

I have suggested above, customarily ignored in catalogues of this type, includes a stock with a distinctive watermark, a rather saucy Mermaid, unparalleled before 1458. (Recall the discussion of paper as a means of dating, pp. 41–42.) The logical inference is that the dating colophon has been copied from another book, probably the scribe's exemplar, and that the book should be dated only broadly, s. xv med.

There are also innumerable volumes of plates that reproduce scribal hands across the centuries. Most of these, like Parkes's *ECBH*, include commentary and at least partial transcriptions, which you will find useful for training purposes. (Take a stab at transcribing what you see, and then check it against what the experienced scholars who collected these images saw. Just one caveat: you must write what you see – if it seems difficult, look for other examples that resemble it on the same page; they may appear in forms you can recognise and sort your problem quickly. And, if what you have copied doesn't make any sense, your first impulse should be to recheck what you have written against the image; scribes do try to write sensible clauses and sentences, and it's almost certainly your misperception.)[79] A few classic volumes with extensive ranges of examples include:

Franz Ehrle and Paul Liebaert, *Specimina Codicum Latinorum Vaticanorum*, 2nd edn (1912; Berlin and Leipzig, 1932);

Joachim Kirchner, *Scriptura Gothica Libraria* (Munich and Vienna, 1966);

S. Harrison Thomson, *Latin Book Hands of the Later Middle Ages, 1100–1500* (Cambridge, 1969); and

Helmut van Thiel, *Mittellateinische Texte: Ein Handschriften-Lesebuch* (Göttingen, 1972).

(1431×43). But, equally, notice Linne R. Mooney and Estelle Stubbs, *Scribes and the City: London Guildhall Clerks and the Dissemination of Middle English Literature, 1375–1425* (Woodbridge, 2013), plate 4.2 (at 70): John Shirley, who was not trained as a formal scribe, but as a domestic secretary, was using the form in manuscript copying, but again only for household consumption, in the 1420s.

[79] Copying what someone else has written may seem simple, but … . Another Parkesian dictum, 'To transcribe accurately, you have to already know what it should be saying.' A single but repeated example: Latin scribes routinely write dm: but is it 'deum' or (as dni) 'Domini'? If you're actually following along, you won't have a problem, because you'll know whether to expect an accusative (deum) or a genitive (dni).

While I think that anyone interested in manuscript study should be able to handle texts in Latin, a few useful collections address English vernacular examples only:

> Walter W. Skeat, *Twelve Facsimiles of Old English Manuscripts* (Oxford, 1892);
>
> C. E. Wright, *English Vernacular Hands, from the Twelfth to the Fifteenth Centuries* (Oxford, 1960); and
>
> Jane Roberts, *Guide to Scripts Used in English Writings up to 1500* (London, 2005).

Moreover, every Early English Text Society volume for nearly a century has included an image from a relevant manuscript as a frontispiece (and obviously, at some point, transcribed its textual contents).

Anyone who can write can, of course, make a book, for personal use or, as John Shirley (see n.78) did, for an audience. However, you should realise that in the Middle Ages vastly more people could read (an intellectual/spiritual activity) than could write (a handicraft). As a result, the great majority of surviving books appear to be professional products, produced by people who lived by their writing skills – far from always in text-copying, but in various administrative roles. For a classic demonstration of this expected multiple employment (presumably legal copying is the day job, formal scribal work moonlighting), see Carter Revard's detailed discussion of the scribe responsible for BL, MS Harley 2253, 'Scribe and Provenance', *Studies in the Harley Manuscript: The Scribes, Contents and Social Contexts of British Library MS Harley 2253*, ed. Susanna Fein (Kalamazoo MI, 2000), 21–109.

As a result of this professionalisation, these people potentially exist in more than one manuscript. The most prolific example I know personally is John Dyg(g)on, the fifth recluse of Sheen (a Carthusian house now in suburban London); while he is responsible for some extensive scribal (and artistic) work, he's most frequently present as an arranger of a personal library – and in 21 books. His activity pales, however, beside two scribes identified by Jeremy Griffiths. One of them was a specialist in roll-chronicles, c. 1475–85, in more than 50 copies (see SJ 23 and 58, catalogue 39–40, 77–79). The second, equally a specialist, just at the end of the century, copied more than 20 manuscripts of the Statutes of the Realm (including SJ 257, catalogue 325–27 and plate 18).

There is a lengthy, and sometimes contentious, tradition of writing about scribes, their texts, and their employers (much of it extremely valuable as one comes to consider book history). A modest sampling of such materials, mainly discussions of s. xv copyists, would include:

Mynors, 'A Fifteenth-Century Scribe: T. Werken', *Transactions of the Cambridge Bibliographical Society* 1 (1949–53), 97–104;

Parkes, 'A Fifteenth-Century Scribe: Henry Mere', coll 249–56;

Peter J. Lucas, 'William Gybbe of Wisbech: A Fifteenth-Century English Scribe', *Codices Manuscripti* 11 (1985), 41–64; and 'An Author as Copyist of his Own Work: John Capgrave OSA (1393–1464)', *New Science*, 227–48, full reference at n.64;

Doyle, 'The Work of a Late-Fifteenth-Century Scribe, William Ebesham', *Bulletin of the John Rylands Library* 39 (1957), 298–325;

Doyle, 'An Unrecognised Piece of *Piers the Ploughman's Creed* with Other Work by Its Scribe', *Speculum* 34 (1959), 428–36; with Linne R. Mooney's coda, 'A New Manuscript by the Hammond Scribe: Discovered by Jeremy Griffiths', *The English Medieval Book: Studies in Memory of Jeremy Griffiths*, ed. A. S. G. Edwards *et al.* (London, 2000), 113–23;[80]

Doyle, 'More Light on John Shirley', *Medium Ævum* 30 (1961), 93–101, with the codas Jeremy J. Griffiths, 'A Newly Identified Manuscript Inscribed by John Shirley', *The Library* 6th ser. 14 (1992), 85–93; and Margaret Connolly, *John Shirley: Book Production and the Noble Household in Fifteenth-Century England* (Aldershot, 1998);

Doyle, 'Stephen Dodesham of Witham and Sheen', *Of the Making of Books: Medieval Manuscripts, Their Scribes and Readers: Essays Presented to M. B. Parkes*, ed. P. R. Robinson and Rivkah Zim (Aldershot, 1997), 94–115.[81]

---

[80] As well as, foreshadowing a topic to which we will turn shortly, her 'Scribes and Booklets of Trinity College, Cambridge, Manuscripts R.3.19 and R.3.21', *Middle English Poetry*, ed. Minnis, 241–66 (full reference at n.4).

[81] I took a preliminary run at an earlier period in 'Pre-Fifteenth-Century Scribes Copying Middle English and Appearing in More than One Manuscript', *Journal of the Early Book Society* 14 (2011), 131–42. For another widely attested scribe, mainly as textual annotator (on Bishop's plate xx, for example), see Ker, 'The Date of the "Tremulous" Worcester Hand', coll 67–70; Christine Franzen, *The Tremulous*

There is also a large literature on pre-1170 book production in monastic surroundings, where a handful of the community may have been devoted to providing books and repeated hands are thus expected:

> Mynors, *Durham Cathedral Manuscripts*; with the coda Michael Gullick, 'The Scribe of the Carilef Bible: A New Look at Some Late-Eleventh-Century Durham Cathedral Manuscripts', *Medieval Book Production: Assessing the Evidence*, ed. Linda Brownrigg (Los Altos Hills CA, 1990), 61–83;
>
> Elaine M. Drage, 'Bishop Leofric and the Exeter Cathedral Chapter, 1050–1072: A Reassessment of the Manuscript Evidence', Bodleian Library, MS D.Phil. c. 2650 (Oxford, 1978);
>
> R. M. Thomson, *Manuscripts from St. Albans Abbey, 1066–1235* (Woodbridge, 1982);
>
> Teresa Webber, *Scribes and Scholars at Salisbury Cathedral, c. 1075–c. 1125* (Oxford, 1992);
>
> Jennifer M. Sheppard, *The Buildwas Books: Book Production, Acquisition and Use at an English Cistercian Monastery, 1165–c. 1400*, Oxford Bibliographical Society 3rd ser. 2 (Oxford, 1997).

For one very elaborate monastic book, already mentioned, see *The Eadwine Psalter: Text, Image, and Monastic Culture in Twelfth-Century Canterbury*, ed. Margaret T. Gibson *et al.* (London, 1992). See further Doyle's essays on late medieval monastic copying:

> 'Publication by members of the religious orders', GP 109–23; and
>
> 'Book Production by the Monastic Orders in England (c. 1375–1530): Assessing the Evidence', *Medieval Book Production*, ed. Brownrigg, 1–19;

Hand of Worcester: A Study of Old English in the Thirteenth Century (Oxford, 1991). The scribe's oeuvre was recently augmented; see Rodney Thomson, *A Descriptive Catalogue of the Medieval Manuscripts in the Library of Peterhouse, Cambridge* (Cambridge, 2016), 24–25 and plate 65 (b) (MS 44, a Bible, s. xiii med.).

and his studies of two monastic scribes copying after the coming of print:

'Books with Marginalia from St Mark's Hospital, Bristol', *New Directions in Medieval Manuscript Studies and Reading Practices: Essays in Honour of Derek Pearsall*, ed. Kathryn Kerby-Fulton et al. (Notre Dame IN, 2014), 177–91 (primarily on John Coleman); and

'William Darker: The Work of an English Carthusian Scribe', *Medieval Manuscripts, Their Makers and Users: A Special Issue of Viator in Honor of Richard and Mary Rouse* (Turnhout, 2011), 199–211.[82]

In my introduction I mentioned Jeremy Griffith's effort at producing a list of scribes recorded in more than one book. Jeremy's materials were taken over by the industrious Linne Mooney, and, with others, she has continued to expand these records online. A selection of the materials the group has collected, limited to five major English authors, appears at the website https://www.medievalscribes.com. David Rundle's study of humanistica in England (n.74) similarly offers extensive examples of scribes repeatedly engaged by one or another patron.

Two scribal features, beyond letter formation, are of potential importance. Latin was no one's native tongue and had to be acquired by grammar-school instruction; as a result, it had a reasonably fixed spelling system, based on late classical usage. However, such was not true of vernaculars, and a scribe's spelling, even of very common items (e.g. 's(c)he' v. 'heo' SHE), is geographically distinctive. The guide to such matters is *LALME*, Angus McIntosh et al., *A Linguistic Atlas of Late Mediaeval English*, 4 vols (Aberdeen, 1986), now available online with a variety of helpful features: www.lel.ed.ac.uk/ihd/elalme/elalme.html. This concentrates on materials from c. 1350 to c. 1450; the earlier period is covered by *Linguistic Atlas of Early Middle English*; http://www.lel.ed.ac.uk/ihd/laeme2/laeme2.html.

Spelling allows individual scribes writing English to be placed at least in a single county, and often more narrowly still. For the technique involved, see Michael Benskin, 'The "Fit"-Technique Explained',

---

[82] In addition, there's a more globally conceived library history, including an important statement on the effects of the Dissolution: Alan Coates, *English Medieval Books: The Reading Abbey Collections from Foundation to Dispersal* (Oxford, 1999).

Regionalism in Late Medieval Manuscripts and Texts: Essays Celebrating the Publication of The Linguistic Atlas of Late Mediaeval English, ed. Felicity Riddy (Cambridge, 1991), 9–26. Because of this localism in presentation, it is very likely that scribal graphic dialects identify an initial audience sharing the same features and may suggest your manuscript's imbrication in some provincial local community.[83]

Second, in addition to copying, scribes typically punctuate their texts. For example, later medieval scribes usually have a system of three signs: the point for a heavy stop at the end of a unit (a 'period', hence the North American name for the symbol); the '/' ('slant-bar' or 'virgule', Latin *virgula* 'a small staff', for a comma-like pause);[84] and a sign like an inverted semicolon (the 'punctus elevatus', usually setting off contrasts or 'if-then' constructions). As this brief description will indicate, the system differs from that conventional today; a 'period', for example, is not the same as a modern 'sentence'. As Parkes argues in the authoritative *Pause and Effect: An Introduction to the History of Punctuation in the West* (Aldershot, 1992), in contrast to modern grammatical punctuation, the medieval system is rhetorical. Some forms of punctuation are distinctive – a specifically Cistercian system, for example – and you should always notice how the scribe points his text.

As I have implied in introducing the monastic studies just above, you should not be surprised to find, as you advance in your manuscript, that the hand changes, that you find that your manuscript has been copied by more than one person. The classic account, for students of the later English Middle Ages, is Doyle and Parkes's seminal 'The Production of Copies of the Canterbury Tales and the Confessio Amantis in the Early Fifteenth Century', *Medieval Scribes, Manuscripts and Libraries: Essays Presented to N. R. Ker*, ed. Parkes and Watson (London, 1978), 163–210. There Doyle and Parkes identified five scribes combining on a copy of John Gower's *Confessio amantis*, Cambridge, Trinity College, MS R.3.2, as well as numerous other examples of the

---

[83] But see the cautionary analysis of Benskin's method: Anne Hudson, 'Observations on the "Wycliffite Orthography"', *Pursuing Middle English Manuscripts and Their Texts: Essays in Honour of Ralph Hanna*, ed. Simon Horobin and Aditi Nafde (Turnhout, 2017), 77–98; and on the potential localism of scribe and patron: Revard on Harley 2253 (full reference at p. 71); and, volubly, Michael Johnston, 'Copying and Reading *The Prick of Conscience* in Late Medieval England', *Speculum* 95 (2020), 742–801.

[84] Occasionally also known as a *solidus* 'shilling', since it was the punctuation that conventionally separated shillings from pence.

same individuals working separately. Beyond the identifications, the essay includes a sagacious analysis of the situation in which such collaboration might have occurred, as well as provocative comments on commercial scribal work. This essay has deservedly inspired many sequels, perhaps most notably (and controversially) Linne Mooney and Estelle Stubbs' *Scribes and the City*, another example, like Revard's Harley scribe, of the blending of documentary and formal manuscript copying.[85]

You may recall that I have alluded to such a situation previously, in the discussion of the erratic foliation assigned Magd lat. 162 (p. 44). In that book, a group of university scholars combined to produce an anthology of logic texts, each of the participants generally copying one text. (Presumably, just as they had shared the copying, they intended to share access to and use of the manuscript.) The primary motive underlying such activity is temporal economy; as with lat. 162 or Doyle and Parkes's Gower manuscript, multiple hands can copy out a full text much more quickly than an individual scribe working alone. The model underlying such behaviour is monastic, and well illustrated in MSS such as SJ 63, 89, and 158, all of which provide examples of varying situations: individual scribes copying protracted segments or whole texts, scribes wandering in for relatively short stints consecutive within a single text, and varying evidence of close supervision of the work.

But similar situations appear elsewhere. BL, MS Sloane 2275, was copied in a monastic cathedral, s. xv med. Because the exemplar for most of its textual core survives – it is now Paris, Bibliothèque nationale, MS lat. 15700 – one can identify both the supervisor of the operation and his initial parcelling out of the desired texts. Contemporaneously, an anonymous group of four scribes undertook a small anthology of texts by Richard Rolle in SJ 127, parcelling out the desired items one apiece. Neither production was, in the end, entirely straightforward, but both achieved the desired result, more or less: an extensive anthology in reduced time.[86]

---

[85] One might also here draw attention to Robinson's London 'Dated and Datable' volumes, which innovatively (and constructively) include a range of documentary copying. Mooney and Stubbs have attracted a fair amount of negative feedback, much of it marked by a gratuitous viciousness no responsible editor should have allowed in print; for a sober assessment, here of Mooney's identification of a single scribe, see Jane Roberts, 'On Giving Scribe B a Name and a Clutch of London Manuscripts from c. 1400', *Medium Ævum* 80 (2011), 247–70.

[86] See my 'Making Miscellaneous Manuscripts in Fifteenth-Century England:

How did a scribe proceed, once he had ruled a sheet? This question introduces what one might describe as palaeography's analogue to the 'wave-particle dilemma' in physics: skins or bifolia? The issue may be exemplified in the contrasting analyses of Gilissen, 'La Composition' (cited p. 61) and J. P. Gumbert, 'Sizes and Formats', *Ancient and Medieval Book Materials and Techniques*, ed. Marilena Maniaci and Paola Munafò, Studi e Testi 357–58 (Vatican, 1993), 227–63. Did scribes, after pricking and ruling, write on a single skin, whether the full sheet open before them or folded to make a small booklet, a quire (Gilissen), or did they cut a skin into pieces, 'bifolia', a joined pair of leaves, and arrange these into small bookets for copying (Gumbert)? Ultimately, as Gumbert implies, definitive answers to these questions may emerge from scientific scanning.

The images that appear at text-openings (variously of authors composing or scribes copying) appear to offer a range of options. However, as images, one doesn't know whether they are, as it were, 'naturalistic', describing actual behaviours, or imaginative. For the latter view, that a 'book', usually shown as already bound, or as a scroll, is an emblem for completed authorial/scribal work, not a descriptor of an actual process, see the most extensive analysis: Kathleen L. Scott, 'Representations of Scribal Activity in English Manuscripts c. 1400–c. 1490: A Mirror of the Craft', *Pen in Hand: Medieval Scribal Portraits, Colophons and Tools*, ed. Michael Gullick (Walkern, 2006), 115–49.

Evidence from the membrane of the glossed Luke I have already discussed (pp. 33–34) would confirm Gumbert's analyses. Most quires (see pp. 90–91) here alternate leaves from the skins of distinct beasts, C (calf) and S (sheep). The usual ordering of the two types, CSCSSCSC, indicates that the sheets were cut into bifolia before copying, for that is the only way to achieve that alternation. You cannot fold the uncut sheets to produce anything other than CCSS/SSCC or CSSC/CSSC (this last a widely attested form in manuscripts that mix membrane and paper, analogously MppM/MppM). The same must be true of the single sheep-skin bifolia inserted in two of the manuscript's quires. This

---

The Case of Sloane 2275', *Journal of the Early Book Society* 18 (2015), 1–28; and for SJ 127, catalogue 178–79, which is not entirely accurate, and needs to be supplemented by *Editing Medieval Texts: An Introduction, using exemplary materials derived from Richard Rolle, 'Super Canticum' 4* (Liverpool, 2015), 159–60. As that supplementary discussion indicates, the apparent plan for this manuscript was not fulfilled, and failure of supervision, with consequent lack of communication between participating scribes, is always a potential danger in such shared work.

evidence requires a quire that is a little book. On the other hand, the quires fully sheep could have been copied on the open sheet, although, given the evidence elsewhere in the MS, are unlikely to have been so. I would suppose, as Gumbert argues, that the most fundamental unit of a manuscript is the 'bifolium', not, as Gilissen argued, the quire produced by folding a single sheet.

However, there is a small literature on books certainly copied on open sheets. See G. I. Lieftinck, 'Medieval Manuscripts with "Imposed" Sheets', *Het Boek* 3rd ser. 21 (1961), 210–20; Charles Samaran, 'Manuscrits "imposés" à la manière typographique', *Recueil d'études …: Une longue vie d'érudit*, 2 vols (Geneva, 1978), 2:547–61 [originally 1957]; and 'Manuscrits "imposés" et manuscrits non coupés: Un nouvel exemple', *Codices Manuscripti* 2 (1976), 38–42; Doyle, 'Further Observations on Durham Cathedral ms. A.iv.34', *Varia Codicologica: Essays Presented to G. I. Lieftinck I*, ed. J. P. Gumbert and M. J. M. de Haan (Amsterdam, 1972), 35–47. These examples universally appear in small books, although there is evidence for open-sheet copying in the full-sized Merton College, MS 68.[87]

Equally, there are certainly examples of copying into a purchased prepared book. However, with only one exception I know, these are late and devoted not to literary copying but to legal record. BodL, MSS Tanner 194 and 224, with accounts from Hickling priory (OSA, Norfolk), c. 1509 and 1519, are pre-prepared paper books, both on a single stock, apparently acquired bound – and the greater portion still blank. MS Tanner 221, fol. 1ᵛ, c. 1507, again mainly accounts, in this case of a religious guild, is similar and yet more explicit about procedures: 'This booke *bought* and ordeigned by maister iohn collett doctour of diuinite and deane of the cathedrall chirche of poules and rectour of the fraternite and guilde of iesus in the croudes of the seid chirche' (my emphasis). The one possible literary example I have run across, on membrane, is BodL, MS Rawlinson C.894, where 24 leaves prepared for writing in the same way as the rest, but completely blank, appear at the end of the book.

On copying generally see Michael Gullick, 'How Fast Did Scribes Write: Evidence from Romanesque Manuscripts', *Making the Medieval*

---

[87] The use of 'imposition' here (as also in Gilissen's title, p. 2/2) is unfortunate. All these authors meant to suggest an analogy with the most familiar method of producing a text on a full open sheet. However, that process, in which a text is quite literally imposed on the full sheet, but multiple pages simultaneously, not successively, is proper only to the world of print. On evidence for this feature in Merton 68, see *Bodleian Library Record* 27 (2014), 135–36.

Book: Techniques of Production, ed. Linda Brownrigg (Los Altos Hills CA, 1995), 39–58; Ker, 'Eton College MS 44 and its Exemplar', coll 87–99; 'Copying an Exemplar: Two Manuscripts of Jerome on Habbakuk', coll 75–86; S. J. P. van Dijk, 'An Advertisement Sheet of an Early Fourteenth-Century Writing Master at Oxford', *Scriptorium* 10 (1956), 46–64 (and de Hamel, *Scribes*, 1st edn, plates 30 and 31). One matter of particular interest, accuracy of copying, can be assessed through scribes' multiple copies of the same material (often through a repetitive error); see Beadle, 'Some Measures of Scribal Accuracy in Late Medieval English Manuscripts', *Probable Truth* (full reference at n.2), 223–39.[88]

What texts does it contain?

Finally (you will be saying), we can get down to what everyone has books for, the contents. Perhaps your primary obligation, once you take up any book, is to prepare a listing of its texts. You should identify each text in the book, as you come upon it, in a page by page examination. Initially, because only experience will allow you to recognise any text readily, you are required to transcribe, – that is, copy down – the text's limits, its 'incipit' (from the Latin opening *Hic incipit* 'Here begins') and its end, the 'explicit' (a hangover from books on scrolls, *explicitus* 'it's unwound'). These, as we will see – the incipit in particular – are the most ready identifiers of texts.

At both points you are apt to find more than the text itself, most conventionally (although far from universally) something you will recognise from your inner image of the first page, a heading or rubric. You must transcribe this as well, although italicised or underlined, to indicate that it is a scribe's identification, not an integral part of the text, and not necessarily the way in which that text is known to a modern audience.[89] Following the rubric, you should transcribe about

---

[88] This kind of error occurs fairly frequently in short, especially repetitive passages. For an extensive example, see *Speculum Vitae: A Reading Edition*, EETS 331–32, 1:101–08, where the scribe of BL, MS Royal 17 C.viii, having apparently lost his place in his exemplar, repeats nearly 200 lines.

[89] For example, at Cambridge, Queens' College, MS 10, fol. 29 (pp. 134, 137), the scribe identifies a new text as 'Scintillarum poetarum Alexandri Nequam'. As my finished description there indicates, the authorial ascription is commonplace, but incorrect, although the title ascribed is probably the one the actual author

ten words – and at the conclusion again ten words plus any concluding rubric (often referred to as a 'colophon'). Do pay attention at the end, however; a great many texts, whether their authors intended it or not, conclude formulaically, some version of 'Qui cum patre regnat, etc.'. That is obviously not particularly distinctive, and you should start your transcription of the incipit ten words or so before the concluding formula begins.[90]

A brilliant guide to transcription appears at Parkes's *ECBH*, xxvii–xxx. It will not solve all your problems, many of which will concern decipherment, recognising the scribe's intended spelling and word. Most immediately, you will be faced by the fact that the proverbial 'Time is money' applies to scribal activity. The faster you copy (and the less membrane or paper you use), the more you are going to profit. As a result, if they can avoid it, scribes, particularly ones copying Latin, are loath to write out many words in full. (Scribes copying vernacular texts customarily limit themselves to a substantially reduced selection of the multiple 'shorthand' forms ubiquitous in Latin manuscripts, originally a product of taking dictation, or notes during a lecture.)[91] There is an extensive guide to the commonest abbreviated forms: A. Cappelli, *Dizionario di Abbreviature latine ed italiane*, 6th edn (Milan, 1967). You should add a copy to your scholarly library, and you should try to internalise the most common examples, the ones you run across more than once, just as you would 'the thousand basic characters' were you setting out to learn Chinese.

Unfortunately, Cappelli's examples are primarily drawn from Italian manuscripts, and abbreviation is subject to local variations, both temporally and spatially (if not, as I'll suggest, complete personal

---

intended (although far from that universally reproduced). This information may prove valuable should you investigate the circulation of your text, because catalogues of lost libraries customarily refer to their texts by contemporary, rather than modern, titles. On this subject, see Sharpe's brilliant *Titulus: Identifying Medieval Latin Texts. An Evidence-Based Approach* (Turnhout, 2003).

[90] Similarly, the incipits of sermons and other biblically predicated texts require extra care. These invariably start with a biblical verse (something likely to be widely repeated, and thus not distinctive). One can cite it, or a portion, but the incipit of the sermon is what follows. See the model presentation, Siegfried Wenzel, *Latin Sermon Collections from Later Medieval England* (Cambridge, 2005), 403–671 passim.

[91] Cf. Parkes, 'Tachygraphy in the Middle Ages: Writing Techniques Employed for *Reportationes* of Lectures and Sermons', coll 19–33.

whim).⁹² You should never be surprised (although you may be irritated) to run across something completely unrecorded that you must somehow interpret. For example, English scribes routinely use 'the common mark' not as the customary instruction 'add a nasal here' but as 'go to the next nasal in this word': so *com̄da-* for *com(m)enda-*. I recall coming upon the abbreviation 'm̄ia', which everywhere in Europe represents *misericordia* 'pity' (and is one of your 'thousand basic characters'), but in a context – the insanity of heretics – where it could not possibly mean the expected. My best guess is that the scribe was well aware of the conventional form, and, given the senselessness of that form in this context, abbreviated following the common English rule; he expected his readers to understand *mania* 'madness'. (An alternative puzzler involving the same abbreviation: occasionally, but nonetheless repeatedly, English scribes use 'the common mark' to indicate 'supply u', since it's, after all, the same letter-form, two minims, as the customary 'n'.) Or again, in a rule for nuns, I ran across *legōnis*, a form I've never seen before (nor had Capelli); after thinking about the context, that the rules emerge from a bishop's visitation, I finally hit upon *legacionis*. So, sometimes, you're just stuck with mother wit and imagination.

Scribes, of course, make mistakes – and, indeed, one common image assumes they will. In this conventional depiction, the scribe writes right-handed and holds in his left a penknife, both the implement for sharpening his goose-quill pen and his eraser, used for scraping an errant reading from the sheet. Of course, this presupposes that, as a conscientious labourer, he will correct his gaffes.

Indications of correction appear frequently in manuscripts. The most universal sign that an effort has been made is the abbreviated form 'corr²', less frequently 'ex²', usually unobtrusively at the foot of a

---

[92] Thus, Auguste Pelzer, *Abbréviations latines médiévales: Supplément au Dizionario* ... (Louvain and Paris, 1964), adds mainly items you will find only in 'scholastic' books, manuscripts of Aquinas, for example. Although it was constructed for other purposes, as the title indicates, frequently Charles T. Martin, *The Record Interpreter: A Collection of Abbreviations, Latin Words and Names Used in English Historical Manuscripts and Records*, 2nd edn (London, 1910), offers aid in English situations neither of these scholars saw. On early systems of abbreviation, for example, see W. M. Lindsay, *Notae Latinae: An Account of Abbreviation in Latin MSS. of the Early Minuscule Period (c. 700–850)* (Cambridge, 1915); and Lowe, 'Nugae Palaeographicae', *Palaeographical Papers*, 1:315–25.

page.⁹³ These are the abbreviations for *corrigitur* 'it is corrected' and *examinatur* 'it is examined'; both indicate that some protracted effort at proofreading has gone on, the copied text being compared with its exemplar. This was not necessarily the same isolated activity as copying the text may have been; at least, the easiest way to envision the process is as one person reading the exemplar, the copy from which the scribe has made his new one, aloud, while the scribe holds his copied text and ensures that what he has written corresponds to what he hears. As such, these marks may then testify to cooperative endeavour and to the existence of at least quasi-formal associations between scribes. For example, both ChCh Allestree F.1.1 and L.4.1 have been extensively corrected, with both marginal notation of errors and erasure. Markings that corrective procedures have been undertaken appear page by page in SJ 134, 153, and Magd lat. 6, fols 164–73, as well as on several folios of BodL, MS Bodley 16, fols 27–48. In MS Bodley 549 (II), most quires are marked 'co²' in the gutter at the foot of the last verso.

Corrections, however the need for them is identified, follow certain conventions. The full range is on display at Cambridge, Emmanuel College, MS 35, fols 63–99, a copy of Rolle's *Incendium amoris*, s. xv med. Here the text has been edited and corrected later to accommodate it to a different version.⁹⁴ Similarly, CUL, MS Ll.1.15, fols 202ᵛ–3ᵛ, s. xiii ex., exhibits a wide range of conventional markings. Again, these are later corrections of a previously copied text, Walter Map's *Dissuasio Valerii*, read against a copy very different from the exemplar the original scribe had copied.

Some corrections, such as erasures, are simply imposed on the copied text itself. However, as a scribe, you needn't erase an error; if it is simply an extra word you shouldn't have written, you can cancel it, with a cross-hatch of lines, a *cancellus* 'a lattice-work'. Alternatively, extra erroneous letters can be removed while still remaining visible and legible; the corrector accomplishes this by placing a dot beneath the portions of a word that are to be ignored, sometimes called 'subpunction', but more usually 'expunction' (and the offending elements are said to be 'expunged'). Very large erroneous insertions are frequently also legible, but marked, in this case, with the word *vacat*

---

⁹³ You might notice, again, that this location means that notation of this activity may have run foul of the binder's plane; in any event, the absence of such marks does not mean that the activity has not occurred.

⁹⁴ One leaf from the MS with extensive examples of this work appears as the cover image to *Richard Rolle: Unprinted Latin Writings* … (Liverpool, 2019).

'it's void/empty'; sometimes it appears whole near short omissions, but more frequently as 'va' at the head of offending matter, 'cat' at the end (which may be some distance away). This instruction appears on a rejected erroneous leaf in SJ 153, and a spaced 'va ... cat' corrects a bit of repeated text at the boundary between two scribes' stints at BodL, MS Bodley 43, p. 105.

If a leaf is considered too erroneous to bother with correcting, it is excised, a 'cancel(ed leaf)', and sometimes a replacement provided. This has clearly occurred in places where you'll discover a missing leaf (see further p. 91), but where the text is continuous. For example, BodL, MS lat. th. d.15 (Rolle tracts, s. xvi med.) has three cancelled leaves with no loss of text, including a 'ghost-leaf', fol. 56.[95] On a few occasions, you'll find that the offending leaf is still present in the book, although not in its original position. In Magd lat. 127 (glossed Job, s. xii ex.), fol. 144 appears originally to have been a ruined copy of fol. 2, but removed and reused as part of the final portion of the book, where it was not needed for copying.[96] In Oxford, Keble College, MS 49 ('The Regensburg lectionary'), the original fol. 116 was deemed unfit for use in the book but was replaced and subsequently recycled as the front pastedown. In Cambridge, Jesus College, MS Q.B.18 (James 35), two rejected text-leaves (Latin *Mandeville's Travels*, s. xv) are tucked in among the rear flyleaves.

Just as frequently as adding what they shouldn't have, scribes also omit. Short examples typically are signalled with the mark '∧', a *caret* (Latin 'it is lacking') and supplied by interlineations (words between the original writing lines) or in the margins. In transcriptions, these are customarily set off by '\ ... /'. But more flagrant examples frequently require extensive surgery. In the Bodleian's 'Great Bible', MS Auct. E. inf. 2, during the repetitive 'begats' at the head of Matthew, the original scribe omitted clauses; the text has been scraped, and a different hand has squeezed in the much more extensive materials that should have appeared here. Similarly, in BodL, MS Oriental 62, an Anglo-Hebrew MS, at a page-boundary, a frequent locus of scribes' distraction (as

---

[95] I.e. the leaf-number was omitted when BodL foliated the manuscript, but the continuous text shows the leaf was cancelled during copying and never present in the manuscript (which remains in its contemporary, probably original, binding).

[96] The transposition here obviously required moving the other half of the bifolium as well; in its original position, at the head of the book, it had not been copied on and remained blank, but, when moved to near the end, it bears consecutive text.

is, more frequently – and surprisingly – the end of a line), the scribe returned to his exemplar at Ezechiel 30:13, rather than 30:10, as he should have done. (The verses open with the same words.) He was followed by the scribe who provided the Latin Vulgate version in a marginal column, and the omitted text(s) have been supplied in the lower margin.[97]

In MS Oriental 62, this correction is signalled by what may be a double 'signe de renvoi'. These are matching arbitrary signs at the point of an omission and at the head of the text to be inserted, to indicate 'this text should go here', here a sideways 'V' and a mark 'o–o'. (What I describe as a 'sideways V' may simply be a large caret to indicate an omission, and only the second mark a signe de renvoi.) Other examples of such arbitrary signs to redress serious textual dislocations include examples pointing the proper order for sheets reversed in the binding in SJ 7 and 78; in SJ 198, the point to insert material on an added bifolium with corrections is indicated by signes de renvoi. Most vertiginously, in ChCh 152 (Chaucer, *Canterbury Tales*), a previous – presumably the first – binding, one that preceded the foliation now affixed in an early modern hand, had reversed the leaves in two different places. These bear notes (s. xv) with signes de renvoi to direct a reader through the text, such as 'turne over v. lefes to thys sygne [a diamond]' (fol. 21ᵛ). In the rebinding, the order of the leaves was corrected, so that now the answering signs appear on the immediately following leaves.

Finally, scribes routinely correct words they have transposed while copying; the conventional mark for the instruction, 'reader, reverse these two words', is the paired marks //...// written at ascender height at the head of the two words affected.[98]

But not so fast ... Remember: patience is a virtue. Besides an incipit, there's one further thing to notice at textual openings: devices in the book to supplement a contents table or other aid, ways of

---

[97] For images of both these contretemps see N. R. Ker, *English Manuscripts in the Century after the Norman Conquest* (Oxford, 1960), plate 22a (and discussion at 50–51); and Judith Olszowy-Schlanger, *Les manuscrits hébreux dans l'Angleterre médiévale: étude historique et paléographique* (Paris, 2003), plate 16 (p. 232), respectively.

[98] See further Gameson, *Trinity* 51, for a discussion of corrections in that College's MSS. There is a, to my mind ineffectual, discussion in Daniel Wakelin, *Scribal Correction and Literary Craft: English Manuscripts 1375–1510* (Cambridge, 2014); the monolingual author would have done better to include Latin MSS in his survey, where such features are vastly more extensive.

making a text immediately locatable and available for consultation. These usually take the form of small pieces of waste vellum pasted to the edge of the first leaf of a text. Such finding tabs appear, for example, at SJ 29, 85, 96, 101, etc.;[99] and similar tabs are virtually universal in manuscripts at Jesus College, Cambridge, although here mainly part of extensive library revision, s. xvii/xviii. Other forms of marking text heads for ready consultation occur here and there. ChCh 91 and Allestree M.1.10 have sewn-in bits of string along the leading edge. In Magd lat. 43 strips have been cut and turned out from the leaves to mark the heads of the individual texts and in BodL, MS Wood empt. 19 small parchment strips inserted through slits in the relevant leaves. Other books feature such finding features as attached bookmarks or inserted straws.

Having copied out your incipit and explicit, you have to identify the text. In many prominent cases, things like *The Canterbury Tales*, *La roman de la rose*, or Gregory the Great's *Moralia in Iob*, it's like falling off a log, but the greater majority of contents will send you on a bibliographical stroll to make an identification. I'd recommend one book, not produced to help here but inspirational in a variety of discussions and educative about the expected circulation of a large number of texts: Jacques Berlioz *et al.*, *Identifier sources et citations* (Turnhout, 1994).

Generally speaking, texts are identified by their incipit. The most extensive collection, although with limited references to relevant MSS, is Jacqueline Hamesse with Slawomir Szyller, *Repertorium Initiorum Manuscriptorum Latinorum Medii Aevi*, 4 vols (Louvain, 2007-10). In addition, for Latin texts, there is the very useful Brepols website 'In Principio'; this now appears to be a closed file, but similar listings have been continued in successive issues of the journal *Bibliographie annuelle du moyen-âge tardif*. Beyond general listings like these, numerous topically limited examples of *incipitaria* exist, such as Morton W. Bloomfield *et al.*, *Incipits of Latin Works on the Virtues and Vices, 1100-1500 A.D.* (Cambridge MA, 1979), now with Richard Newhauser and István P. Bejszy, *A Supplement* (Turnhout, 2008). (This tool has a far broader catchment, across a wide range of late medieval spiritual texts, than the title would suggest.) For medieval Latin verse, everyone takes as a standard Hans Walther and Alfons Hilka, *Initia carminum ac versuum medii aevi posterioris Latinorum*

---

[99] An example in SJ 167 typifies library practice in the great Bridgettine house Syon Abbey; see the reference to de Hamel's discussion, catalogue 232.

(Göttingen, 1959). There's an extensive bibliography of finding tools of all sorts in Sharpe, xxix–xxxvii, often suggestive of places to look for identifications.

All these sources will direct you to a published edition, or at least to another manuscript, and you should verify your identification (and the textual materials you cite) through comparison with it. Although I suspect that few cataloguers ever do this, believing it the province of editors, you should also verify the run of the text in your manuscript. Checking every folio-boundary is probably supererogatory, but at least ascertaining that the text remains continuous by checking your manuscript against an edition every eight folios or so is, at the very least, prudent. (In the absence of an edition, with an unpublished text you should check against an available second manuscript of the work in question; incipit lists will usually identify such an available copy for you.)

There are also numerous studies, ranging from book-length to brief articles, directing you to full manuscript lists of single authors or texts, frequently with additional information more helpful than printed editions. One of the most useful, because covering commonly repeated texts of great authority (and thus numerous copies), is Eligius Dekker *et al.*, *Clavis Patrum Latinorum*, 3rd edn (Turnhout, 1995), perhaps easiest to use in conjunction with J. M. Clément, *Initia patrum Latinorum*, 2 vols (Turnhout, 1971–79). Examples of book-length studies dealing with complicated texts include Reginald Gregoire, *Homéliaires liturgiques médiévaux* (Spoleto, 1980), esp. 423–86 (on 'Paul the Deacon''s highly variable *Homiliarius*); and Columba M. Batlle, *Die 'Adhortationes Sanctorum Patrum' ('Verba Seniorum') in lateinischen Mittelalter: Überlieferung, Fortleben und Wirkung*, Beiträge zur Geschichte des alten Mönchtums und des Benediktinerordens 31 (Münster i. W., [1972]). As one example of a useful article-length listing, see Louis J. Bataillon, 'The Tradition of Nicholas of Biard's *Distinctiones*', *Viator* 25 (1994), 245–88.

For texts in English, a good deal fewer of them than of Latin ones, there are well-known standard bibliographical guides, again keyed to incipits. Verse is covered in Carleton Brown and Rossell H. Robbins, *The Index of Middle English Verse* (New York, 1943), extended by a number of supplements, of which the most responsible, although incomplete, is 'The digital index', https://www.dimev.net, which is scrupulous in its attention to manuscript sources. Prose has been only fitfully covered, most globally by R. E. Lewis *et al.*, *Index of Printed Middle English*

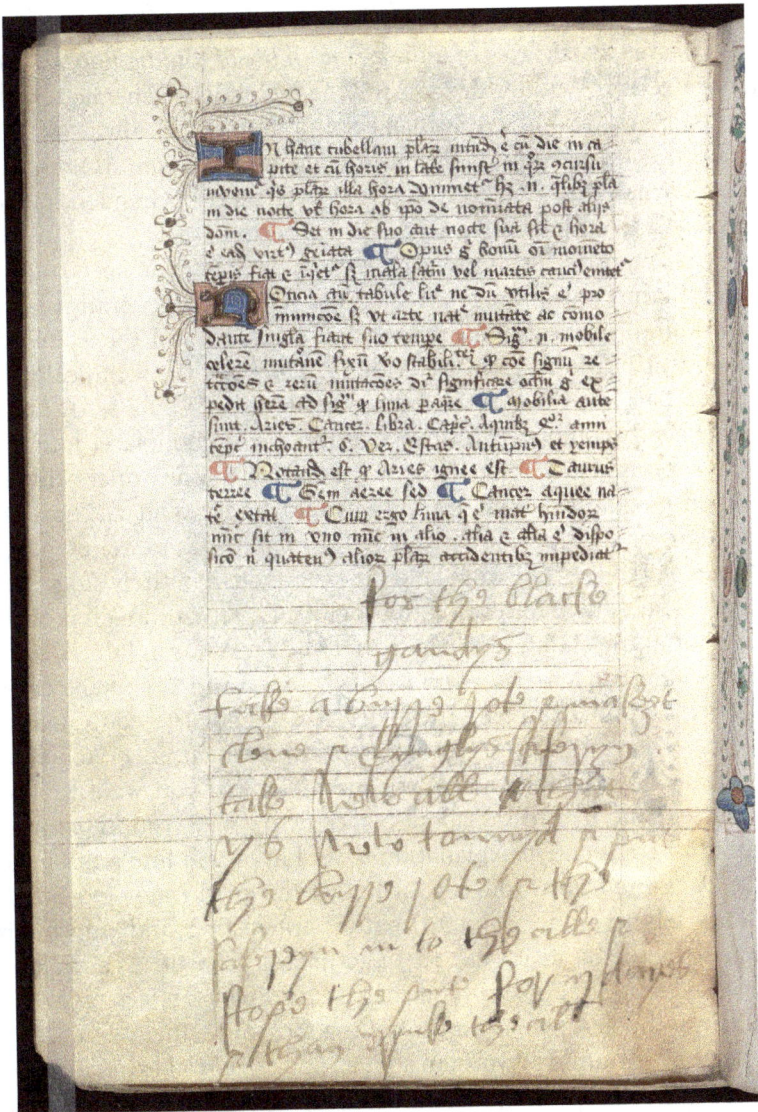

Filling blank space: While not Luxford's 'busy flyleaf', this image illustrates the fate of blank spaces in manuscript. Here, in a volume, s. xv ex., largely devoted to an English version of the pseudo-Aristotelian *Secreta Secretorum*, allegedly the philosopher's instruction to his pupil Alexander the Great, a blank page-foot has been filled by a reader's addition, s. xvi. This is a common type of text frequently added by later hands, a medical recipe 'for the blacke gandys' [i.e., 'jaundice'], and, like most such, begins 'Take a', the English equivalent of Latin 'Recipe'. (New Haven, Yale University Library, MS Takamiya 33, fol. 29ᵛ, reproduced at 56%).

Prose (New York, 1984).[100] Collection indexes of contemporary prose have appeared as fascicles of an ongoing *Index of Middle English Prose* (Cambridge and Woodbridge, 1984–); the incipit lists generated by this series, ed. Kari A. Rand, are available online at imep.lib.cam.ac.uk. Ruth J. Dean, *Anglo-Norman Literature: A Guide to Texts and Manuscripts*, Anglo-Norman Text Society occasional publication 3 (London, 1999) is exhaustive and authoritative.

If your manuscript contains more than one text, you keep running through to the end, looking for breaks between texts (generally marked by a heading), transcribing incipits and explicits, and then pursuing textual identifications from a relevant *incipitarium*, the technical name for collections like those I have been describing.

One nearly completely uninvestigated, yet commonplace, accompaniment to texts is the *tabula* 'table or list of words'. Many micro-divided texts come equipped with what we would understand as the lineal descendant of such devices, a 'table of contents'. But more interesting and unexplored are indexing tables; these are often entirely *sui generis*, an individual's guide to reading the book, but many, although probably not authorial, are standard appendices to their texts, as in John Trevisa's translation of Higden's *Polychronicon*, where it translates an antecedent Latin version, for example. These devices are not the equivalents of modern full-text indexing. Generally speaking, the users of 'tabulated' texts know how to find their main discussions: if you want to know what an exegete had to say about a specific passage, you know where to go in his consecutive explanation to find it, or you find a discussion in the *Polychronicon* through your knowledge of chronology. *Tabulae* are thus selective and point to matters interesting and informative that arise by the by, as it were, in an author's argument. As such, these devices present material for considering reading practices (as well as indicating a book's status as a continuing tool for textual reference).

But, having found all you can about a book's central texts, you aren't done yet. Recall my citation of Julian Luxford (p. 25). No blank space, whether in the text or binding leaves, is immune to being filled, and you have a responsibility to note and consider such things as marginalia and texts added by later hands. (These are particularly important, like *tabulae* are, when you come to consider a manuscript's use, readership, and post-production history.) The usual case is straightforward; for

---

[100] See also 'Extending the *Index of Printed Middle English Prose*', *The Medieval Journal* 9.1 (2019), 41–107, a preliminary survey of texts published since the original publication.

example, in medical manuscripts and books of remedies you can expect users to fill spaces with their own recipes, as in virtually any blank space in BodL, MSS Greaves 56 or Wood empt. 18.

At the opposite extreme, some producers, probably most frequently of manuscripts for personal use, will continue copying on any open surface, not necessarily adjacent to where they last left off. At *PH* 28–29 I described one persistent example of this behaviour in BodL, MS Ashmole 751. However, this scribe's practice is scarcely unique. In Magd lat. 93 John Dyg(g)on began copying what's now the unique surviving copy of Thomas Gascoigne's *Vita Sancti Hieronymi* (Sharpe 658) at fol. 233; he appears to have run out of writing material at the end of this segment on fol. 236. However, he had some textual material with a blank leaf at the end and resumed copying there, concluding the text on what's now fol. 226 of the MS, ten folios *ahead* of where he had broken off. Similarly, in Merton College, MS 68, a scribe, s. xv ex., began copying the unique copy of William Butler's 'determination' against translating the Bible into English within a block of blank leaves at fols 113–20ᵛ. Again, like Dyg(g)on, he ran out of space, and continued at the next available blank leaf he could find, about 80 folios later (fols 199–201).[101]

How has it been put together?

Unless the first text in your manuscript is very short, your search for its explicit/end is going to run you past features that are probably, from the point of view of the manuscript, as important as the text. In an s. xii or early s. xiii book, for example, you'll come to a mid-text verso that will have a large roman numeral 'I' centred at the foot and perhaps an apparently extraneous word written over toward the gutter. These form examples of a 'signature' and 'catchword'.

Whether a folded skin or a booklet formed from cut sheets, all books are constructed from small discrete units, their 'quires'. The

---

[101] See *Bodleian Library Record* 27 (2014), 130–31. The disruption between these two portions of the text was so severe that an incensed later reader who excised the scribe's initial copying never realised that the text continued far, far away, and we thus receive a partial copy of Butler's attack, ed. Anne Hudson *et al.*, *From the Vulgate to the Vernacular: Four Debates on an English Question c. 1400*, British Writers of the Middle Ages and the Early Modern Period 7 (Toronto and Oxford, 2020), cxviii–xxii, 115–49.

word is a derivative of Latin *quaternus* 'a group of four', and it is describing the simplest, and most common, case. The scribe takes up four sheets, folds them parallel to the short side, and produces a demi-book comprised of eight leaves, 16 'pages'. After cutting, these begin as four independent pairs, bifolia, the first and 8th leaves, the second and 7th, etc., which remain physically joined. In your inspection of the book, a basic responsibility is to identify all these smaller bunches of leaves and ascertain their limits.

Your guides in this regard are two features associated not with copying per se but with a topic treated above, binding the book. As you saw in that discussion, the fundamental purpose of binding is to preserve the copied pages – and, one should add, in an appropriate or desired order. Peculiar to binding is securing the individual quires in the overall binding structure; this requires sewing each quire, down its central fold, to the horizontal bands or thongs. Because the sewing has to secure all the leaves, it shows, at the centre of each quire, as a heavy thread in the gutter. Thus, in the simple case of a *quaternus* proper, four bifolia/eight leaves, you should be able to look down at the opening between fol. 4 and fol. 5 and see this sewing. If the sewing does not appear there, you are probably looking at a larger quire, one of five or six or more bifolia (ten or 12 leaves, etc.), and you should continue looking for sewing down the gutter. (If your MS is on paper, you may have to go on for quite some way, as paper books frequently and notoriously include very large quires; see Gumbert, 'Thick Quires in Italy', *Vernacular Manuscript Culture 1000–1500*, ed. Erik Kwakkel (Leiden, 2018), 219–32, a study that could be significantly extended by much larger English examples, such as Robert Thornton's propensity for quires of 26 leaves in folio.)

An immediate caveat: on many occasions, you won't be able to find these central sewings easily. Often books are tightly bound, and won't open fully. In a minority of cases, mainly examples of restoration from s. xvii or xviii, the book will have been 'over-sewn' or 'stab-bound'; a later binding will have involved sewing the book not from quire-centre to spine but end to end, above whatever sewing was there originally. This new sewing will prevent your seeing down to earlier sewing in the gutter. (One classic example is Cambridge, Emmanuel College, MS 35, a substantial collection of Richard Rolle, s. xv med.) In spite of the frustration you may feel in these circumstances, you must never open a book past 120–150 degrees; if you do so, you will put undue pressure on the spine and perhaps break it. A number of libraries provide book-rests or -cradles that will restrain your aggressive search for the sewing (most notoriously, the Pierpont Morgan Library in New York). But you must remember that you are not the only researcher who may be interested in this manuscript, and you owe it to all your successor colleagues to leave the volume in the state you found it.

It follows that, as you run through a book, the sewn quire centres should create their own rhythm. If you found sewing between fols 4 and 5, and if the book has been constructed in a consistent fashion, sewing should appear again between fols 12 and 13, fols 20 and 21, etc. And, consequently, quires should end at fols 8, 16, 24, etc. Recall my earlier comment that you should check the book's foliation at least every eight leaves; in addition to keeping track of anomalies in foliation, this will also alert you to an aberrations in a book's quiring (which occur frequently). Scribes do not always produce quires consistent in size, and any quire with an odd number of leaves is missing at least one somewhere. (Moreover, as Queens' College 10, quire 1, shows, simply an even number of leaves is no guarantee that everything originally there is still present; see p. 133, an erroneous first perception, corrected p. 137.)

This investigation will also solve one conundrum where my earlier treatment (p. 93) may have left you perplexed: how do you identify leaves added in binding? If you find the first text leaf, and if the sewing follows the fourth leaf, and if there is a catchword on the eighth leaf, you have identified the book's first quire. That being the case, everything preceding the first text leaf is binding material, not integral with the book's textual portions. (It's on this basis that I earlier identified the blank leaf in ChCh Allestree L.4.1 as part of the book, not the binding; without it, the first quire there would have had only seven leaves, and I could see, in the binding, that this leaf comprised a bifolium with the eighth, that they were 'conjoint'.) The same sort of procedures will sort this problem when you come to the end of the book.

Sewing secures the quires in the binding. But how did they pass, as loose materials, at best the small booklets of the quires, to the binder? And how did he know what order to sew them in? The answer is that, in addition to copying, the scribe, just as he may have provided guides for headings or initials, left signs in the book to direct the binder's activities. These are an important, if subsidiary, aid in separating the quires; often, they do not appear to be part of the scribal work (not in the same ink, for example) and, in some cases, may represent much later additions.[102]

---

[102] For example, Robert Cotton's binder, s. xvii in., routinely disposed of existing bindings, but ensured he kept the constituent quires in order by writing

There are two forms of such marking. First of all, nearly universally, on the final leaf of a quire a scribe provides a 'catchword'. This is the first word of the next leaf, which is the first of the following quire. This marking is quite sufficient to ensure that quires remain in order; the binder simply looks at the foot of the final leaf he has sewn in and knows that he must next find the quire that begins with the word signalled there to proceed in sewing the book accurately.[103] Rather obviously, in any manuscript you examine, you should ensure that the catchword at the end of one quire matches up, as it should, with the first word on the next folio. (If it doesn't, most probably, a quire has been either lost or misbound – in the latter case you'll find another disruption like this later – although it is not unknown for scribes to offer erroneous inaccurate catchwords. To uncover that possibility, you will need to investigate whether the text appears to be continuous.)[104]

However, scribes regularly provide a second – a fail-safe, if you will – marking. Quires are also 'signed' – that is, given an ordering, in either the capital alphabetical series 'A, B, C, ... ' centred at the foot of the first leaf of each quire, e.g. in MS Titus D.xviii (*Ancrene Riwle*, s. xiii ex.). In his rebinding of Magd books, Robert Way often left similar notations, e.g. 12 extant examples in MS lat. 34. There are sporadic signs of similar added signatures in ChCh 111 to facilitate a partial rebinding, s. xx; and in Oxford, New College, MS 93, another binder, s. xvii, wrote a sequence of arabic numerals in the same position as Cotton's binder on nearly 30 quires.

[103] On only a handful of occasions have I run across a book with catchwords that did not place them in this final position, running ahead to connect one quire with the following one. In BL, MS Sloane 2275, a book on any number of counts erratically produced, the catchwords regularly appear on the first leaves of quires and run backwards, as do three added examples in SJ 95. In Cambridge, Jesus College, MS Q.G.13 (James 61), there's one 'backward-reading' catchword to accommodate a single leaf oddly bound in. There is one peculiar placement of these signals to watch out for: many continental books, s. xv, have vertical catchwords along the gutter rule, e.g. SJ 68 and 82, ChCh 113+114 and 508.

[104] For example, in Dublin, Trinity College, MS 69, fols 65–72 should be bound between fols 104 and 105 (and, in their current position, interrupt a clearly integral series of texts that otherwise runs from fols 1 to 82). In Magd lat. 198, fols 17–28 and 29–40 were once bound in erroneous reverse order, signalled by signes de renvoi; like ChCh 152, discussed at p. 84, this misordering has been corrected in the current, later binding. Oxford, Balliol College, MS 26 shows no such overt disruption, but either its scribe or a predecessor had spilled quires of his exemplar and, in restoring them, exchanged leaves between two of them; as a result, the textual materials at fols 29–33 and 53–57 have been (silently) transposed.

a numerical or an alphabetical sequence. If there isn't a catchword, or if the binder has missed it, he's doubly protected against misbinding. In early books these signatures appear, usually as large roman numerals, on either the first or the last leaf of a quire, at the page-foot. There are abundant examples at St John's, on, for example, the last verso in MSS 21, 24, 26, 29, 34, etc.; and on the first recto in MSS 60, 96, 118, 126, 165, etc. In two books, MSS 111 and 152 (I), the roman quire number appears on both the final verso and the first recto.

Two comments. First, neither of these markings should be foreign to your experience, since both are longstanding components of print-book culture (where they reflect carryovers from that of manuscript). A great many books, down to s. xviii, have catchwords, although most frequently for pages, not quires, as an aid to continuous reading (so that one doesn't lose track of the drift when distracted by having to turn the page). And British books, well past the middle of the last century, have the equivalent of quire signatures. For example, Beryl Smalley's *English Friars and Antiquity in the Early Fourteenth Century* (Oxford, 1960) has a tiny B at the foot of p. 1, C at p. 17, D at p. 33, etc., all the way to Z at p. 337, and then subsequent AA (p. 353), etc. (In this case, the marks indicate the printed sheets, eight pages on each side, that had to be folded and cut to produce the bound book.)

Second, you should not be surprised to find neither of these helpful markers in your book. As I have suggested, both catchwords and signatures appear low on the leaf; as a result, they frequently fall victim to the binder's plane, part of his process of creating for you the semblance of a clean page. On many occasions you will be able to intuit their original presence, since, just as the binder may not have been scrupulous about preserving running titles or top of the page decoration, he may not have been fastidious about removing all signs of production detail. Even if nearly all the signatures and catchwords may have been cut away, you may still run across the tops of roman numerals or catchwords at the page feet.

The destructive efforts of binders in effect produce, accidentally or not, a 'clean book'. But many scribes were not content to leave their catchwords as unostentatious markers of incompleted production. Perhaps initially as an aid to binders, they emphasised their catchwords through minor bits of decoration, often with colour (the 'finisher's' red or ochre) for emphasis. Utterly commonplace are boxed catchwords, ones enclosed in rectangular frames, as in SJ 7*, 10, 76, 108*, 130* (the starred examples with red). Perhaps nearly so frequently, the catchwords appear on scrolls, as in SJ 2, 144 (quite elaborate), 179, 197, or ChCh 90 (with a wash and red). Half-boxes or cartouches appear somewhat less frequently, as in SJ 142 or 197 (red). And odd shapes like ellipses (SJ 25) or an interlace pattern (SJ 109), or examples with an ochre slash or wash (SJ 79, 101, 131, etc.) are reasonably routine.

A good many decorated catchwords are associated with drawings, ranging from the kind of doodling often left by readers in margins up to fairly artistic examples. In Magd lat. 9 and 155, boxes round the catchwords attract extra strokes that covert them into dogs or boats. One scrolled catchword in SJ 14, fol. 36^v, has an associated drawing of a snake's head (in red). In Magd lat. 97, drawings, in ink with some red highlighting, appear associated with the catchwords: for example, a pope (fol. 10^v), a virgin and child (fol. 30^v), a knight in a castle (fol. 100^v), a mounted king (fol. 120^v), an eagle (part of a series of symbols of the evangelists; fol. 130^v), (?) *La roman de la rose*'s Oiseuse with her mirror and comb (fol. 150^v).[105]

I have described these quire-differentiating production marks in terms of final (or sometimes first) leaves, and I've rather ambiguously noted that that is where they appear in 'early books'. But signature systems provide another example of the book revolution that occurred s. xii/xiii. My colleague Rod Thomson universally describes, without further comment, 'signatures of the usual late medieval form': from s. xiii in. it became customary to sign not the first or last page but all the leaves in the first half of each quire, and to assign each quire in sequence either a letter or, as previously, a number. These marks, usually in a form like 'a iij', customarily appear low on the outer corner of rectos, another detail for you to notice (and to aid you in your examination of the book's quiring – you should most normally observe a sequence like 'i–iiij' before you find the quire-sewing). But again, this is detail that, given its placement, you should not be surprised to find that the binder has removed. These notations, of course, appear only in the first half of quires, because they are identifying the bifolia that make up the quires (and that almost always remain joined and intact in the binding today).[106]

---

[105] For analogous examples, see K. L. Scott, 'The Remains of a Missal: Chetham's Library MS 6713', *Tributes to Lucy Freeman Sandler: Studies in Illuminated Manuscripts*, ed. Kathryn A. Smith and Carol H. Krinsky (Turnhout, 2007), 299–314, at 301 n.14.

[106] In this regard, you should ignore J. P. Gumbert, 'Skins, Sheets, and Quires', *New Directions in Later Medieval Manuscript Studies*, ed. Derek Pearsall (Cambridge, 2000), 81–90, who's following Michael Gullick, 'From Scribe to

Rod Thomson's 'usual ... form' only summarises a multitude of practices. What he signals is that this system marks both the order of the quire and the order of bifolia within the quire. (And may well, if the order isn't followed, alert you that something's gone amiss – bifolia bound in the wrong order within the quire, for example.) The exact form of marking is highly various, and the only thing that seems to have interested scribes is that signing follow an identifiable sequence, whether alphabetical or numerical (and whether imposed in roman or arabic, or some combination of both), or occasionally just a sequence of strokes '/–////' at the feet of the leaves.

You have an obligation to keep track of the signatures in your book. For example, a jump in a sequence, one quire 'xii'/'12' and the next 'xiiij'/'14', will alert you to a possible textual omission – and potentially that the quire numbered 'xiiij'/'14' isn't a continuation of the text you've been reading, but the middle of something entirely new. (Of course, it may, on inspection, just turn out to be a scribal lapse – they are just as apt as manuscript foliators to nod here and there.)

This aid would be unproblematic (you can count), but for one thing. How many letters are there in the alphabet? Wrong answer. A medieval Latin alphabet has only 23 letters, with an optional 24th. In medieval scripts, the letters 'j', 'v', and 'w' 'do not exist'. That is, 'j' and 'v' are what are considered 'positional variants'; they exist as alternatives to 'i' and 'u' in specific contexts, 'v' at the head of a word, and 'j' at the end of a sequence of 'i''s (as in my roman rendition of '14' in the last

---

Binder: Quire Tackets in Twelfth-Century European Manuscripts', *Roger Powell: The Compleat Binder: Liber Amicorum*, ed. John L. Sharpe (Turnhout, 1996), 240–59. Gumbert argues that the end of tacketing (a membrane tab sewn through the quire-centre) was responsible for the switch to a different system of signing, since the absence of tackets left scribes no way to keep bifolia in order otherwise. Although an outstanding continental platonist, Gumbert seems to have forgotten that *post hoc, ergo propter hoc* is a logical fallacy. Traditional twelfth-century signing appears long after any evidence for tacketed quires, e.g. first-leaf quire signatures only in Merton College, MS 2 (s. xiii ex.); CUL, MS Ff.2.20 (s. xiii/xiv); Magd lat. 27 (s. xiii^1); or final-leaf quire signatures only in Magd lat. 54 (s. xiii^2) and lat. 69 (s. xv^2); quire signatures in both positions in Merton College, MS 19 (s. xiv), Magd lat. 66 (s. xiii med.), and many examples one would date to the transition, s. xiii in., as well as many more with mixed forms, both single quire numbers at head or end *and* leaf-numbering. Clearly, scribes had found some means of holding a quire's leaves together less ostentatious than tacketing, perhaps just a single looped thread that would be obscured by the binder's later sewing.

paragraph). And, of course, 'w' does not exist in the Latin alphabet.[107] Thus, alphabetical signatures always run *ghikl* and *stvxyz* – nothing's been left out here.

The optional 24th element comes at the head. In many manuscripts with alphabetical signatures, the second quire, not the first, will be signed *a*. In the first quire, you may see no quire-signature, or a small cross (+). This reflects the fact that children, when taught the alphabet, were supposed to cross themselves in hope of divine aid before beginning their recitation. Indeed, one synonym for 'alphabet' was 'cross-row', or 'Christ-cross-row'.[108] At the other end of the alphabet, manuscripts with 24 or more quires typically continue the sequence with signs, usually the abbreviations that indicate *et*, *est*, and *con* (usually a 7-shaped sign, ē, and a high loop), before going on to aa, bb, cc, etc.[109]

Only very occasionally will you run across odd-ball forms of leaf-signing. For examples – mainly matching arbitrary or alphabetical signs in the gutters of versos and the opposite rectos through the first half of the quire – see the catalogue descriptions of SJ 16, 63, and 113; ChCh 88 and 123; Magd lat. 192 (II). These are sufficient to ensure that the quire's leaves remain in the order intended. Rarely, you may run

---

[107] Which is why Old English scribes had to import the rune *wynn* 'ƿ' to represent the sound. And English, of course, at various times uses other letters alien to the Latin alphabet: æ, þ, ð, and ȝ. You will occasionally see 'w' in Latin scripts, invariably to represent a form like *vult/uult* (as *wlt*), where the letter represents its alphabetical name 'double u'. Confusingly, although 'v' is only a positional variant form of 'u', it, rather than 'u', is the usual signature, since it is, in a signature, standing at the head.

[108] Cf. the little poem at '*On the Properties of Things': John Trevisa's Translation of Bartholomaeus Anglicus De Proprietatibus Rerum: A Critical Text*, ed. M. C. Seymour *et al.*, 2 vols (Oxford, 1975), 1:40/3–5: 'Croys was maad al of reed / In þe begynnynge of my book – / That is cleped God me spede'.

[109] Just a small note. I'm sure you haven't run out to check a copy of Smalley's *English Friars*, mentioned above as a modern book fully signed by the quire. But if you were to do so, you'd discover very quickly that, as late as 1960, the publisher Basil Blackwell's compositors were still using a medieval alphabetical system. Hint: if p. 1 = B and p. 352 = the end of Z, and each sheet has 16 leaves, there are only 22 sheets. Figuring out things like this isn't just an idle operation; at the end of your examination of a manuscript you need to make sure that your total count of leaves (the manuscript's foliation, as corrected) equals the total you have counted in assigning the leaves to each quire. Little multiplication exercises – and learning to think in eights or dozens, not fives and dimes – like this are integral to the procedure.

across examples of overkill, signatures through the full quire. In SJ 75, for example, all the quire's leaves have received letters (here 'a–m', in a book with 12-leaf quires; notice: no 'j'); similarly parts of Magd lat. 111. In ChCh 92, signatures appear in upper corners on both rectos of the bifolia, probably because this opulently painted book was sent out, by the bifolium, to a group of artists to be illuminated. Occasionally, rather than signatures, catchwords in the gutter join leaves in the first half of the quire, as in Magd lat. 96 and 112.

There is a standard shorthand format for reporting how a manuscript is quired, often called a collation. A good discussion appears at BH 23–25 and, lest you think the attention there to notation of quires inserted in quires truly baroque, see the references to CUL, MS Ff.1.6 in n.113. SJ 84 (Sallust, s. xv med.) offers a further straightforward example. The MS includes 76 folios; these are disposed in nine quires of eight leaves and a concluding one of six. This last unit is sewn and signed as if it were of eight leaves, like the remainder, but, as frequently happens, blank leaves at the conclusion have been cut away. Again, although many have been cut away, the book was once fully signed, with a letter and arabic numeral on all leaves in the first half of each quire, from 'a 1' to 'k 4' (again, notice: no quire 'j'). Thus, the catalogue reports the book as constructed '1–9^8 10^8 (lacks 7 and 8, blank leaves)' – and something like 'i–ix^8, x^8 (-7, -8)' should have been just as effective and accurate a report.[110]

Determining the quire structure of paper books often involves difficulties. These stem from several facts: their quires are often supersized; they often represent relatively informal productions, frequently lacking signatures; their bindings have proven fragile and unstable, leaving piles of loose sheets (recall pp. 42–43). Conversely, through its watermarks, the paper itself often offers provocative evidence to help you through. Here the classic demonstration, focussed on the *Ludus Coventriae* or *N-Town Plays*, BL, MS Cotton Vespasian D.viii, is Stephen Spector, 'Symmetry in Watermark Sequences', *Studies in Bibliography* 31 (1978), 162–77.

I offered a pendant to Spector's study in 'The London Thornton Manuscript: A Corrected Collation', *Studies in Bibliography* 37 (1984), 122–30. That essay will suggest to you how to sequence watermarks:

---

[110] If you read catalogues of continental collections, be prepared to find quires designated by the number of their bifolia, as 'quaternions', etc. While this may draw attention to the basic construction (a bifolium, not a leaf, is the basic unit), the need to mark a single missing leaf as such is potentially a source of confusion here. If you're going to provide a formal description, help your reader!

notice and record the relevant folio for each watermarked leaf; use the pattern of paired leaves to identify a quire centre; and display the leaves in pattern.[111] Here's another example, from BL, MS Sloane 3489, fols 12–28, leaves that represent an independent manuscript with a copy of the popular herbal *Agnus Castus*, s. xv ex. This segment is on paper marked with Mountains (M), with an attached cross on the chainline (+) and folded in quarto. Partial watermarks appear on fols 18 M, 19 M, 21 M, 24 +, 25 +, 26 M, and ?28 M. However, the text is discontinuous, with material lost after fols 13, 15, 16, 23, and 24. The watermarks allow one to construct a collation (// = the quire centre, x = a missing leaf):

[1] a quire of 10: 12 13 x 14 15 // x 16 x 17 **18M**
[2] a quire of 8: **19M** 20 **21M** 22 // 23 x x x
[3] a quire of 6: **24+** x **25+** // **26M** 27 **28M** [including the only signed bit in the whole production, with c j and c iij on fols 24 and 25]

As I suggest in the essay on Thornton, you should try to construct a symmetrical diagram that will account for both marked sheets and unmarked ones. To do this, you diagram the folios while folding the leaves back over on themselves, so that your notation of the leaves in the first half of the quire will face their bifoliar mates in the second half. If you then add notations to indicate the marks you see, the sheets will reveal themselves nearly automatically. The easiest example here is the third quire; this is the founding example, since in this case, given losses, one needs to work backward:

24+ x **25+** //
28M 27 **26M**

---

[111] The essay also addresses Thornton tailoring quires from within by inserting extra sheets. My discussion preceded John J. Thompson's protracted study of this book, *Robert Thornton and the London Thornton Manuscript: British Library Additional 31042* (Cambridge, 1987), which came to slightly different, but analogous, results. For some further suggestive studies of paper quiring, see I. C. Cunningham, 'The Asloan Manuscript', *The Renaissance in Scotland: Studies in Literature, Religion, History and Culture Offered to John Durkan*, ed. A. A. MacDonald et al. (Leiden, 1994), 107-35; Bruce Barker-Benfield, *The Works of Geoffrey Chaucer and* The Kingis Quair: *A Facsimile of Bodleian Library, Oxford, MS Arch.Selden.B.24* (Cambridge, 1997), 35-60 (with beta radiograph images); 'Humphrey Newton and Bodleian Library, MS Lat. misc. c.66', *Medium Ævum* 69 (2000), 279-91.

As one would expect in a quire of six leaves, there's a half-sheet here (the full sheet in this fold provides only four leaves). In any case, it is this half-sheet that bore one of the watermarks. One can't be sure which of the watermarked bifolia is from the full sheet (and thus the rest of fol. 27's partially lost bifolium) and which from the half-sheet.

Working analogously, on this basis, one would identify in quire 1 the missing leaves 3+8, after fols 13 and 16, respectively, as a watermarked bifolium; the unwatermarked half of their sheet as fols 14 and 16; leaves 12+13+17+18 as a sheet surrounding them (the '+' on fol. 12 illegible); and fol. 15 the remains of a half-sheet without watermark. Were one to believe the production utterly rational (a view for which there is no evidence), one might suppose this half-sheet to be a pair with the marked half-sheet now in the third quire. And quire 2, although no longer intact, presents the normal case, two sheets, the first and third lost folios at the end with '+' to match fols 21 and 19, respectively.

Are there other discontinuities?

Finding the boundaries of quires is basic, but you'll frequently run upon something that appears to be a much more abrupt hiatus. The utterly seminal contribution in this regard is P. R. Robinson, 'The "Booklet": A Self-Contained Unit in Composite Manuscripts', *Codicologica* 3 (1980), 46–69. Robinson offers a further example in 'Self-contained Units in Composite Manuscripts of the Anglo-Saxon Period', *Anglo-Saxon England* 7 (1978), 231–38. In the first essay, Robinson's central exhibit was BodL, MSS Douce 132 + 137, a case of a single volume comprised of several discrete chunks, assembled by a private owner early s. xiv, dismembered by an early modern owner, and reassembled in her essay.

At a certain level, Robinson's findings – that many manuscripts are composites, assembled after the fact and joining originally independent books – is no big discovery. Cataloguers have routinely marked books as comprised of diverse elements for nearly two centuries, in Bodleian catalogues from the 1840s (William H. Black on the Ashmole MSS) on, and James regularly did so in his numerous catalogues of Cambridge libraries. It is commonplace to find these, for example:

> SJ 126: five separate MSS, of various dates, ss. xii ex. and xiii in., at least two portions probably joined contemporaneously (with more or less consecutive signatures);

SJ 178: six separate MSS, of various dates, ss. xiii¹ to xiv²/⁴, certainly together in this form since s. xv²/⁴, according to a contents table on the flyleaf, fol. iii;

ChCh 91: four separate MSS, the first three relatively contemporary with a contents table on fol. iᵛ, s. xv³/⁴, joined with the last, a book of s. xiii med. or xiii², in a binding contemporary with the contents table and majority contents;

ChCh 99: five separate MSS, of various dates, ss. xiii ex. to xiv²/⁴, together since the date of the current binding, s. xiv;

Magd lat. 6: six separate MSS, of various dates, ss. xiii/xiv to s. xv¹, certainly together in this form since s. xv med., according to a contents table on the first text-leaf (now fol. 3).[112]

Congeries like these reflect varying historical situations and, as we will see, in discussing 'provenance' below, it will be important for you to consider the mechanisms of juncture. Two of the books certainly represent library activity at medieval institutions, consolidating loose items within a single binding: SJ 178 is from Westminster Abbey and ChCh 91 from Crediton collegiate church, Devon. ChCh 99 certainly appears an institutional historical collection, but has no secure provenance. SJ 126 is a little more problematic; much of it, but not necessarily all, is certainly from Southwick (Hants, OSA), but the donor to St John's was the first Dissolution owner of the house's properties and the collection may reflect his depredation of the house library, possibly grouping his spoils with alien materials.

However, institutions are not the only responsible parties. Private citizens also collect what was loose around the house into a single book, as in Robinson's most extensive example.[113] Magd lat. 6 is clearly a

---

[112] This book is another fine example of misleading Oxford foliation (recall p. 44), numbered 3–233, but actually 244 leaves, with unnumbered blank leaves at the ends of units.

[113] Some well-known examples involve private parties gathering up loose bits they had produced into larger units, as famously with Robert Thornton; or Phillipa Hardman, 'A Medieval "Library *in Parvo*"', *Medium Ævum* 47 (1978), 262–73, and her *The Heege Manuscript: A Facsimile of National Library of Scotland MS Advocates 19.3.1* (Leeds, 2000). For further discussion, see Thompson and Julia Boffey, GP 279–315; Deborah Youngs, 'The Medieval Commonplace Book: The Example of the Commonplace Book of Humphrey Newton of Newton and

collection made for a priest's use, and designed to be passed on through a succession of such individuals. The second old front flyleaf (fol. 2ᵛ, at the foot) bears an inscription of about 1425: 'Whoever receives this book is bound to pray for the soul of Mr John Martell and for the souls of all the faithful; as well as, on receiving it, to give sixpence to poor people; and, after his death, to assign it to another virtuous priest, one who preaches God's word or plans to do so; so that this book may pass from one preacher to another, always preserving those conditions mentioned above.'[114] John Martell was born c. 1381 and was a fellow of Oriel College 1410×26. He donated to Oriel its MS 43 (Richard Fishacre on the *Sentences*) in 1430, and might be associated with assembling Magd lat. 6 (*BRUO* 1231).

However, as I have suggested of John White, looting Southwick and possibly other collections, modern owners have also found creating composite books a convenient mode of preservation. For the continuation of medieval practices into the early modern period, see Watson, 'A Sixteenth-Century English Sammelband', coll XII. In the process, loose fragments achieve some integrity as bound volumes. For a famous example, in this case a collector assembling fragments, including 'The

---

Pownall, Cheshire (1466–1536)', *Archives* 25 (2000), 58–73, with abundant further references; 'The Production of Cambridge University Library MS. Ff.i.6', *Studies in Bibliography* 40 (1987), 62–70, again with further references, particularly to Kate Harris's discussion.

[114] 'Quilibet hunc librum recipiens tenetur pro anima Magistri Iohannis Martyll specialiter et animabus omnium fidelium orare; in recepcione eiusdem libri, vj. d pauperibus distribuere; et eundem librum post decessum suum alteri honesto sacerdoti, verbum dei predicanti vel predicandum proponenti, assignare; ita quod iste liber sic transiat ab vno predicatore ad alium, predictis condicionibus semper saluis'. Injunctions of this type are commonplace; they appear frequently in John Dyg(g)on's books, e.g. SJ 77 or Magd lat. 77; see further Jo Ann H. Moran, 'A "Common Profit" Library in 15th-Century England and Other Books for Chaplains', *Manuscripta* 28 (1984), 17–25. Moran's title stretches the meaning of 'common profit book'; see Wendy Scase's discussion, heavily indebted to Doyle, 'Reginald Pecock, John Carpenter and John Colop's "Common Profit" Books: Aspects of Book Ownership and Circulation in Fifteenth-Century London', *Medium Ævum* 61 (1992), 261–74, as well as Sheila Lindenbaum, 'London after Arundel: Learned Rectors and the Strategies of Orthodox Reform' and James Willoughby, 'Common Libraries in Fifteenth-Century England: An Episcopal Benefaction', both in *After Arundel: Religious Writing in Fifteenth-Century England*, ed. Vincent Gillespie and Kantik Ghosh (Turnhout, 2011), 187–208 and 209–22, respectively.

Macro Plays', s. xv moralities, see Beadle, 'The Manuscripts of James Cobbes of Bury St Edmunds (c. 1602–1685)', *The Medieval Book and a Modern Collector: Essays in Honour of Toshiyuki Takamiya*, ed. Takami Matsuda *et al.* (Woodbridge and Tokyo, 2004), 427–42; and his elaborate essay on Cobbes's (and others') activities with one such book, 'Macro MS 5: A Historical Reconstruction', *Transactions of the Cambridge Bibliographical Society* 16 (2016), 35–77 (as well the Rouses' description of one component, now UCLA, MS Rouse 51, at 128–36).

Thus, Robinson's most salient contribution was in trying to offer signals for identifying such subsidiary units. However, the issue is more complicated than Robinson imagined. For it is not just 'composite manuscripts' that display discontinuous features. Subsidiary units, independent chunks of a single quire or of a good deal more, provide a commonplace method for making a book. Rather than a feature of reception, part of the manuscript's ongoing history, as in the examples I cite above, it is a feature of production, marked in many books. I tried to make this point in an early essay, with a good many examples, *PH* 21–34.[115]

There I pointed out that Robinson's tool might be more powerful as a way of understanding book production. I offered a prioritisation of categories for recognising that such divisions had occurred in the process of making books. The most powerful indications of piecemeal production in 'booklets' or 'fascicles' seemed primarily breaks in consecutive presentation, particularly where the conclusion of a quire and of a text coincide. But I went on to suggest that this might be shown as non-accidental on the basis of several persuasive signs: sequences of quires with independent signature systems,[116] variation in the size of unit-ending quires (the essay emphasises the final quire, but I would now add the penultimate one as well), and blank leaves at quire-ends (often cut away). (You've already run upon this last feature in the vicissitudes of Oxford foliation, with Magd lat. 162 and 6.) Obviously enough, variations in the scribal hand and format are further indicators, although secondary ones, since both often shift within books continuously produced.[117]

---

[115] A revised and expanded version of 'Booklets in Medieval Manuscripts', *Studies in Bibliography* 39 (1986), 100–11.

[116] Thus, it's important to supplement Rod Thomson's general statement of 'late medieval signing' by attending carefully to the sequence(s) of marks assigned.

[117] See further Gumbert, 'Codicological Units: Towards a Terminology for the Stratigraphy of the Non-Homogeneous Codex', *Segno e testo* 2 (2004), 17–42, a continental platonising initiative taken up in spades in Patrick Andrist *et al.*, *La*

We might examine two simple cases, SJ 15 and SJ 16, which are structurally rather similar. Both manuscripts involve single scribes copying a succession of texts, apparently books continuously produced. However, on examination each falls into separable units, in which individual texts have quasi-independent status, each demonstrably in a separate unit of production. Yet, as we will see, this generic similarity might obscure the conclusions you would draw about the production of either. I offer the brief overviews (full accounts at catalogue 23–26):

SJ 15, fols 257, copied s. xv$^{2/4}$

[1] Fols 1–120: Augustine, epistles (fols 114^v–20 indexes to the texts, two of these not the original scribe, but added on the originally blank fols 116–20; much of fol. 120 and all of fol. 120^v blank) = quires 1–10, fol. 120 an extra leaf at the end;

[2] Fols 121–82: Ambrose, epistles (fol. 182^{rv} an index, which appears added, in the same scribal hand, but in a much larger script, to fill the leaf) = quires 11–16, fols 181–82 a concluding bifolium; and

[3] Fols 183–257: Thomas Becket, epistles (fols 253–57 an added index in a later hand) = quires 17–23, fols 255–57 a concluding four with the final blank leaf cancelled.

Continuous original signatures: the quires lettered [+], a–f, [g], h–i ∥ k–l, [m], n–o ... ∥ y on the penultimate quire 22, indicating a skip in the sequence somewhere.

SJ 16, fols 132, copied s. xiii med.

[1] Fols 1–33: Joshua, with the ordinary gloss = quires 1–4, the concluding quire of ten leaves, not eight as the preceding ones, and the last (probably blank) leaf excised;

[2] Fols 34–79: Judges, Tobit, Judith, and Esther, with the ordinary gloss = quires 5–10 (with probably three missing quires in the middle), the last quire of six leaves, not eight as the preceding ones;

syntaxe de codex: essai de codicologie structurale, Bibliologia 34 (Turnhout, 2013). More generally helpful and suggestive is Gumbert's 'C Catalogue and Codicology – Some Readers' Notes', *A Catalogue and Its Users: A Symposium on the Uppsala C Collection of Medieval Manuscripts*, ed. Monica Hedlund, Acta Bibliothecae R. Universitatis Upsaliensis 34 (Uppsala, 1995), 57–70.

[3] Fols 80–132: Acts, with the ordinary gloss = quires 11–16, the last leaf with the end of the text, but probably mostly blank, now lost.

There are no signatures, but all the quires are joined by catchwords. The missing quires may have included a further division in production, Judges copied apart from the consecutive presentation Tobit–Judith–Esther.

Signatures and/or catchwords show the integrity of both productions, always planned to be joined. However, both books display those concluding features that I have suggested initially mark separable production: final quires of a shape unusual in the continuous production appear in SJ 15/1–3 and SJ 16/1–2, and originally blank leaves at the conclusion in SJ 15/1 and 3; SJ 16/1–2.[118]

The comparable shapes of production, however, obscure certain contrasts one would wish to make in discussing the books. The first is a deliberate generic or thematic collection, of a sort one can imagine being used by a bishop or archdeacon seeking models for ecclesiastical administration, and its divisions correspond to materials derived from different authors. It had to be gathered, and its juxtaposition of 'the modern instance', Becket, with the two great Fathers is certainly provocative (cf. Henry VIII's effort at expunging Becket from memory in the 1530s). The second is a selection, essentially substantial excerpts from a much larger text (a full set of glossed biblical books at Magd runs 12 volumes, MSS lat. 121–32). Although additional pieces may now be missing, the manuscript would always have been a partial representation of the full text. The pieces may have been selected to concentrate on biblical history, perhaps especially episodes when the *numen* has just departed and there are consequently threats to holy community.

It is important to recognise such features. Discontinuity of this sort indicates the potential separability of any manuscript's contents. Analogously to those textual grabbags with which we began this discussion, the conjunction of texts in manuscript may be arbitrary. If it isn't simply a thoroughly arbitrary procedure (loose bits I found lying around), it is more apt to tell one about the interests of a manuscript's patron, perhaps intuitable (as the last paragraph may suggest), than it is

[118] For further discussion, see the elaborate presentation of SJ 94 at catalogue 125–30 (perhaps especially 128), and the provocative presentation of books once from Herne, Kwakkel, *Die dietsche boeke die ons toebehoeren: de Kartuizers van Herne en de productie van Middelederlandse handschriften in de regio Brussel (1350–1400)* (Louvain, 2002).

about inherent or historical connections between texts. However, there is no hard and fast rule for dealing with such collocations. In addition to the example I cite in the next paragraph, one might consider two contrasting studies. The first chapter of Jeremy Griffith's unfinished dissertation examined, among a range of similar books, SJ 257 (*Statutes*, s. xv/xvi). The work is clearly fascicular (catalogue 325–27, esp. the collation at 326), but the division into such booklets is simply imitating the scribe's source, the great roll of the Statutes, where these materials appeared on separate rolls. Conversely, the Rouses demonstrate that two texts of Cicero, traditionally considered separately by classicists, had actually been fused in their earlier transmission and were never so thoroughly independent as fifteenth-century scholars believed (along with the moderns who follow them).[119]

One should also notice that SJ 15 and 16 were produced about two centuries apart. This kind of production does not present a chronological development; it is simply a means of making a book available to copyists at any point during the Middle Ages. For an example of a sort one might not have expected, consider Cambridge, Peterhouse, MS 11. This is a book from relatively late in manuscript culture, s. xv in., and of a sort one would not expect to have required any production breaks: an 'author-anthology' joining works by the same person, Ambrose of Milan. However, although this manuscript is consistently produced, the works were dispersed, assigned to and produced as three separate fascicles.

In these examples you can see a juncture of multiple texts. But, *pace* Robinson, producing a book in this way does not necessarily respect textual boundaries, a point illustrated in my discussion in *PH*. For example, SJ 2, a 'coucher book' with William of Nottingham's enormous commentary on Clement of Lanthony's diatesseron, s. xv in., was produced as two large chunks (the break at fols 169–70, exactly halfway through).[120] Similarly, the copy of Peter Lombard's *Sentences* in SJ 50, s. xiii^1, was probably produced as three separate fascicles. In SJ 74, Italian, s. xv med., John de Turrecremata's extensive *De ecclesia* was copied in fascicles corresponding to the book-divisions of the

---

[119] See 'The Medieval Circulation of Cicero's "Posterior Academics" and *De finibus bonorum et malorum*', *Authentic Witnesses: Approaches to Medieval Texts and Manuscripts* (Notre Dame IN, 1991), 61–98.

[120] It is just possible that the intent was to have this large text in two volumes, but the current binding, although the covering leather has been refreshed, is contemporary.

text (a marginal case, which might be construed as 'respecting textual boundaries').

This procedure frequently occurs to enable speeded-up, apparently simultaneous production by a scribal team, as in Doyle and Parkes's famous example, 'the Trinity Gower'. The situation may be readily paralleled in manuscripts produced by multiple scribes. See, for example, SJ 96, saints' lives, s. xii ex., four or five scribes across three booklets, perhaps at Pershore (Worcs., OSB) (catalogue 131–33); or SJ 102, French didactic treatises, s. xv med., five scribes at a booklet each (catalogue 138–39). BodL, MS Bodley 43, again with multiple scribes and booklets, has separate signatures for each unit, with traces of what appears a consecutive set to join them, but, if so, ignored at least in the current early modern binding.

Equally, fascicular production is a method for piecing together a miscellaneous book eventually imagined to be continuous. Here the state of books now assigned five separate shelfmarks at Princeton UL, MSS Garrett 66, 75, and 85–87, is telling.[121] These were apparently in a single binding as late as s. xix, and are certainly companion productions. They are all in the same scribal hand, c. 1425 or s. $xv^{2/4}$, on the same greenish membrane that Parkes identified as 'Oxonian' and with fairly identical dimensions, the leaves all c. 365–70 mm × 240 mm, the writing area c. 270 mm × 175 mm. Even within the now separated segments, the number of lines per page varies slightly, but within narrow commensurate limits, all five in 42–46 lines. All five segments share the s. xv return to writing above the top ruled line. What results is tolerably gargantuan, 337 folios of moderately sophisticated parochial texts with an emphasis on sermons that might be used as models, each title produced as an independent unit:

Garrett 66: ps.-John Chrysostom, *Opus imperfectum* (a collection of homilies on Matthew);

Garrett 75: Hugh Ripelin of Strasbourg/ps.-Aquinas, *Compendium theologie*;

Garrett 85: William Peraldus, sermons on the Sunday gospels;

---

[121] All are described at Don C. Skemer et al., *Medieval and Renaissance Manuscripts in the Princeton University Library*, 2 vols (Princeton NJ, 2003), 1:128–31, 152–53, 173–78, respectively. Notice that, as Skemer points out, the original order before dismemberment appears to have run 75, 86, 66, 85, 87. In addition to my correction of Skemer's dating of the hand, see further pp. 128–29.

Garrett 86: James of Varezzo, sermons for Lent;

Garrett 87: Richard Rolle, on the nine lessons for the Office of the Dead.

Yet each of these segments is textually self-contained; in addition, each shows another keynote to booklets, individual sets of signatures for each portion:

Garrett 66: a–m, I [13 quires, fols 103^v–4^v with the scribe's additional texts]

Garrett 75: in red [+], a–g [8 quires, fols 62^v–64^v originally blank, filled by a later hand]

Garrett 85: a–h, k [9 quires, fols 71–72^v with the scribe's additional texts]

Garrett 86: in red a–h [8 quires, fols 62^v–64^v with the scribe's additional texts]

Garrett 87: in red h, f, g [3 quires, fols 17^v–23 with the scribe's additional texts and a final blank leaf cancelled, at what was apparently the end of the conjoined book].

Even in a manuscript like these, where there are no deviant quires at all – the entirety is in eight-leaf quires – the separate signatures are revealing.[122] However, if you recall my comments above about blank spaces in manuscript (pp. 88–89), you'll see another, not quite so persuasive, identifier of booklets. The scribe here copied large continuous texts, but had a few blank leaves at the end of his segments. Had he left them in that state, one would easily recognise these as concluding units. However, he chose to piece out his script with brief note-like texts to the end of his materials. Another sign of booklet-production is provided by such short materials, often called 'filler'. In

---

[122] These may imply something like an order of copying: Garrett 75 ends 'g'; Garrett 87 begins 'h', but in the (in-progress?) Garrett 66 signing jumps to 'I', and in the (similarly in-progress?) Garrett 85 signing jumps to 'k'. But signatures in red in only some units imply that Garrett 86 must be contemporary with 75 and 87. You might compare the accounts of SJ 173 (a religious miscellany, s. xvi in.: nine booklets, two of only a quire each) and SJ 179 (a portable breviary, s. xv in.: five booklets) at catalogue 240–43 and 255–56, respectively.

this case, where it is apparently original (although not so in Garrett 75), the behaviour offers a reasonably persuasive indication of intended common binding. Such oddments are designed to give the impression that what had begun separably actually forms a continuous production. You could compare SJ 200 (catalogue 291–95), although comprised of much smaller and informal units.

As Skemer indicates, only letters affixed on these manuscripts' s. xix rebinding indicate the ordering of the segments – and those may not have corresponded to the original form of the book. However, it is fairly routine to find fascicular books where the bindings and the signatures affixed to the quires are not aligned. We don't know whether such signatures actually correspond to the scribal copying order, or whether the scribe may have imposed them on his quires as a way of indicating that totality that would go into a consecutive binding. But, in any event, there are commonplace slips between signatures and bindings, a sign that what the scribe thought an appropriate order often did not correspond to the opinions of his patron.

In a few cases one can discern a motivation for the binding decision. For example, both Magd lat. 98 and 99, on the basis of their consecutive signatures, have been bound with the head of the book, signed beginning 'a', displaced; in both cases, this reversal of parts buries a work by the heresiarch John Wycliffe carefully out of sight. On the other hand, it may simply be a question of a patron's having had a different conception of a useful book than did the copyist. In Merton College, MS 68, the MS retains the order indicated by an s. xv contents table, but the signatures indicate a different ordering during production.[123] Perhaps informatively, in SJ 147, William Ebesham provided an index to the volume, corresponding to its bound form but not the order of the signatures he imposed while copying (see catalogue 208–12).

As a further example, consider the state of BodL, MS Bodley 52. The manuscript, which has an original, if sloppy and erroneous, medieval foliation, as bound, was produced by a single scribe as five booklets, s. xv$^{2/4}$, with consecutive signatures:

---

[123] See *Bodleian Library Record* 27 (2014), 132, 137–38. Occasionally, you will find overt evidence of changing plans about binding order scattered through the book, various signature systems advanced and cancelled, as in a pair of multi-fascicular, multi-scribe monsters, BL, MS Sloane 2275 (see n.86) or a Royal MS discussed in '"Classicizing Friars", Miscellaneous Transmission, and MS Royal 7 C.i', *Journal of the Early Book Society* 19 (2016), 97–123.

[I] fols 1–60 = quires 1–5 = *o–s*, all 12s
[II] fols 61–108 = quires 6–9 = *k–n*, all 12s
[III] fols 109–14 = quire 10, leaf numbers only, a 6
[IV] fols 115–25 = quire 11, signed *t* , a 12
[V] fols 127–257= quires 12–22 = [+], *a–I*, -, all 12s

These clearly indicate a different earlier sequence: [V] now fols 127–257, [II] now 61–108, [I] now 1–60, [IV] now 115–25; the sequence of signatures only allows [III] now 109–14 a place at the end. This may be a case analogous to the Wycliffite examples I have cited above. At least the deferral of [V] to the end allows Richard Rolle's popular (and anodyne) *Parce michi*, a commentary on the lections from the Office of the Dead, to stand at the head. This placement obscures the fact that a good portion of the volume is a collection of anti-mendicant and implicitly anti-papal materials.

Elsewhere, signatures reveal things about 'the hoole booke'. BodL, MS Rawlinson C.397 (Latin Rolle and Walter Hilton, s. xv in.) has two sets of signatures. In the first, in faded text-ink, quires 1–10 = g–q; in the second, in red, quires 1–10 = a–k, corresponding to the current book. These indicate that the current manuscript represents a fragment abstracted from a larger (discontinuous) copying job. Magd. lat. 79, sermons, s. xv¹, probably was always intended to be a unit (on a single paper-stock), although in a range of hands. In one protracted stint, fols 98–225ᵛ (quires 8–15), the scribe, perhaps simply to keep his copying in order, assigned the quires the signatures *a–h*. When this freestanding portion was incorporated into the whole, these were cancelled in favour of the volume-consecutive *h–p*, part of the patron-owner John Dyg(g)on's persistent rearrangement, sometimes over several decades, of apparently loose quires into more substantial volumes.

While recognising clear booklet presentations in independent (sequences of) quires like these is fairly easy, there are commonplace examples where booklet production has been obscured. In the Garrett MS the scribe avoided visible breaks by providing continuous filler. Very frequently, however, what began as booklet production is extended through adjusting the blank ends of standing quires, what I called in *PH* 'codicising' or 'codicisation': that is, thinking of a whole book, rather than just a part. There's only a modest economy to this gesture – it saves a little membrane and may reduce the number of in-progress quires by one. Its gains are in imposing continuity on the production. In a very simple example, BodL, MS Rawlinson poet. 175, s. xiv ex., a scribe had copied *The Prick of Conscience* into a sequence of five 12-leaf quires, with a blank side and five further blank leaves at the end. A close colleague – the two appear to have been trained in the same school – simply took up his fragment and used his blank leaves to continue, adding rather more miscellaneous texts in seven additional quires on to the end of the current manuscript.

One might contrast this rather neat handover with that in another *Prick of Conscience* manuscript, a bit older, c. 1375, BL, MS Additional 33995. Here two scribes worked simultaneously on what were originally separate runs of quires, separate booklets, one with the poetic derivative of *Somme le roi*, *Speculum Vitae*, one with *The Prick*. They had clearly planned this work out in advance, because the second scribe's first full quire begins his *Prick* in mid-text. The two segments were intended to be joined by a bridging quire, at the end of which the second scribe would copy his retained head to his text. This was all fine, except … To effect their join, the scribes constructed a quire of dimensions unparalleled elsewhere in the book, ten leaves rather than the usual 12, and with some short filler texts. Moreover, this abbreviation wasn't quite enough to make a clean join; there was too little copy reserved from the head of *The Prick* to fill the space, and the appearance of clean continuity was achieved only by cancelling a blank leaf in this portion.[124]

One should probably consider the Additional MS a book produced as two fascicles with an effort at 'codicising' the result. One occasionally runs across overt evidence for such superseded and now 'codicised' fascicles. In SJ 113, the original fol. 49, now the flyleaf, fol. iii, was a fascicle-concluding single leaf; it was cancelled, its text rewritten to include following materials, and the booklet extended a further quire (catalogue 158). At BodL, MS Bodley 61 (II), fol. 79, another fascicle-ending leaf, the scribe erased the colophon for the text ending here and inserted the heading for the following one, which begins at the head of what had been a new, independent sequence of quires. In SJ 98, a sequence of seven separate MSS written in France, s. xiii med., there have been later efforts, some in English hands, to join originally separate textual units (catalogue 136–37).

In some instances, codicising involves what I would describe as 'near breaks'. The quires are complete, but of erratic construction and with texts ending and beginning at some point near the end. Books like these appear to have been, perhaps at several points during manufacture, considered to be complete, yet then subject to extensions, like that

---

[124] For descriptions of both MSS see *Richard Morris's Prick of Conscience*, EETS 342 (Oxford, 2013), xxi–iv.

provided by the second scribe of the Rawlinson MS. I discussed some prominent examples of s. xiii at 'Lambeth Palace Library, MS 487: Some problems of early thirteenth-century textual transmission', *Texts and Traditions of Medieval Pastoral Care: Essays in Honour of Bella Millett*, ed. Cate Gunn and Catherine Innes-Parker (Woodbridge, 2009), 78–88.

However, not all quire variations nor all quire-ending breaks are automatically explicable as examples of such procedures. SJ 1 is an extremely large book, s. xiii/xiv, 460 mm × 325 mm, originally 315 fols, with an extensive text (Augustine on John, s. xiii/xiv). It is constructed completely in quires of 12, with the exception of quire 16 (a six, fols 181–86). This corresponds to a textual division between Augustine's homilies 47 and 48, the heading for the latter on fol. 186, the text beginning on fol. 187. Very shortly, but not immediately (at fol. 196), the handling of major initials shifts slightly: the gold leaf in the champs is no longer plain, but tooled or 'diapered'. Like many examples of variant quiring you may find, this doesn't seem to me a booklet-boundary. The odd quire may simply reflect a decision not to split a big book for a two-volume presentation.[125] But, given the shift in decoration, this disruptive quire may simply reflect a production economy, an effort at overlapping 'finishing', by the quire, with continued copying.

A somewhat more vertiginous form of codicising is worth mentioning. This involves taking a quire in which only the first half has been written and refolding it so that the original first leaf now follows the centre sewing. Thus, what had been the blank second half of the quire becomes its head, and can now receive a continuation of a text from another quire. A fine description of Dublin, Trinity College, MS 115 appears at Marvin L. Colker, *Trinity College Dublin: Descriptive Catalogue of the Mediaeval and Renaissance Latin Manuscripts*, 2 vols (Aldershot, 1991), 1:238–44. The manuscript is comprised of booklets the Cambridge Augustinian friar Adam Stockton copied separately over at least the period 1375–77 (with later additions, 1379–80), and in a variety of places, presumably during down-time as he pursued preaching duties. The separability of these units is shown by the fitful signatures, which are strokes counting leaves in the first halves of quires but without ordering letters.[126] However, the volume was early

---

[125] Such multi-volume presentation occurs frequently with long texts – Gregory's *Moralia in Iob*, Aquinas's *Summa*, or the extensive chunks of Vincent of Beauvais's *Speculum maius*, for example.

[126] What I would call 'open signing', leaving room for a later determination of a desired bound order. In a fair number of MSS you'll examine, different inks

'codicised', as a contents table on p. 1, s. xiv ex., giving the texts in their current ordering, would indicate.

Colker's four-part division of the production, into the units A–D, is accurate enough for what remains, although it obscures some signs of adjustments to plan. There are actually six original units, rather than the apparent four. A small concluding bit of Walter Map's *Valerius* appears at the top of p. 175 (quire 8, leaf 1), and there is no catchword on the preceding p. 174; the subsequent leaves have texts not in Stockton's hand, are dated after his work (1379–80), and are followed by an entirely blank second half of the quire (pp. 187–98). Not only should this be construed a separate booklet (perhaps originally only the outer bifolium of quire 8), but the following copy of John Ridewall's *Fulgencius* (pp. 199–252) is certainly such.

At the end of *Fulgencius*, quire 11 (pp. 251–74) has the look of a unit in which copying began on what is now the first page of its second half (p. 263), the whole then reversed to accommodate, as in my preceding example, a relatively brief conclusion to the preceding *Fulgencius* (pp. 251–52 only), followed by blank leaves to p. 262, the centre of the now-reversed quire. In addition, one might note the provision of a contents list and table for Malachy the Irishman's *De ueneno* at pp. 156–60, following Pierre Bersuire's *Ovidiana*, while Malachy's text itself appears at the head of Colker's D/booklet 6 (p. 371). This certainly suggests that the copy of Map forms an intrusion into a different order earlier envisioned.

For other examples of adjustments like these, see John J. Thompson, 'The Compiler in Action: Robert Thornton and the "Thornton Romances" in Lincoln Cathedral MS 91', *Manuscripts and Readers in Fifteenth-Century England: The Literary Implications of Manuscript Study*, ed. Derek Pearsall (Cambridge, 1983), 113–24; George Keiser, '"To Knawe God Almyghtyn": Robert Thornton's Devotional Book', *Spätmittelalterliche geistliche Literatur in der Nationalsprache* 2, ed. James Hogg, Analecta cartusiana 106 (Salzburg, 1984), 103–29; and A. E. Kraebel, 'Rolle Reassembled: Booklet-Production, Single-Author Anthologies, and the Making of Bodley 861', *Speculum* 94 (2019), 959–1005; and again, *Bodleian Library Record* 27 (2014), 133–35 (a short fascicle-ending quire probably supplemented at the centre, a feature also of Robert Thornton's work).

for signatures for quires (1, 2, 3 … , or a, b, c … , etc.) and for leaves (i, ii, iij …) probably reflect this situation.

Where's it been all this time?

You're never a manuscript's first reader/user. It was made for someone, on their orders and at their expense; having cost money, it was there to be used; and it's unlikely to have been a unique possession of this sort, but will have sat in a library with other volumes. Whatever its original owner thought they were doing, it may have been used by others for several centuries after production and purchase – and, arguably, not with the same motivations as had inspired the original production. Eventually it had to have been preserved, perhaps as a treasure, perhaps just as a sign of acquisitiveness (one among many), before it's pitched up in the book presses of the library where you have gone to inspect it.

Medieval Bibles, which I mentioned near the start of the book (pp. 17–18), offer a striking instance. The production of small Bibles, s. xiii, was so extensive as to render further efforts otiose, and thus, late medieval copies of the Latin Vulgate are extremely rare.[127] The supply produced during this spate was sufficient to last people through into the Renaissance, some books being in use for more than three centuries.

UCLA, MS Rouse 50, affords a telling example. In a binding of s. xvi/xvii, the book is a colossal mess. This is not a tribute to its production, but to long abuse and later careful use. The book represents an effort at constructing a full Vulgate to complete one of several water-damaged originally independent fragments, activity one imagines occurred before 1550. This involved gathering not simply the ten fragments highlighted in the Rouses' catalogue description but a range of other materials. Another ten to a dozen copies were pillaged to fill in small passages completely destroyed by damp; these were pasted to the leaves to fill lacunae (where they, obviously enough, provide continuous text on only one side). Damage was especially acute at the tops of the leaves, leading the owner to cannibalise running titles from other copies; although many of these have been pasted in to complete leaves eaten away, a number of these cuttings still survive loose in the manuscript. This was someone's massive effort to construct a usable text, clearly for detailed consultation.[128]

---

[127] Not so, of course, the vernacular Wycliffite version, the commonest surviving Middle English book. For the most recent list of manuscripts, see Solopova, *Wycliffite Bible*, 484–92 (for a peripheral copy, heretofore overlooked, see p. 131).

[128] See the Rouses, *Medieval and Renaissance Manuscripts*, 118–28.

I might offer two contrasting narratives. On the one hand, consider Cambridge, Jesus College, MS Q.G.15 (James 63). Shortly after 1600, this book, with humanist epistles, was in a community of Catholic 'husbandmen' near Whitby (NRY).[129] It is unclear where they might have acquired the book, and even more unclear as to what they wanted with it (other than record their names in it). What could the apparently aged widow Margaret Duck of Goathland, way out in the moors, whose son's name appears here, have wanted with Poggio Bracciolini? This community, while fervent in its attachment to the old faith, is unlikely to have been blessed with the grammatically trained, and one's best guess is that the volume was simply 'a treasure', in its Latinity a connection with a threatened, persecuted, and vanishing past.

At the other extreme, I once went to look at the manuscripts of the duke of Gloucester, at that time in Kensington Palace. The duke threw open a ceiling-high cabinet that occupied one wall of his living room; piles of released books tumbled out across the floor. The duke looked at them with disgust, 'I suppose the manuscripts are in there somewhere; I never look at them, but the old man was into books about blood-sports.' It is perhaps unnecessary to add that the duke shortly after disposed of 'the old man''s books at auction.[130]

Books aren't just blocky jobbies sitting on shelves in a library. They communicate, even if, as with the Whitby peasants, what one imagines as only a quasi-literate reverence or veneration. In doing so, they convene communities. These are always conditional and temporary,

---

[129] The book includes letters by Poggio Bracciolini, the person who discovered the surviving copies of Lucretius's *De natura rerum*, and by Duke Humfrey of Gloucester, famous for his interests in Italian books and his large donations to the university library in Oxford. On these owners, see *The Library* 7th ser. 21 (2020), 62–65; eventually, c. 1650, the MS was scooped up by a book-collecting clergyman from Northallerton.

[130] A day memorable for a variety of other experiences: Pam Robinson earnestly explaining to me the night before that I could not appear at a royal palace in my usual trainers, but had to wear leather shoes; being told by security that my admission would be through 'downstairs'; the duke's adjutant – of course, a retired RAF colonel – forcing me to have a cuppa, while I examined the books on a gleamingly polished dining table that had every sign of being a Chippendale; the one time I saw Princess Diana in the flesh (as she and spouse decamped from the helicopter that was conveying them to an adjacent royal garden party). Not all one's exposure to manuscripts is the kind of thing that a description or article will reveal.

and, when what binds the community passes, the book exchanges that value for a potentially very different one, in some new context.

All these matters concern what is called a book's 'provenance', its history. It is not just an object that had value for the person who commissioned it, but one with a perhaps traceable line of descent and use. At least part of your inspection of any manuscript is attempting to discover evidence of this passage and to use that to construct a history of the book through time, from its production to its appearance on the library lectern where you are studying it. Ideally, you would like to construct a smooth and connected narrative, from production to the present, but this remains a goal only infrequently realised.

All these endeavours begin with marks you should notice in the books. Although the study focusses on post-print ownership and transmission, there's a wealth of information, provocative and suggestive, in David Pearson, *Provenance Research in Book History* (London, 1994; new rev. edn, with references to online materials, Oxford, 2019). For example, Pearson discusses heraldry, one topic I'll take up below in passing, at 1st edn, 41–44, 97–115, 274–86, and offers a wealth of references to places you might go to identify arms, should you find examples in your manuscript.[131] You do have to remember that, whatever its vicissitudes during the Middle Ages, in which I imagine most of my readers have primary interest, the volume has had to subsist somehow, somewhere, for another five centuries, which may throw up matters of considerable interest.

First of all, the MS had to be produced. Thus relevant to any investigation are studies of the book trade. At the very opening of my discussion I mentioned (n.6) a classic, Pollard on the early London trade. Supplementing Pollard are Howard Winger, 'Regulations Relating to the Book Trade in London from 1357 to 1586', *Library Quarterly* 26 (1956), 157–95; and C. Paul Christianson, *A Directory of London Stationers and Book Artisans, 1300–1500* (New York, 1989), as well as his essay, GP 87–108. An overview of the trade elsewhere appears as Doyle, 'The English Provincial Book Trade before Printing', *Six Centuries of the Provincial Book Trade in Britain*, ed. Peter Isaac (Winchester, 1990), 13–29. On the trade in Oxford, there is a wealth of unpublished material in Pollard's papers, deposited in the Bodleian (160 shelf-feet and more than 400 assigned shelfmarks); and see Parkes, 'The Provision of Books', *The*

---

[131] To his 44 and n.20 there, one could add a further example of Archbishop Thomas Morton's rebus, at ChCh 104, fol. 1, where it appears with his coat of arms.

History of the University of Oxford: Volume II Late Medieval Oxford, ed. Jeremy Catto and Ralph Evans (Oxford, 1992), 407–82; as well as his 'Thomas Hunt and the Oxford Book-Business in the Late Fifteenth Century', and 'A List of Medieval Oxford Stationers', *The Library* 7th ser. 17 (2016), 28–39, 167–78.

That there was a commercial trade indicates why there is so much interest in scribes and illuminators, the subject of the large number of studies I have cited above. The repetitions gathered in such studies are apt to point to possible book patrons and/or owners and their reliance on repeated experiences with the same book producers. For one example, Thomas IV, Lord Berkeley's probable relations with Doyle and Parkes's 'scribe delta', s. xv in., see 'Sir Thomas Berkeley and His Patronage', *Speculum* 64 (1989), 878–916, at 909–13.

Also of potential interest are two early sets of bookmen's accounts. Both chronicle post-print activities, but early ones (thus, with potential overlap of manuscript and print trades), and they provide ample information capable of imaginative reconstruction as to processes: F. Madan, 'The Daily Ledger of John Dorne, Bookseller in Oxford, A.D. 1520', *Collectanea First Series*, ed. C. R. L. Fletcher, Oxford Historical Society 5 (Oxford, 1885), 71–177 (Madan's presentation requires the supplementary comments of a great student of manuscripts and early print, Henry Bradshaw's 'A Half-Century of Notes on the Day-Book of John Dorne, Bookseller in Oxford, A.D. 1520 – as edited by F. Madan for the Oxford Historical Society' [(Oxford), 1886]);[132] and E. S. Leedham-Green et al., *Garret Godfrey's Accounts, c. 1527–1533*, Cambridge Bibliographical Society Monographs 12 (Cambridge, 1992).[133]

Manuscripts often include indications of the prices one or another owner paid for them, the medieval examples customarily introduced by 'prec' or 'pret' (Latin *pretium*). I've noted above (pp. 20, 47–48) a couple of accounts for incidental work, binding, and decoration.[134] There's a

---

[132] See further Beadle, 'Henry Bradshaw and the Foundations of Codicology' (Cambridge, 2017).

[133] Godfrey was a widely attested binder and an entrepreneur with a substantial shop. Among its relics are the leaves he used in constructing a cover, now BodL, MS Eng. poet. d.208, one example of a 'useless' medieval book consigned to binders' waste; see 'Unnoticed Middle English Romance Fragments in the Bodleian Library: MS. Eng. poet. d.208', *The Library* 6th ser. 28 (1999), 305–20.

[134] See further the discussion of one of the few surviving contracts for producing a book, *Introducing English Medieval Book History: Manuscripts, Their Producers and Their Readers* (Liverpool, 2013), esp. 184–90.

vast amount of information of this sort about book prices, potentially informative, when one considers who might afford and own a volume or how much an owner might have invested in a library. The only protracted studies of the issue are H. E. Bell, 'The Price of Books in Medieval England', *The Library* 4th ser. 17 (1936), 312–32; and Wilbur L. Schram, 'The Cost of Books in Chaucer's Time', *Modern Language Notes* 48 (1937), 139–45. But see also Joanne F. Overty, 'The Cost of Doing Scribal Business', *Book History* 11 (2008), 1–32.

However, a great deal of relevant data has never been collected, much less subjected to analysis. For example, a huge amount of information survives in notations of the amounts loaned on the security of a (used) manuscript (see further pp. 120–21). Nor has anyone systematically examined the information in accounts: see, for example, Michael Gullick, *Extracts from the Precentors' Accounts Concerning Books and Bookmaking of Ely Cathedral Priory* (Hitchin and London, 1985); or R. M. Thomson, *A Descriptive Catalogue of the Medieval Manuscripts of Merton College, Oxford* (Cambridge, 2009), 269–81 (the presentation hopefully a sign that this information will become publicised in future). For example, in 1502, Magd purchased a seven-volume printed edition of Hugh of St Cher's *Postilla in totam Bibliam* (now Arch. B.II.4.1–7) for 46s 4d, and the following year spent a much smaller amount to have these books chained to lecterns.[135]

Original, or at least early, owners may be identifiable through their inscriptions of ownership and/or old library marks written into the manuscript. Here, as I pointed out in the discussion of binding (pp. 25–26), flyleaves deserve particularly close inspection, for they are more apt to bear information than the actual leaves of the manuscript itself. In general, although there are still plenty of unrecognised examples waiting to be added to standard accounts, institutional collections have been very well served, individuals (and the commercial trade) considerably less so.[136]

This state of affairs is largely owning to the great Oxford troika whom I mentioned in my introduction: Ker, Mynors, and Hunt. The initial inspiration for their project came from James's early writings, notably *The Sources of Archbishop Parker's Collection of MSS at Corpus*

---

[135] For the record, see the account-book, MS LCE 2, fol. 128ᵛ; the purchase is mentioned by William D. Macray, *A Register of the Members of Saint Mary Magdalen College, Oxford ... New Series*, 8 vols (London, 1894–1915), 1:32.

[136] The point trenchantly argued in Sharpe's brilliant 2019 Lyell Lectures, now edited by Willoughby and forthcoming, Oxford, 2023.

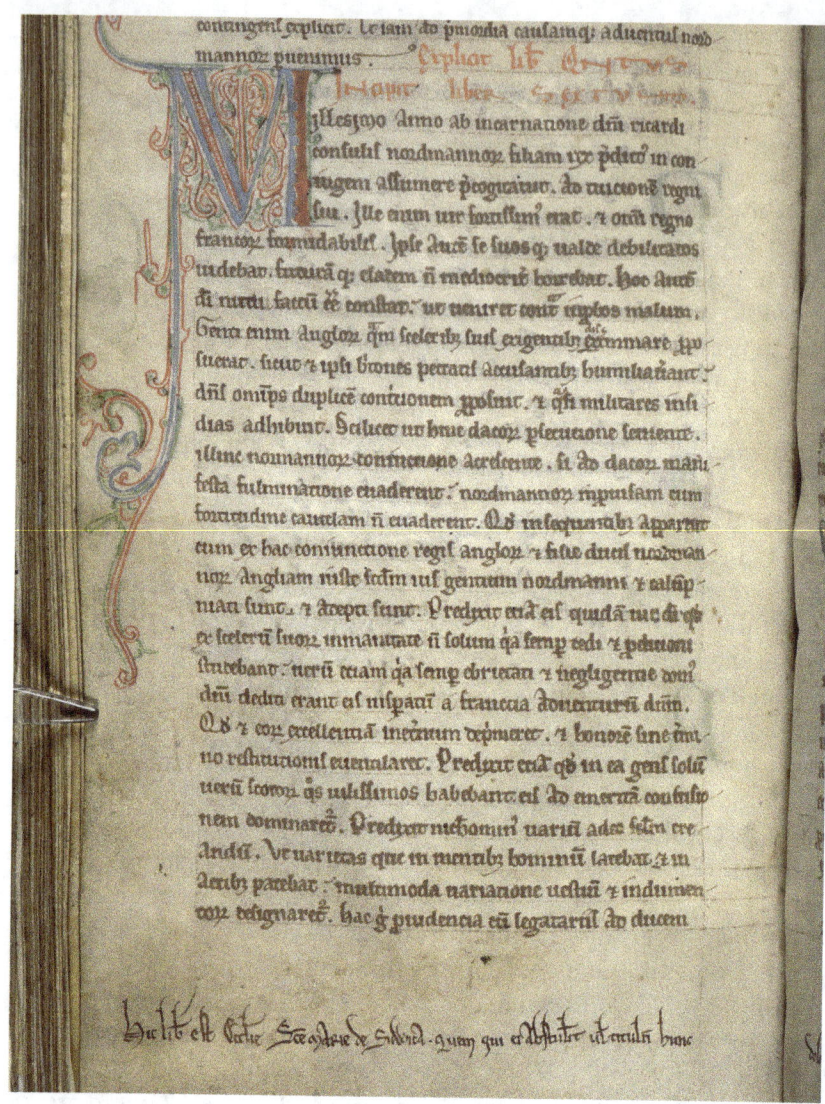

A Southwick constat (and book-curse): As the inscription at the page foot (and across the opening) shows, this copy of Henry of Huntingdon's *Historia Anglorum*, s. xii/xiii, was once in the library of the Augustine canons of 'Suwica', Southwick (Hants). As in other books from the house, the inscription is not simply an indication of communal property but continues to pronounce a curse ('anathema sit') on anyone so bold as to try to remove the volume – or the inscription itself. Such curses are scarcely limited to institutional owners, e.g. BodL, MS Tanner 201, fol. 107: 'Thys ys Rychard Borne boke / wosoeuer stele it sal be … ', on the basis of many other examples, to conclude, 'hanged by a hook/on a crook'. (London, British Library, MS Arundel 48, fol. 84ᵛ, reproduced at 65%).

Christi College Cambridge ... (Cambridge, 1899), followed by his *The Ancient Libraries of Canterbury and Dover* (Cambridge, 1903), a study still not fully replaced. Another model that must have inspired these giants, then fledglings, will have been Powicke's *Medieval Books of Merton College*. The most extensive and definitive progeny of this project are the two *sine qua nons*, MLGB and 'The Corpus'. The latter is particularly important, because, for included libraries, it offers extensive and authoritative headnotes on library history.

The core of these studies is provided by surviving books that bear monastic 'constat inscriptions' (Latin *constat* 'it pertains/belongs to'). For example, the canons of Southwick (Hants, OSA) were either unusually scrupulous or unusually paranoid about possible theft. Their ownership inscriptions are lengthy and quite deliberately placed unobtrusively at page-feet, as well as scattered through the book in not altogether obvious places. The one in SJ 62 that's cited at catalogue 83 is typical and analogous to those in SJ 185. Both occur on three occasions, at the head of the manuscript (the most usual notation universally), near the end, and once toward the middle.

Rather frequently, however, one will meet examples of erasure (a reason for using ultraviolet light on any book you handle) or excision. Later owners often scrupulously remove evidence of origin from their books. (As a consequence, prominent collectors have frequently been charged with having obtained their libraries through questionable means, among them Robert Cotton and Bishop John Moore, who assembled the core of CUL's historical collection.) Consider Wellesley MA, Wellesley College, MS 8, with a succession of cancelled owners, the oldest possibly indicating that the book had migrated from Byland (OCist, NRY) even before the Dissolution.[137] Or BL, MS Cotton Vespasian A.ii, fol. 2, where the previous ownership inscription of St Augustine's Abbey, Canterbury (OSB) has been excised, but is at least intuitable from offset left on facing pages by its red ink.[138]

---

[137] See *Richard Morris's* (full reference at n.123), xxvi. Cf. Michael A. Hicks, 'John Nettleton, Henry Savile of Banke, and the Post-Medieval Vicissitudes of Byland Abbey Library', *Northern History* 26 (1990), 212–27, one of many analogous studies and an example of the information to be gained from publications associable with local or regional history.

[138] A larger portion of this library probably survives than of that of any other monastic house. This is largely owing to post-Dissolution institutional stability (converted to the still surviving King's School) and intelligent, if topical, plundering by the Elizabethan collector John Dee, who owned the library

The other great institutional collections of the Middle Ages were in university contexts, primarily the colleges in Oxford and Cambridge. On this subject, Emden's registers include a huge amount of information on scholarly book ownership, and of donation, with indication of surviving items: *A Biographical Register of the University of Oxford to A.D. 1500*, 3 vols (Oxford, 1957–59); *A Biographical Register of the University of Oxford, A.D. 1500 to 1540* (Oxford, 1974); and *A Biographical Register of the University of Cambridge to 1500* (Cambridge, 1963).[139] For example, MS Bodley 52, described above (pp. 108–09), was copied by John Maynesford. He was a Fellow of Merton College, 1425–40, and eventually subdean of Chichester Cathedral. MS Bodley 52 is the single survivor of four books he donated to Merton in 1488 (see *BRUO* 1250–51; entered *MLGB* 147 as a college book).[140]

A feature unique to university books is one frequent kind of flyleaf notation, the indication of *cauciones* and *elecciones*. Both Latinisms refer to distinctive university institutions, the latter an inheritance from ancient monastic practice. A *cautio* is a security or pledge; it refers to loan-chests operated for the whole community at both universities.

---

catalogue and constructed a wish-list from it. See A. B. Emden, *Donors of Books to S. Augustine's Abbey, Canterbury*, Oxford Bibliographical Society occasional publication 4 (Oxford, 1968), with Andrew Watson's 'John Twyne of Canterbury (d. 1581) as a Collector of Medieval Manuscripts: A Preliminary Investigation', *The Library* 6th ser. 8.2 (1986), coll IV. There are extensive further materials in Bruce Barker-Benfield's magisterial *St Augustine's Abbey, Canterbury*, 3 vols, Corpus 13 (London, 2008).

[139] There are continuations to both Joseph Foster, *Alumni Oxonienses: The Members of the University of Oxford, 1500–1714*, 4 vols (London and Oxford, 1891–92) and his *Alumni Oxonienses: The Members of the University of Oxford, 1715–1886*, 4 vols (London and Oxford, 1887–88); and John and J. A. Venn, *Alumni Cantabrigienses: A Biographical List of All Known Students ... , from the Earliest Times to 1900*, 2 parts in 10 vols (Cambridge, 1922–54). These offer accounts considerably less extensive than Emden, although they may identify for you a later owner and, through their typically single-sentence summaries of his career, offer hints as to where you might seek further information.

[140] There is an abundant literature on books in university contexts, e.g. Ker, 'Oxford College Libraries before 1500' and 'Oxford College Libraries in the Sixteenth Century', coll 301–20, 379–436. On monasteries, required to send select students for university training, see Joan Greatrex, *The English Benedictine Cathedral Priories: Rule and Practice, c. 1270–c. 1420* (Oxford, 2011), 126–59; and Henry Wansbrough and Anthony Marett-Crosby, eds, *Benedictines in Oxford* (London, 1997).

Typically students were given loans in exchange for the deposit of books as security until repayment. On the workings of the system, see Graham Pollard, 'Mediaeval Loan Chests at Cambridge', *Bulletin of the Institute of Historical Research* 17 (1940), 113–29; there is a more extensive unpublished essay on the institution in Oxford in BodL, MS Pollard 253.[141] For examples of *cauciones*, see M. R. James, *A Descriptive Catalogue of the Manuscripts in the Library of Gonville and Caius College*, 2 vols (Cambridge, 1907), the index entry at 2:709. James there gathers references to 31 *caucio*-inscriptions in that library alone, all cited in full in the text, but generally formulaic, as befits legal inscriptions.

As I mentioned in discussing bindings (pp. 29–30), medieval institutions typically had a double library, chained and circulating. One practice within this system, first mandated as a Lenten observance in St Benedict's Rule, was the annual distribution of reading matter to the monks (or college Fellows); each was allowed to choose (*eligere*, past participle *electus*) books from the circulating stock as private reading material. A good many college records of the procedure survive, and it is occasionally recorded in books. For example, Magd lat. 17, fol. iii, is inscribed 'Liber Collegij sancte Magdalene de sorte Collett'; lat. 174, the rear flyleaf^v, 'Liber domus beate marie magdelene de eleccione thome Kerver' (his name over an erasure, so he was not the first to have the book in his rooms); and BodL, MS Bodley 2, fol. ii^v, has two such inscriptions, '6 Flowr x^i <...> 1504', '10 de sorte hyll 2° fo graui (indeed the reading of the second folio).[142]

There is a rich multi-volume survey of libraries and later collectors, *The Cambridge History of Libraries in Great Britain and Ireland*, the most

---

[141] Having paid a great deal of attention, here and there, to the unscrupulous, I should draw to your attention BodL, MS Bodley 132, fol. 228 (*SC* 1893), copied for and donated to Robertsbridge (Sussex, OCist) (so *MLGB* 160, 296). However, the book ended up in an Oxford loan-chest on three occasions before being purchased by a great collector, John Grandisson, bishop of Exeter 1328–69 (on his books see *BRUO* 800–01, an incomplete listing). Below the now-cancelled house inscription of ownership he wrote, 'I, John, bishop of Exeter, don't know where that religious house is, nor did I steal this book, but acquired it by legitimate means' (Ego Johannes, Exoniensis episcopus, nescio ubi est domus predicta, nec hunc librum abstuli, set modo legitimo acquisivi).

[142] For biographies of these lucky winners see *BRUO* 474, 366 (s.v. Carver), 702, and 934–35, respectively. *sors* 'allocation' is, in the context, synonymous with *eleccio*. A number of records of *elecciones*, primarily documents from Merton College archives, appear in R. M. Thomson et al., *The University and College Libraries of Oxford*, Corpus 16, 2 vols (London, 2015).

relevant Teresa Webber and E. S. Leedham-Green, eds, *Volume I: To 1640* (Cambridge, 2006). Some provocative essays on later developments appear in Annika Bautz and James Gregory, eds, *Libraries, Books, and Collectors of Texts, 1600–1900* (New York, 2018).

Manuscripts often contain informative detail about librarianship in the form of shelfmarks, sequences of often unexplained letters and numbers.[143] These are of various dates, from the Middle Ages until the present, and thus present various information on stages of book ownership and preservation. Most modern libraries simply impose arbitrary numerical marks, in many cases simply order of acquisition (as at HEH or BL's Additional MSS); at Oxford, St John's College, the current marks, before a few later acquisitions, simply indicated the manuscript's size (MS 1 the largest, and so on). Equally, books show signs of other orders; Cambridge, Gonville and Caius College has double shelfmarks, one set James's new consecutive numbering, the other an older order, and the 1630 catalogue of Oxford, Magdalen College (see pp. 21–23) had grouped books under the university's traditional four faculties (arts, theology, law, and medicine).

Most libraries imposed two- or three-segment shelfmarks. Robert Cotton's system is perhaps the quirkiest, yet best known. The *Beowulf* MS is Vitellius A.xv because it sat in a bookcase with a statue of that emperor on top, on the top shelf (A), the 15th book along, counting from the left. Such triple marking is still in use at Durham and Hereford Cathedrals; CUL; and Cambridge, Jesus College, for example. Two-segment marking, here a letter and number, appears frequently in older collections such as that of Norwich Cathedral, illustrated in Ker's 'Medieval Manuscripts from Norwich Cathedral Priory', coll 243–72. See further Pearson, 1st edn, 45–50, 171ff., with information on modern collectors.

Medieval private book ownership among laypersons is the subject on which we would like to know most, and about which we are least well equipped. There is no tool comparable to the magnificent bibliography Sears R. Jayne, *Library Catalogues of the English Renaissance* (1956; Winchester, 1983).[144] Further extensive listings of lay collections from this later period include R. J. Fehrenbach and E. S. Leedham-Green,

---

[143] See Richard Sharpe's pioneering study 'Accession, Classification, or Location: Pressmarks in Medieval Libraries', *Scriptorium* 50 (1996), 279–87.

[144] Although Jayne will not offer you information about medieval owners, it remains an extremely valuable resource for tracing early modern ownership of medieval books.

eds, *Private Libraries in Renaissance England*, currently 10 vols, MRTS variously (Binghampton NY and Tempe AZ, 1992–) almost exclusively printed books, but potentially useful for identifying owners who have left their names in manuscripts. Leedham-Green has also reported on the private libraries of learned men, *Books in Cambridge Inventories: Book Lists from Vice-Chancellor's Court Probate Inventories in the Tudor and Stuart Periods*, 2 vols (Cambridge, 1986).

There are a few inspirational initial surveys of medieval private ownership, beginning with Kate Harris, 'Patrons, Buyers, and Owners: The Evidence for Ownership and the Rôle of Book Owners in Book Production and the Book Trade'; and Carol Meale, 'Patrons, Buyers, and Owners: Book Production and Social State', both in GP, 163–99 and 201–38, respectively. There is an extraordinarily useful tool for investigating such transmission: Susan H. Cavanaugh, 'A Study of Books Privately Owned in England 1300–1450', 2 vols (University of Pennsylvania PhD thesis, 1980). This is an extensive 900-page (unindexed) monster, but with two unfortunate limitations. Cavanaugh assembled material well worthy of more than one degree, but only by restricting her searches. Her study cuts off around 1450 and thus does not treat what one might think the most productive (and best-recorded) period, the last century of English manuscript circulation. Second, Cavanaugh gathers, in the main, previously published materials, rather than searching archives. But she offers a healthy trove of published testamentary evidence, typically only part of a library, but often suggestive. The inventories that traditionally accompanied probated wills are more inclusive and helpful, including an assessment of value, but tend not to survive, and, as Pearson points out (173–76), are increasingly less detailed.[145]

Flyleaves not infrequently include booklists of various extents. In addition to a number of published examples,[146] consider Magd

---

[145] A couple of examples: Henry Thorlthorpe, a vicar choral of York Minster (1427), discussed 'An Unanalysed Yorkshire Booklist', *Journal of the Early Book Society* 25 (2022), 195–208; Sir Richard Brereton 'of the Ley' (Chs.) (1558), discussed 'Two New (?) Lost *Piers* Manuscripts (?)', *Yearbook of Langland Studies* 16 (2002), 169–77.

[146] E.g. from an institution, an early Rievaulx (NRY, OCist) library list at Cambridge, Jesus College, MS Q.B.17 (James 34), fols 1–7ᵛ, ed. David N. Bell, *The Libraries of the Cistercians, Gilbertines and Premonstratensians*, Corpus 3 (London, 1992), 89–121; Mary Hamel, 'Arthurian Romance in Fifteenth-Century Lindsey: The Books of the Lords Welles', *Modern Language Quarterly* 51 (1990),

lat. 114, Peter Lombard's *Sentences*, s. xiii ex. This is one of 60 books donated to the college by Mr Richard Laugharne in the 1480s (the leaves include a note of his purchase in 1468). Not much of his gift survives, but one can retrieve some of it from a note on the first flyleaf (fol. 1): 'Libri dimissi apud Mastiton' [? Masurton']: iste M sentenc' [i.e. this volume], liber epistolarum pauli, liber sermonum babion', liber metaphisice <...>, summa Iohannis filij serapionis, quaternus metaphisice M Ricardi, Ouidij Methamorph'. Item <quaternus> de hosp' cum diuersis compilat".

At the head of specific studies stands a distinguished series of contributions on the famous Yorkshire bookman Robert Thornton: George Keiser, 'Lincoln Cathedral MS. 91: Life and Milieu of the Scribe', *Studies in Bibliography* 32 (1979), 158–79; and 'More Light on the Life and Milieu of Robert Thornton', *Studies in Bibliography* 36 (1983), 111–19. Keiser here shows the provocative power of the legal record, to which I will return. Perhaps more significant, in book-historical terms, is Keiser's effort to explain the passage of one of Thornton's books from Yorkshire to Lincoln Cathedral: 'A Note on the Descent of the Thornton Manuscript', *Transactions of the Cambridge Bibliographical Society* 6 (1976), 346–48.

Of particular interest, although not necessarily tied to exact provenances, are marginalia. These often remain obscure, an inscription, 'Nota' or a 'manicula' (a pointing hand) beside a passage, but perhaps capable of eliciting some patterning imposed to offer a provisional reading. Cf. the introductory descriptions of one such annotator at work: Ker, 'Robert Elyot's Books and Annotations', *The Library* 5th ser. 30 (1975), 233–37; and Beadle, 'Robert Elyot – Another Manuscript', *The Library* 5th ser. 32 (1977), 371–72. For a great note-taker, chancellor of the University of Oxford, s. xv med., see R. M. Ball, *Thomas Gascoigne, Libraries and Scholarship*, Cambridge Bibliographical Society Monographs 14 (Cambridge, 2006); and for his notebooks, *Loci e Libro veritatum: Passages Selected from Gascoigne's Theological Dictionary ...*, ed. James E. Thorold Rogers (Oxford, 1881). Gascoigne's notes, copied from autograph manuscripts, provide our only entré to the full extent of Robert Grosseteste's glosses on the Pauline epistles. (Only the reading of Galatians survives more or less continuously, in Magd lat. 57 (I).)

Moving toward the descent of medieval libraries, as my introduction will have indicated, the Dissolution of the monasteries

341–61; or 'Medieval Lay Libraries: The Example of Thomas Stotevyle's Books', *Journal of the Early Book Society* 22 (2019), 155–81.

has always loomed large and has been the subject of extensive studies of despoliation: Ker, 'The Migration of Manuscripts from the English Medieval Libraries' and 'Sir John Prise', coll 459–69 and 471–95; C. E. Wright, 'The Dispersal of the Libraries in the Sixteenth Century', *English Library* (full reference at p. 9), 148–75; Christopher de Hamel, 'The Dispersal of the Library of Christ Church, Canterbury, from the Fourteenth to the Sixteenth Century', *Books and Collectors, 1200–1700: Essays Presented to Andrew Watson*, ed. James P. Carley and Colin G. C. Tite (London, 1997), 263–79; Nigel Ramsey, '"The Manuscripts flew about like Butterflies": The Break-up of English Libraries in the Sixteenth Century', *Lost Libraries: The Destruction of Great Book Collections since Antiquity*, ed. James Raven (Basingstoke, 2004), 125–44; James P. Carley, 'The Dispersal of the Monastic Libraries and the Salvaging of the spoils', *Cambridge History of Libraries I*, 265–91; Richard Sharpe's forthcoming 'Dissolution and Dispersal in Sixteenth-Century England: Understanding the Remains', *How the Secularization of Religious Houses Transformed the Libraries of Europe, 16th–19th Centuries*, ed. Cristina Dondi et al. (Turnhout, 2022).

The grand connoisseur of this subject, the gathering of spolia into more permanent collections, is Ker's student Andrew Watson, author of numerous studies on the dispersals and their early receivers. These individuals importantly preserved what remains during the half-century between Dissolution and the foundation of modern collections. See especially Watson's *The Library of Sir Simonds D'Ewes* (London, 1966); *The Manuscripts of Henry Savile of Banke* (London, 1969, rep. as coll XVI), and, with R. J. Roberts, *John Dee's Library Catalogue* (London, 1990). Watson coll also includes his fine study of the Oxford collector Thomas Allen (from s. xvi ex., VII), to be supplemented by his extensive Appendix to W. D. Macray, rev. R. W. Hunt and A. G. Watson, *Bodleian Library Quarto Catalogues: 9, Digby Manuscripts* (1883; Oxford, 1999).

The two greatest private collectors have a literature all their own:

> Colin G. C. Tite, *The Manuscript Library of Sir Robert Cotton* (London, 1994); *The Early Records of Sir Robert Cotton's Library: Formation, Cataloguing, Use* (London, 2003); Tite's re-edition of the 1696 collection catalogue (a valuable report preceding the destructive fire of 1731) (Cambridge, 1984); and his '"Lost or stolen or strayed": A Survey of Manuscripts Formerly in the Cotton Library', *Sir Robert Cotton as Collector: Essays on an Early Stuart Courtier and his Legacy*, ed. C. J. Wright (London,

1997), 262–306. For a broader assessment, see Kevin Sharpe, *Sir Robert Cotton, 1586–1631: History and Politics in Early Modern England* (Oxford, 1979).

C. E. Wright, *Fontes Harleiani: A Study of the Sources of the Harleian Collection ...* (London, 1972), as well as studies of the greatest English palaeographer, Harley's librarian, Humfrey Wanley: C. E. and Ruth C. Wright, eds, *The Diary of Humfrey Wanley, 1715–1726*, 2 vols (London, 1966); P. L. Heyworth, ed., *Letters of Humfrey Wanley: Palaeographer, Anglo-Saxonist, Librarian, 1672–1726: with an appendix of documents* (Oxford, 1989).[147]

While not a personal library, Elizabeth's archbishop of Canterbury, Matthew Parker, and his collection at Cambridge, Corpus Christi College, particularly strong in pre-Conquest materials, have also attracted extensive notice. For a general view, see R. I. Page, *Matthew Parker and His Books: Sandars Lectures in Bibliography ... 1990 ...* (Kalamazoo MI, 1993), as well as Simon Horobin and Aditi Nafde, 'Stephan Batman and the Making of the Parker Library', *Transactions of the Cambridge Bibliographical Society* 15 (2015), 561–81. Batman provides a classic example of the search for an early modern private owner/user, largely dependent on finding signatures or annotations in a recognisable hand in the books; see Parkes, 'Stephan Batman's Manuscripts', *Pages from the Past* X. Given the need for meticulous searches, Parkes's initial effort is not a complete list; see, for example, A. E. Kraebel, 'A Further Book Annotated by Stephan Batman, with New Material for his Biography', *The Library* 7th ser. 16 (2015), 458–66.

Harris, Meale, and Keiser all direct one's attention to the importance of non-book materials: the administrative and legal record. Local history or 'topography' is a primary resource here, the study of which begins with a sequence of learned gentlemen, ss. xvi and xvii, 'the antiquarian tradition'. A number of these individuals wrote histories of their locale, the shire or county, and were able to draw upon documents now long since vanished. For the author of the earliest of these, *A Perambulation of Kent* (published 1576), see Retha M. Warnicke,

---

[147] Ker described his *Catalogue* of Old English manuscripts as only footnotes to George Hickes and Wanley, *Antiquae literaturae septentrionalis libri duo ...*, 2 vols (Oxford, 1705). For a taste of Wanley's breadth, see his precise and still useful notes on Sir Henry Spelman's manuscripts, auctioned in London, 1709, at BL, MS Harley 7055, fols 232–38.

William Lambarde, Elizabethan Antiquary, 1536–1601 (London, [1973]), including references to an extensive library only dispersed s. xx in. and with no modern study.[148] See further Graham Parry, *The Trophies of Time: English Antiquarians of the Seventeenth Century* (Oxford, 1995), carrying the story forward from May McKisack, *Medieval History in the Tudor Age* (Oxford, 1971) and H. B. Walters, *The English Antiquaries of the Sixteenth, Seventeenth and Eighteenth Centuries* (London, 1934). Perhaps the most famous such survey of county community from the earliest records, and certainly one of the most authoritative, is George Ormerod, *The History of the County Palatine and City of Chester; compiled from original evidences ...* , 3 vols (London, 1819).

The modern avatar of such studies is the 'Victoria County History of England' (always just 'VCH'), a county-by-county and, where complete, parish-by-parish and manor-by-manor survey of the entire country. Because the production depended upon multiple hands, particularly those of local archivists, publication has been fitful. For many counties, only the first volume(s), the general survey, typically treating such matters as geology, prehistoric remains, and religious houses, ever appeared. But in some counties research continues, with impressive and useful results, including tracing the ownership of every manor and the incumbents of every parish church.[149] Thus, VCH forms a potentially useful tool for identifying any name one might find scrawled in a manuscript, and offers an overview of connections and affinities in a society largely rural. The entire series so far published is available through an extensive and useful website, 'British History Online', https://www.british-history.ac.uk.

This uneven coverage can be immediately, if a bit unpredictably, supplemented. Virtually every English county has a journal devoted to local history, and very frequently a publication series as well, such as *Transactions of the Bristol and Gloucestershire Archaeological Society* (since 1876) and the Yorkshire Archaeological Society Record Series (and a further series of 'occasional papers') (since 1885). Most distinguished of all is perhaps Durham's Surtees Society (since 1838), the volumes of which are not limited to co. Durham alone, but cover the North of England.

[148] Evidence from the 1560s suggests that he owned, for example, the large historical miscellany mentioned above (p. 17), CUL, MS Dd.1.17.

[149] As an excellent example, see J. Allison and G. H. R. Kent, eds, *A History of the County of York: East Riding. Volume VII: Holderness Wapentake, Middle and North Divisions* (London, 2002).

With publications like these you are rather dependent on what (mainly local) researchers have found of interest, but if you hit paydirt the rewards are rich. Generations of scholars have found valuable materials in the Surtees publication, beginning in the 1830s, of numerous Northern wills, for example. A similar, but perhaps surprising, resource often offers suggestive detail – the numerous histories of their lineage written by family members.[150] As one would expect from a family that sponsors such an enterprise, such people are frequently prominent in their locales and culturally ascendant, the sort of people with whom one might associate book use and ownership. Many of them will have sat as MPs and thus have some biographical notice in volumes such as John S. Roskell *et al.*, eds, *The House of Commons 1386–1421*, 4 vols (Stroud, 1992).

The unedited legal record, while it is often sparse and not very culturally informative (lots of suits over debt, 'detention of indentures', and the like), is potentially useful. For example, persons named as supervisors of wills, or as feoffees of a person's property, are very usually intimates and close supporters, forming part of a network that might be expected to extend to cultural exchange. The great tool here is The National Archives's search engine 'Discovery'; you can insert a name, narrow your search to a single century, if you like, and see what might emerge. One powerful feature of this tool is its inclusion not just of documents held in TNA but in a number of county record offices and similar depositories. Visiting such local archives may also be helpful; customarily, in addition to their document collections, they hold extensive publications on their locale that may not be available elsewhere. Through such materials, one can begin to glimpse affinities and family connections, the bedrock of medieval society.[151]

I offer a couple of examples where discussions of books I have already cited might be supplemented from materials of this sort. In his description of the five Garrett MSS I have discussed (pp. 106–08), Skemer notes, but does not actively pursue, an s. xv signature that appears on the putative final leaf of the collection, MS Garrett 87, fol. 23^v, 'W. Taylard'. Skemer does cite *MMBL* 4:235, which describes a similar signature and armorial in Saffron Walden Town Hall, MS E.1104/3476 (a liturgical

---

[150] E.g. Henry E. Chetwynd-Stapylton, *The Stapeltons of Yorkshire, Being the History of an English Family from Very Early Times* (London, 1897).
[151] See, for example, tools like these in use in 'Extending *MLGB*: The Case of Vossianus latinus F.81', *Journal of the Early Book Society* 23 (2020), 203–11; or 'The Descent of Some Chester Libraries', *The Library* 7th ser. 22 (2021), 57–68.

manuale with extensive prayers, s. xiv/xv). However, some basic tools might fill this reference in a good deal more fully. Both books are probably to be identified with a William Taylard, who was a Cambridge MA by 1496, later a student of canon law, and subsequently a minor church official and rector in his native Hunts. (*BRUC* 578). His memorial brass is still in the church in Offord D'Arcy, where he served until death, 1502-32. His armigerous family was from neighbouring Diddington (he was also rector there, 1500-02); his father, also William, is buried in that church, his arms, 'quarterly argent and sable, a cross paty quartery sable and argent', on the tomb. See William Page *et al.*, eds, *VCH Hunts.*, 3 vols (London, 1926-38), esp. 2:271-72, 327 and nn.5-6.

This is fairly sparse stuff, but there's further evidence for Taylard engagement with fancy service books, important collections, and persons of prominence. An earlier William Taylard from this family, s. xv med., was engaged in the transmission of BL, MS Harley 2942. This is a very nice Sarum processional from a well-known (and extensively annotated) collection, that of Thomas of Woodstock, duke of Gloucester (d. 1397). Taylard presented it on behalf of himself and others to a newly constructed chapel at St Bartholomew's priory, West Smithfield (OSA), and someone certainly his relative, Walter Taylard, simultaneously offered the priory a substantial cash donation (10 marks). Among Taylard's co-donors, persons whose funds had been used to purchase the book, were John Lorde and Simon Briggeman. They are identifiable as prominent persons, the former called 'curie Cant' procurator generalis', and the latter a London fuller who owned suburban properties. Further extended researches might show both their and their families' relations with the Taylards, as well as uncover further hints of book use and possibly libraries.[152]

A further example: the Rouses describe their *schedula* (mentioned p. 14) as recording 'tenants of an unidentified English ecclesiastical institution (abbey, cathedral)'. However, not all the entries record tenants, but some include the place-name 'Brisingham', a detail that would help clarify the Rouses' statement. This is a village, today

---

[152] The most convenient version of the inventory of Thomas of Woodstock's books (which also included BL, MSS Egerton 617+618, mentioned p. 17), made on his attainder for treason, appears at Cavanaugh, 'A Study', 844-51, the chapel books (among which this copy cannot be identified) at 849-50. My information about Briggeman is derived from a quick check of 'Discovery'. The book does not appear in *MLGB*, which only intermittently lists liturgical books, from the church, not the library.

Bressingham, just west of Diss, on the Norfolk–Suffolk border. One might look at the account offered by the great local antiquary Francis Blomefield (d. 1752). At *An Essay Towards A Topographical History of the County of Norfolk: Volume 1* (London, 1805), 49–73 passim, he cites a document contemporary with the *schedula* (c. 1360) indicating that the manor of Bressingham was held by Sir John Verdon as a sub-tenant of the Earl Marshall (usually the dukes of Norfolk), in his turn a sub-tenant of the great abbey of Bury St Edmunds (OSB).

Signatures like those prominent in pursuing Batman's books serve to identify a small, apparently local collection that appears to have remained together for perhaps as long as 75 years before its donation to a library. This is a largely unnoticeable sequence of seven volumes, one an *MLGB* book, that first appears in records of Bodleian collections only about 1655. It includes the following Bodleian manuscripts:

MS Auct. D.1.3 (*SC* 2532), s. xiii: Matthew and Mark with the *glossa ordinaria*;

MS Bodley 428 (*SC* 2513), French, s. xiii in.: penitential tracts, the Gospel of Nicodemus, Anselm;

MS Bodley 687 (*SC* 2501), s. xv in.: *Fasciculus morum*, John Waldeby OESA's *Novum opus dominicale* (one of only two surviving copies of this sermon cycle), Peter Aureole on the Decalogue;

MS Bodley 701 (*SC* 2542), s. xiii in., probably French: Gregory the Great's homilies on Ezechiel;

MS Bodley 702 (*SC* 2548), s. xiii$^{1/2}$, French: Jerome's epistles;

MS Bodley 771 (*SC* 2553), s. xiv/xv: the Wycliffite *Oon of Foure*, from the Shrewsbury Franciscans; and

MS Bodley 844 (*SC* 2577): five manuscripts of s. xv: a verse life of Alexander the Great, Innocent III's *De miseria*, Pierre Bersuire's *Ovidiana*, Aristotle commentaries.[153]

---

[153] For these books, see respectively *SC* 2.1, 413, 404–05, 398–99, 424, 420, 422, and 434–35. For Bodley 771, see also Solopova, *Manuscripts of the Wycliffite Bible*, 87. Gameson takes up an informative analogy, one Thomas Unton, in "'Pope's Chaucer'", *Middle English Manuscripts* (full reference in n.3), 237–54.

Although a single cluster, one should notice that that these seven books are a rump, the remains of something larger. A contemporary donation to the Bodleian indicates that at least portions of the collection had been dispersed into some general circulation. This is MS Selden Supra 87 (SC 3475), s. xiii ex.: Raymund de Penyaforte, *Summa*, which came to the library with Selden's other books in 1659. This book offers an interesting echo of the core collection, since on fols 207ᵛ–9 a sixteenth-century hand has offered an excerpt from the Wycliffite Bible.[154]

This sequence of books belongs together because they all are signed by the same individual, one Thomas Cardiff or Kerdiff (Bodley 702 not so, but a companion volume to 701). One knows next to nothing about him, save for his notes in the books. He was born in 1540 and by 1570 was a merchant of the Staple with a London shop. However, he appears to have removed to the Shrewsbury area, and his inquisition post mortem (Kew, The National Archives, Public Record Office C142/258/7) shows that he died as a Shropshire landowner in 1598/9. A few years later, a Roger Cardiff, presumably his heir, was sued over a lease in Isombridge (Salop, 11 miles east of Shrewsbury) (*ibid.*, C2/Eliz/P1/45).

Given this information, Cardiff plainly acquired the vernacular *MLGB* volume, Bodley 771, locally. But he was rather late in the game, since the MS includes a succession of a half-dozen previous signatures of owners/users (beginning with a 'frater Thomas Rydwar', presumably from the conventual owners). One should think that Bodley 687 (and perhaps the Bersuire portion of Bodley 844) had similar mendicant origins. However, the former has a sequence of notes indicating that the book was earlier in Exeter diocese, and it had also passed through the hands of 'Ralph Hassoll de Hankelow'. This is an east Cheshire locale, but within Shrewsbury's 'catchment area'; that fact might indicate that he was the last intermediate owner before Cardiff.[155]

Four of Cardiff's remaining volumes certainly look as if they should have been monastic books (and it is important to see that his

---

[154] See *SC* 2.1, 649. The rubric, 'Here suen foure full notable Prologis upon the Sauter', in spite of the truncated reproduction (only the first such prologue is copied here), indicates that the scribe/owner had access to a Wycliffite Psalter; the only surviving books with this sequence are Dublin, Trinity College, MS 75; and HM 501.

[155] Ralph appears in local litigation of the 1540s and 1550s at The National Archives, C 1/1301/27–29, C 1/1347/57, C 3/81/75, and STAC 2/16. Again, all these references are derived from a search on TNA's 'Discovery'.

vernacular materials were a minority of his collection). Indeed, Bodley 701 has a note (s. xvi) reporting the opinion of William Granson of Upton (Upton Magna, nr. Shrewsbury) concerning a rental in 'Boulwas manor', probably Buildwas (Salop), site of a Cistercian house. Yet this is scarcely the only possible source for such materials; the Benedictine Shrewsbury Abbey was a pilgrimage site (the abducted remains of St Winifred of Holywell in north Wales), and other Shrewsbury religious houses, as well as Haughmond (home of the English authors John Mirk and 'blind John' Audelay), are also nearby. But whatever sort of rump this book-stash may represent, it testifies both to the late sixteenth-century availability of books (to someone with an apparent interest in *biblia* and their public promulgation, as well as classical materials) and to continuous collection descent that held a substantial portion of this small, yet far from insubstantial, group together for well over half a century.

Studies like these frequently plunge you into an arena a good deal removed from the customary pursuits of academics, contact with the rich and famous. I'll close this survey of the pursuit of medieval private libraries with someone at the opposite end of the scale, a professional poor person, Henry Chambron (Champernon). Henry was a Franciscan and a minor author (not in Sharpe); he left behind a handful of Latin sermons, some including English bits, and a brief Middle English tract. Like all mendicants, he basically sought a life of obscure service. However, one central piece of his library survives, his Bible (or one of them?), now SJ 48. See *The English Manuscripts of Richard Rolle: A Descriptive Catalogue* (Exeter, 2010), 67–68, with further references, particularly to Wenzel, *Latin Sermon Collections*, 125–31.

Looking at Cambridge, Queens' College, MS 10

The raw file of notes

One introductory caution: in my examination of the manuscript I did not pay much attention to incipits and explicits; I was interested initially in the manuscript because of my familiarity with most of the texts gathered here. Nor did I attend much to the limited decoration: headings in the text hand (often marginally, sometimes added in darker ink), two-line unflourished red lombards at textual divisions, the texts occasionally divided by red paraphs.

Described James, *Queens'* 10–12
Parchment – 6¾ × 4½ – fols 129 + 4 – 40–50 lines, hand s 'xiii, xiv' in Kathleen O. Elliott and P. J. Elder, 'A Critical Edition of the Vatican Mythographers', *Transactions and Proceedings of the American Philological Association* 78 (1947), 189–207, interpreted as s. xiii/xiv, as also by Coulson-Roy and Swanson, below; Sharpe, *Titulus*, gets it right.

Probably given by Francis Tyndal – donor of much of the collection s. xvii: Venn 1, iv:284 was admitted to Caius 1561 (b. 1544), d. a bachelor 1631, will in PCC, admitted Lincoln's Inn 1585 and lived in late xvi in Cambridge.

James divides the book into three parts 1–56v (actually two booklets) and the remainder (James mistook the shape of quire 9 and misfoliated some later portions of the MS, which may have hindered his recognition procedures, but actually six/seven booklets); his third part is the binding materials at the end, separate from the final text quire ... .

Fol. 1 (this part has medieval foliation? they may be chapter divisions? NO) Fulgentius Mythography by Ridewall.

Hand early anglicana, 1300–30, probably earlier rather than later.

Q1 sewn 2/3, CW 4v, there are quire signatures, perhaps contemp, in crayon, the quire's arabic number only, in lower margins of most first rectos, a 4.

Q2 8/9, CW 12v, an 8.

Q3 16/17, CW 20v [name Thomas Wele, upper margins 19v and 20], an 8.

Q4 24/25, breaks off at end 28v, an 8.

Fulgentius ends 27v near foot, followed immediately by copy of Val; it has the look of being filler, and lower half of 28v quite packed in to get as much text as possible, but breaks off in Pacuvius, ' ... arbor illa suspendit et tercio amice ... '.

Q5 32/33, CW 36v, an 8.

Fol. 29 Scintillarum poetarum Alexandri Nequam – not the same hand as the first, but one certainly comparable; at head of leaf 'Assit principio sancta Maria mea'.

Q6 40/41, CW 44v, an 8.

App. name I can't read in margin fol. 37, Edward Phelyps 1552 upside down in lower margin fol. 40 (again vertically in the outer margin fol. 61, similarly fol. 89v [real 91v], 102v and 103 [real 104v and 105]).

Q7 50/51, ends with 56v blank, a 12.

Nequam ends at foot of fol. 55, Secundus philosophus used as quire filler on the remaining blank leaves, fols 55v–56.

Q8 59/60, CW 62v, a 6.

Fol. 57 Ridewall's commentary on Map, ending 62 foot; a superseded booklet boundary with Malachy of Ireland's Venenum beginning 62v – this is probably same scribe as prec. Continuing.

Q9 66/67, text break 70v, an 8.

Malachy ends near foot of fol. 68, Frontinus, *Strategemata* starts there – again, these are quire-filling excerpts of some sort, same form of early s. xiv hand.

Q10 76/77, no CW at 82v, a 12.

More early s. xiv; new text 'Maria thomas katerina Prior sancti (?) eligij super ouidium'; the text ends fragmentarily, and the quire numbering jumps (next marked 'xij' in crayon) – Frank Coulson and Bruno Roy, *Incipitarium Ovidianum* no. 2, Bersuire's *Reductorium* book 15 – note what this says about dating: composition probably c. 1340, and Bersuire was not abbot of Saint Eloi (ile de la cite) until 1354.

Q11 89/90, this is a 14 (the MS is foliated only on first leaves of quires, and MRJ (?) assigned head of medieval Q13 fol. 95, which is wrong – it should be folio 97 (**so +2 in the remainder**).

New text 'exposicio Ouidij' fol. 83, ends on last line fol. 96v – Coulson and Roy no. 257 Arnulf of Orleans, *Interpretationes* – this quire and the last resemble each other closely and are a little more s. xiv-ish in mien than earlier?

Q12 (med. 13) 100/1, breaks off at 105 (i.e. real 107), sewn as a 12, and lacks the 12th leaf.

'Assit principio sancta Maria meo katerina'; 95 (i.e. real 97) the text of Fulgentius proper.

Q13 (med. 14) 111/12 sewn as a 12, lacks the 12th leaf, last 117, but MRJ has guessed here and this is really fol. 116 (NOT real 119 but 118, so his numbering is now only one ahead).

106 [real 108] Seneca the elder Declamationes, ends fragmentarily?

Q14 (med 15) 123/24 a full 12, with CW at the end, but the remainder now lost.

118 (real 119?) John of Wales, Brev on cardinal virtues – so should end with real fol. 130.

At the end three flyleaves of late s. xv stuff, then another flyleaf to match the one in front with late s. xiii anglicana –the top of the recto of this has added superscription 'Schak ye tayl and mak hit wele quod hending in may'.

Provenance stuff: app. name I can't read in margin fol. 37.

[name **Thomas Wele**, upper margins 19v and 20].

Emden BRUO 2007 has a Thomas Well OFM at the Oxford convent 1378 and ordained subdeacon; ibid. 2048 a Thomas Wille, Exeter diocese priest, given licence to study at Oxford 1370×73 and rector of Truro 1370×1412.

BRUC 625 Thomas Wele vicar of Swaffham st Cyriac Cambs 1458×68; another 626 was OESA of Cambridge convent 1498; and 627 Thomas Wellys a canon lawyer (BCL by 1451) mainly in Norwich and Ely dioceses, d. 1476 and who left books to both Queens' and Trinity Hall (all titles cited canonistic).

Venn 1, iv:364 has a number of s. xvi Thomas Wells's, one at Queen's 1660.

Edward Phelyps 1552 upside down in lower margin fol. 40 (again vertically in the outer margin Fol. 61, similarly fol. 89v [real 91v], 102v and 103 [real 104v and 105]).

No Edward P in Venn; the only plausible in AO 3:1156 is an otherwise unknown MA of 1508.

In its medieval binding, scar from clasp-seating in upper board.

A basic organised report

What follows is a scaled-down report of the basics (not all of Ker's 'sixteen points' cited at p. 15), information particularly useful for a literary scholar, or one of history. In teaching, I always gave students, as exemplary models, copies of Ker, *MMBL* 1:422-24 (London, Westminster School, MS 3); Parkes, *The Medieval Manuscripts of Keble College, Oxford: A Descriptive Catalogue* ... (London, 1979), 35-36 (Oxford, Keble College, MS 13); and C. W. Dutschke with R. H. Rouse, *Guide to Medieval and Renaissance Manuscripts in the Huntington Library*, 2 vols (San Marino CA, 1989), 1:205-07 (HM 148). I could well have added numerous examples from Mynors's catalogue of Balliol College manuscripts (cited n.8), or from K. A. de Meyier, *Codices Vossiani Latini*, 4 vols, Bibliotheca Universitatis Leidenensis Codices Manuscripti 13-16 (Leiden, 1973-84).

Membrane. s. xiv med. (not before 1354 – see booklet 5 below – probably 1360s). Fols i+130+iii+i; there is a later medieval foliation, running 1-138, with some omissions, details below. Overall 170 mm × 110 mm, in long lines, but varying formats, as indicated below. In anglicana, probably three hands, quires 1-4 and probably 12-14, 5-9, and 10-11, plus a lost quire; the filler items are in similar hands but not assignable.

Booklet 1 = fols 1–28

Writing area 135 mm × 85 mm, 40 lines.

[1] Fols 1–27^v: John Ridewall OFM, *Fulgencius metaforalis* (Sharpe 301-2, with a full list of manuscripts), ed. from an incomplete MS, only about one-third of the text, Hans Liebeschütz, *Fulgentius metaforalis: Ein Beitrag zur Geschichte der antiken Mythologie im Mittelalter*, Studien der Bibliothek Warburg 4 (Leipzig and Berlin, 1926). The text here is more extensive, but also incomplete, as in two other copies, ending with Perseus (1.12).

[2] Fols 27^v–28^v: Walter Map, *Dissuasio Valerii* (Sharpe 737), added filler, ed. Hanna and Traugott Lawler, *Jankyn's Book of Wikked Wyves*:

Volume 1 The Primary Texts (Athens GA, 1997), 222-47; a list of around 160 manuscripts at 260-73 (capable of considerable extension, both of extant and recorded copies). The text here is excerpted, only lines 1–114, 159–78, 198–203, where it breaks off. There may have been a following quire, perhaps only a bifolium or two (cf. Booklet 5), but it was already lost when the book was assembled with the crayon signatures.

COLLATION 1⁸ (lacks 3 to 6) 2-4⁸. The missing leaves of the first quire are signalled by the skip in the medieval foliation from '2' to '7', and the text indeed lacks material from Liebeschütz 71 (the fourth part of Idolatry) to 83 (the eighth part of Jupiter). Throughout, regular catchwords within continuous portions; quire signatures only, perhaps contemporary, in crayon, the quire's (usually) arabic number, in the lower margins of most first rectos.

Booklet 2 = fols 29–56

Writing area 135–40 mm × 80 mm, 47 lines.

[3] Fols 29-55: Alberic of London/Mythographus Vaticanus III, *Scintillarium poetarum* (Sharpe 35), ed. Georg H. Bode, *Poetarium siue Scintillarium poetarum, Scriptores rerum mythicarum Latini tres Romae nuper reperti* (Zelle, 1834), 152–256, most authoritatively available in the French translation by Philippe Dain, *Mythographe de Vatican III* (Besançon, 2005). Elliot and Elder's list of 40-odd copies is incomplete and frequently erroneous.[156] On the ascription here to Alexander Neckam, see R. W. Hunt, ed. rev. Margaret Gibson, *The Schools and the Cloister: The Life and Writings of Alexander Nequam (1157–1217)* (Oxford, 1984), 24, 148 (and Sharpe 53).

[4] Fols 55ᵛ–56: *Secundus philosophus* (*Altercatio Hadriani Augusti et Epicteti Philosophi*), added filler; the translation by William of Gap, ed. Ben E. Perry, *Secundus the Silent Philosopher* (Ithaca NY, 1964), 92–100. There is a list of 101 extant and seven lost copies at *Altercatio Hadriani ...* , ed. Lloyd W. Daly and Walter Suchier, Illinois Studies in Language and Literature 24 (Urbana IL, 1939), 162–66. Fol. 56ᵛ is blank.

---

[156] E.g. their Durham Cathedral, MS Hunter 15 is, first of all, a wrong reference. The book is MS Hunter 30; moreover, it has no copy of this text, but rather Defensor's *Liber Scintillarum* (see *MMBL* 2:494).

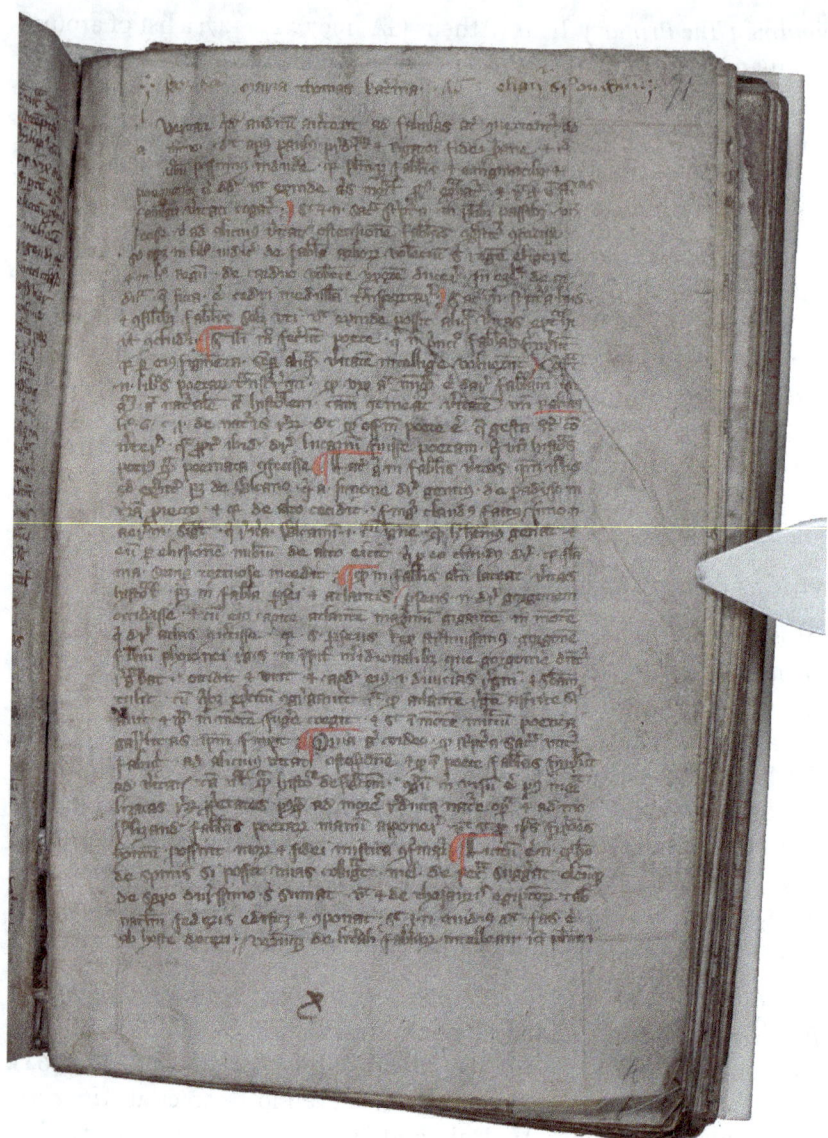

Queens' College, MS 10: The image, the opening of Pierre Bersuire's moralised Ovid, provides the most secure evidence for dating this manuscript. Even the great Montague R. James had thought some portions of the scribal work here to date from s. xiii. However, as the rubric would indicate, the three rather similar hands that produce the collected quires that form the manuscript were probably writing s. xiv med. While their scripts certainly might fit earlier in the century, they are probably mature writers simply reproducing earlier training. (Cambridge, The Queens' College, MS 10, fol. 71, reproduced at 83%).

COLLATION 5–6⁸ 7¹².

Booklets 3+4 = fols 57–62, superseded and extended to fol. 70

Writing area 145 mm × 90 mm, 47 lines; in the continuation, 150 mm × 90 mm, 46 lines.

[5] Fols 57–62: John Ridewall's commentary on Map's *Dissuasio* (Sharpe 301), ed. Lawler, *Jankyn's Book of Wikked Wyves: Volume 2 Seven Commentaries* … (Athens GA, 2014), 52–119, using all known copies.

[6] Fols 62ᵛ–68: Malachy the Irishman OFM, *De veneno* (Sharpe 369), ed. Hanna (Liverpool, 2020), with additions to Sharpe's list, *Titulus*, 218–45, bringing the total to 115 copies.

[7] Fols 68–70ᵛ: Frontinus, *Strategemata*, excerpts, added filler.

COLLATION 8⁶ | 9⁸.

Booklet 5 = fols 71–82

Writing area 135 mm × 80 mm, 39 lines.

[8] Fols 71–82ᵛ: Pierre Bersuire OFM and later OSB, *Ovidius moralizatus* (i.e. *Reductorium morale*, book 15), ed. [J. Engels], *Reductorium morale, Liber XV, cap. I. De formis figurisque deorum naar de Parisije druck van 1509: Werkmateriaal* (Utrecht, 1960), etc. The text is incomplete and a following quire now lost. For manuscripts, see Frank T. Coulson and Bruno Roy, *Incipitarium Ovidianum: A Finding Guide for Texts in Latin Related to the Study of Ovid* … , Publications of the Journal of Medieval Latin 3 (Turnhout, 2000), no. 2 (24–27). The scribe's rubric, 'Prior sancti eligij super ouidium' provides the *terminus a quo* for (at least this portion of) the production, since Bersuire became abbot of Saint Eloi (in Île de la Cité) only in 1354.

COLLATION 10¹² [missing quire]. The original presence of the following quire is indicated by the medieval quire signatures, '10' on fol. 71, 'xii' on fol. 83; this segment was already gone when the book was foliated in the fifteenth century (fols 82 and 83 = '87' and '88').

Booklet 6 = fols 83–94/[96]

Writing area 130 mm × 80 mm, 36 lines.

[9] Fols 83–94ᵛ/[96ᵛ]: Arnulf of Orleans, *Interpretationes* [of Ovid], ed. Fausto Ghisalberti, 'Arnolfo d'Orléans: un cultore di Ovidio nel secolo

XII', *Memorie del Istituto Lombardo di Scienze e Letture* 24.4 (1932), 158–234, at 201–29. For manuscripts, see Coulson and Roy, no. 257 (83–84).

COLLATION 11^{14}. The current foliation, probably imposed by James and generally applied only to the opening rectos of each quire, fails to account for two leaves in this quire.

Booklet 7 = fols 95/[97]–105/[107]

Writing area 140 mm × 80 mm, 41 lines.

[10] Fols 95/[97]–105^v/[107^v]: Fulgentius, *Mithologiae*, ed. Rudolf Helm, *Opera* (Leipzig, 1898), 1–80.

COLLATION 12^{12} (lacks 12).

Booklet 8 = fols 106/[108]–17[118]

Writing area 135 mm × 85 mm, 40 lines.

[11] Fols 106/[108]–17^v[18^v]: Seneca the elder, *Declamationes*, excerpts only.

COLLATION 13^{12} (lacks 12). The current foliation has skipped a leaf in this quire.

Booklet 9 = fols 118[119]–129[130]

Writing area 130 mm × 85–90 mm, 38 lines.

[12] Fols 118/[119]–129^v/[130^v]: John Waleys/of Wales OFM, *Breviloquium de virtutibus* ... (Sharpe 337), ed. *Summa de regimine vitae humane seu Margarita philosophorum* (Venice, 20 July 1496), fols 240–59, here breaking off with a catchword. A list of manuscripts, more than 150 in all, dispersed among the account of Jenny Swanson, *John of Wales: A Study of the Works and Ideas of a Thirteenth-Century Friar* (Cambridge, 1989), 229–89.

COLLATION 14^{12} [lost quire(s)].

BINDING Medieval, brown calf, over wooden boards, a scar from a strap-seating at the centre of the upper board. The front flyleaf and the last at the rear (this a raised pastedown) from a theological (?) discussion, anglicana, s. xiii ex. The rear flyleaf is preceded by three leaves with notes, s. xv ex. At the head of the rear flyleaf, in contemporary Middle English, 'Schak ye tayl and mak hit wele quod hending in may', certainly proverbial and octosyllabic verse, but not from the collection customarily ascribed to Hending (conceivably with reference to the owner 'Thomas Wele'?).

PROVENANCE Certainly a communal production by associated hands, and certainly members of the same religious group. Cf. the invocations at the openings of individual stints: fol. 29 (scribe 2), 'Assit principio sancta Maria mea'; fol. 71 (scribe 3), 'Maria thomas katerina'; fol. 95 (i.e. real 97, scribe 1) 'Assit principio sancta Maria mea katerina'.

A not especially legible inscription, s. xv (fol. 37, in the outer margin), ? 'Ihon de Ihorn<y?->t<'>'; no plausible candidate appears in either *BRUO* or *BRUC*.

'Thomas Wele', s. xv med. (fols 19^v and 20, in the upper margins): probably to be associated with a man of the name, who was vicar of St Cyriac's, Swaffham Prior (Cambs.), 1458×68 (Emden, *BRUC* 625). He is a more likely candidate than Thomas Wellys, a canon lawyer (BCL by 1451, d. 1476), mainly practising in Norwich and Ely dioceses; he left books to both Queens' and Trinity Hall (all the titles cited canonistic) (Emden, *BRUC* 627).

'Edward Phelyps 1552' (variously, fols 40, 61, 89^v [actual 91^v], 102^v and 103 [actual 104^v and 105]). No likely candidate appears in either Venn or *Alumni Oxonienses*. Sir Edward Phelips, Speaker of the Commons and a royal justice under Elizabeth and James I (d. 1614), was born too late and is associated with Montacute House (Somt.), a good deal too far afield to be relevant.

Probably donated by Francis Tyndal (1554–1631), sometime Cambridge resident and source of much of the Queens' collection; for him, see Venn 1, iv:284.

Previously described James, *A Descriptive Catalogue of the Western Manuscripts in the Library of Queens' College, Cambridge* (Cambridge, 1905), 10–12. James there divides the book into three parts: 1–56^v (actually two booklets) and the remainder. James mistook the shape of quire 9 and misfoliated some later portions of the manuscript, which may have hindered his recognition procedures; his third part consists of the binding materials at the end, separate from the final text quire.

Some preliminary analysis

You may have thought that I was trying to turn you into a collection cataloguer. Not so. Trying to describe the manuscript in front of you is basic to organising perception/observation, trying to see what one might want to make of an object, what questions might be asked – and then imagining where you would go to develop answers.

Near the end of my essay, I suggested some ready ways of extending a couple of previous descriptions. Discussing MS Queens' 10 will raise the issue of things you can deal with, and then ones you can't, ones you have to leave in the realm of mystery. It is important to know the difference; there's no use banging your head against a stone wall.

Ideally, one would like to locate where and why a book was made, and, more than that, under what auspices. And then how it has descended to the present.

So I begin with some general statements about MS Queens' 10 as a production. This is a portable, on the person book (though not the utterly minimal size of Paris Bibles). Perhaps in contrast to its learned texts, it is an informal production. The membrane is decidedly down-market: a bit stiff and rather dark on the hairsides, a number of sheets from the edges of the usable skin (no visible follicles, but a good many lower edges are oddly shaped cutoffs, and there are a number of holes). As I noted above, the texts have been copied without much finishing; they're apparently familiar, and titles generally look as if they could have been added. This is distinctly a private consultation volume; although it does have a reasonable binding, it is not one readily datable, and is probably s. xv.

The three scribes must have been mature individuals. At the date of copying, their script should have been slightly archaic (hence a variety of early datings in previous discussions), and the hands are not exceptionally practised, although they are working in relatively small script. That's a strong indication, consonant with the nature of the texts here, that the group may have been more accustomed to informal glossing (rather than text production), indicative of an academic environment. The trio resemble one another closely enough to suggest that they are probably of shared training.

The scribes' textual handling, so far as I have investigated it, might be described as a bit blasé. There's a marked tendency in several texts, at least, to copy for the sense, not the *ipsissima verba*. This implies an interest in textual content, information personally relevant, rather than fidelity. Like the MS of logic texts, Magd lat. 162 (see p. 44), the three appear to be working simultaneously on small booklets. There's been some effort at codicisation: blank leaves at the ends of units have been filled with brief, usually excerpted (this selectiveness is another indication of personal relevance), texts in yet smaller script; at one point (quires 3–4), there is probably a superseded booklet boundary. This is to be some variety of shared book, for consultation by at least the group of three and possibly a broader institutional community.

The texts themselves identify some of the scribes' interests, basically in mythology and classical material. However, you need to be aware that modern characterisations of contents (just like modern identifications of authors and texts, see p. 79 and n.89) do not necessarily map directly on to medieval perceptions. Miscellanies imply some measure of motivation, these texts and not those. The process by which this example has been constructed is most evident, as I'll show in a moment, in the way in which the truncated text of Walter Map's *Dissuasio* has been excerpted.

Here John of Wales's *Breviloquium*, a text utterly ubiquitous, in conjunction with some other items, is suggestive. John presents his work as a handbook for addressing princes on proper conduct; his discussion is organised around the classical cardinal virtues. What ensues is fundamentally a preacher's book of moralisable anecdotes, *exempla*, most drawn from classical sources, particularly Valerius Maximus's *Dicta et facta*. In his brief prologue, John, alluding to the biblical text he cites at his incipit, Proverbs 20:28 ('Mercy and truth preserve the king, and his throne is strengthened by clemency'), says that the four virtues:

> are like four columns or four posts that strengthen the throne I have mentioned. Therefore I have written below a few stories, exemplary and hortatory, about them. These stories are useful for rulers and instructive for those who are enthroned, insofar as they are drawn from the lives of powerful people or of wise worldly philosophers. There are plenty of available stories about holy people in their lives or in the stories related by Holy Scripture.[157]

'Narrationes exemplares et persuasorie'. As always in John's oeuvre, he is producing fodder for preachers, moralisable exemplary material for sermons. His speciality, as Swanson's study points out again and again, is the address *ad status*, speaking to specific professional cadres within

---

[157] 'sunt quasi quattuor columne siue quattuor postes, quibus predictus thronus roboratur. Ideo de predictis virtutibus alique narrationes exemplares et persuasorie ad vtilitatem presidentium et instructionem in thronis residentium subscribantur, prout continentur in gestis potentum siue sapientum mundi philosophorum. Nam exempla sanctorum sufficienter patent in gestis eorum et hystorijs sacrarum scripturarum' (fol. 240ra).

an audience, here rulers. (Given that these individuals are powerful and should be wise – hence the examples of pagan philosophers – the text itself might substitute for a live preacher, be a private-study guide, hence the profusion of surviving copies.) Further, John follows here a conventional injunction to preachers, that unfamiliar materials, his classical bent, are more effective than are those customary, like those you'd find in a saint's life or a biblical episode.

MS Queens' 10's rather obscure classical texts, materials generally not familiar to us, Seneca senior and Frontinus, belong within the same ambit. Seneca sr is a basic handbook for disputation, instruction in how to analyse a given factual situation and then to frame a compelling argument for a specific action on the case. Frontinus is a common alternative to the more widely circulated Vegetius; it's a trove of information on Roman military leadership, but offered as a model for self-governance and considered action.[158]

Both these texts are persistently cited by John Ridewall's Oxford predecessors and contemporaries, the Dominicans Thomas Waleys and Robert Holcot. The two use both texts in ways consonant with John of Wales's suggestion, as exemplary material, brief narratives that encourage wise conduct. A similar interest marks the excerpted presentation of Walter Map. The manuscript, so far as it goes, offers two chunks from the text: the first includes Map's paired anecdotes, biblical heroes and classical gods (usually warnings against sexual licence as inimical to wisdom); the second, until the text breaks off, presents Map's collection of *dicta* ascribed to classical wise men. These are invented anecdotes analogous to what John of Wales (or his source, Valerius Maximus) presents as real historical accounts.[159] Ridewall's commentary, a central text in the volume, as these excerpts are not, offers both moralisations and basic historical information.

Other texts in Queens' 10 are subject to similar analysis. Malachy of Ireland is a manual of moralised natural history, in a traditional seven sins/remedies for sin format, and again is explicitly addressed to preachers. Ridewall's title *metaforalis* identifies his work as presenting moralised mythology; and, like John of Wales, his presentation is

---

[158] On Seneca sr, see Marjorie C. Woods, 'Rape and the Pedagogical Rhetoric of Sexual Violence', *Criticism and Dissent in the Middle Ages*, ed. Rita Copeland (Cambridge, 1996), 56–86, at 66–69; for Vegetius, see n.163.

[159] The gap in presentation, 20 omitted lines following 178, is probably deliberate; the excerpter suppresses Map's interchange between Canius and Livy, ostensibly an (outrageously ironic) encouragement to 'wise' promiscuity.

predicated on the cardinal virtues (or the corresponding sins). For example, Ridewall explains the genre in which his author, Fulgentius writes: 'A mythography ... is a species of writing devoted to fables and anecdotes, constructed to describe sins and virtues. For this reason, the Greek word *mithos* is the same as Latin *fabula* "fable".'[160] I would take this characterisation to draw attention to what always accompanies 'fable' as a Latin genre, for example in the Aesopian texts that medieval people knew from childhood, that they come with attached morals and offer instruction, beyond their narrative delight.

This emphasis would imply the scribes' interest in constructing a volume that would allow flexible encouragement of virtue, within both classical and Christian frameworks, both cardinal virtues and seven sins with their contraries. Moreover, the manuscript provides a range of approaches to the topic. There are materials presenting moralised natural history (a conventional gambit, e.g. the bestiary *Physiologus*), history (Ridewall's examples in his *Fulgencius* run all the way from legendary Rome, derived from Livy's opening book, to stories he found in Marco Polo), mythic poetry, and mythology.

The interest in Ovid displayed in Queens' 10 is certainly striking. However, just as apparently prioritising Ridewall's *Dissuasio*-commentary over Map's text, these Ovidian materials are here to preclude having to engage directly with the classical poem. Ovid is handled in a manner consonant with John of Wales's classical history, for both Arnulf and (much more expansively) Bersuire essentially treat Ovid as an exemplum book. They first, as is customary in a commentary, divide the text. Thus, the *Metamorphoses* becomes a sequence of separable moralisable tales, and both authors, rather than the grammatical analysis traditional in commentaries on *auctores*, offer suggested moral readings. Bersuire, in particular, provides extensive flexible materials (the same story taken both as an account of vicious behaviour and as presenting encouragement to virtue).[161] (Analogously, as an appendix to the author's *Reportorium*

---

[160] ' ... methologiam, sermonem scilicet fabulosum et apologicum, ordinatum ad descripcionem uiciorum et uirtutum. Unde *mithos* Grece idem quod "fabula" Latine' (Liebeschütz 70).

[161] See the selections presented in A. J. Minnis and A. B. Scott, eds, *Medieval Literary Theory and Criticism c. 1100–c. 1375: The Commentary Tradition*, rev. edn (Oxford, 1988), 366–72. Arnulf has somewhat broader, if more elementary, interests, as he points out in his opening statement (p. 201), 'Modo quasdam allegorice, quasdam moraliter exponamus, et quasdam historice'. Thus, in addition to readings like Bersuire's (although usually only one at a time), he summarises

morale, Bersuire's treatment resembles Malachy's work on sin's poison. Both authors re-present, in what they claim, whether explicitly or not, is a more organised, more easily consultable form of a more authoritative text, for both derive substantial materials from Bartholomaeus Anglicus, *De proprietatibus rerum*.)

Queens' 10 also includes 'originalia', and thus offers a reasonably encyclopedic access to yet further mythographic materials. Ridewall's *Fulgencius* is fine stuff, so far as it goes. However, Ridewall engages only with Fulgentius's account of the gods and goddesses, and not with a wider presentation of narrative mythography, individual myths that Fulgentius retells. A good many of these are, of course, Ovidian, but accompanied by proffered moralisations different from those elsewhere. Similarly, Alberic's *Scintillarium* is one of Ridewall's primary sources. Again, the full text offers considerably more detail than Ridewall selects; this introduces a more diverse range of figures and information on a broader range of topics than we might consider strictly mythology, such as divination and astronomy. That is, in addition to 'prepared *praedicabilia*', already moralised anecdotal material, MS Queens' 10 includes sources for a good deal more. Thus, if the identification I have offered above of the Mr Well who signed the MS as a parish priest is correct, one can imagine what he might have wanted the volume for. The one thing certain about this identification, if it is correct, is that it imagines the book as already, a century after its production, dispelled from whatever communal environment it was made for.

However, the manuscript offers no direct information that would allow one to locate a site where the three scribes did their work. The most promising evidence is provided by the prayers the scribes wrote at the start of their stints. These may be generic, but may equally point to the dedication of a religious house of which all were members. The texts included, particularly two works by Ridewall, neither of very wide distribution, would suggest that all were, or had connections with, Oxford Franciscans. But the prayers at the heads of texts do not, as one would expect were this the case, invoke Francis, and they serve only to identify the writers as probably in religious orders (no great advance on what one might have expected). Nor is St Katherine an especially helpful dedication. This was reasonably common in medieval England (and still, s. xxi, affixed to nearly 100 parish churches), but no monastic institution so dedicated seems a very promising locale in which to

---

and provides background to the narrative and is fond of demonstrating the appropriateness of Ovid's transformations to natural processes.

place this activity.¹⁶² However, like the Francis one might expect, were this a Franciscan book, Katherine may represent a generic patron, one attached to a particular order. The Alexandrian virgin-martyr is conventionally a patron of scholars, as well as of the Dominican order, and the book plausibly represents one such house.

Any further discussion has to proceed by inference. Here two related resources may offer suggestive material. First, my description above has, at various points, cited available lists of the manuscripts that provide copies of the relevant texts.¹⁶³ You can gain a sense of terrain from these listings, see whether your manuscript has analogues, ones with more visible contexts, that would allow extended arguments. However, here one may well be routed; Swanson's 150 manuscripts of John's *Breviloquium* will resist any effort at close inspection, and many Queens' 10 texts have similarly extensive circulations. Second, whatever one thinks about editorial procedures, transmission histories turn out to be valuable in terms of linking books. Scholarly editions are committed to outlining for you how the editor believes the text has been transmitted, which manuscripts are most closely related to one another, for example. For two manuscripts to have related versions of texts, they must have shared, perhaps at some remove, an exemplar, a physical object that has to have travelled between them. That simple necessity may allow some inferences about provenance.

Here the two texts by John Ridewall, the *Fulgencius* and the Map-commentary, each extant in a manageable number of copies

---

¹⁶² Examples would include the Gilbertine priory of St Katherine, at the very south end of Lincoln ('without the walls'), VCH Lincs. 2:188–91; Edington (Wilts., Bonshommes), where Katherine is a shared secondary dedication (at the time the manuscript was made, a new foundation, but directly connected to Salisbury Cathedral, where the local founder was bishop), VCH Wilts. 3:320–24; Flixton (Suff., OSA nuns), a joint dedication to the Virgin and Katherine (VCH Suff. 2:115–17); a hospital 'by the Tower' in London, a still extant royal foundation (VCH London 1:525–30).

¹⁶³ In addition to Swanson and other examples cited above, variously relevant are, for Seneca sr, a widely dispersed exemplum book with excerpts, Nigel F. Palmer, 'Das Exempelwerk der englischen Bettelmönchen: ein Gegenstück zu den *Gesta Romanorum?*' *Exempel und Exempelsammlungen*, ed. Walter Haug and Burghart Wachinger (Tübingen, 1991), 137–72; and Charles R. Schrader, 'A Handlist of Extant Manuscripts Containing the *De re militari* of Flavius Vegetius Renatus', *Scriptorium* 33 (1979), 280–305, as well as C. T. Allmand, *The De Re Militari of Vegetius: The Reception, Transmission and Legacy of a Roman Text in the Middle Ages* (Cambridge, 2011), esp. 64, 66–68, 84–91.

(about 15 each), offer the most promising beginning. Comparing the lists of copies, it's immediately evident that the two texts appear together in only a pair of copies, Queens' 10 and a manuscript mentioned above (see pp. 111–12), Dublin, Trinity College, MS 115. Alas. A closer inspection suggests that their relation is, at best, attenuated, and only suggestive. In the Map commentary, both Queens' and Trinity derive from the same ultimate materials, only available to the scribes of about half the copies; however, their immediate exemplars were certainly different, and the two copies have different immediate congeners (Queens', the fragment at HM 30319, from Battle abbey, Sussex, OSB).[164]

The text of *Fulgencius* is more complicated, yet potentially more promising. Adam Stockton's Trinity text represents an example of conflation, visible on the page. Stockton copied the text from one manuscript, so far as its readings are recuperable, unrelated to Queens'.[165] But he then corrected his copy against a second manuscript (persistent erasures, expunctions, obliterations, marginal insertions); this did resemble the materials available to Queens'. Stockton's access to a similar textual version might strengthen the identification of Thomas Well with the Swaffham vicar, since Stockton was based in Cambridge and copied pieces of the MS as he travelled about dispersed villages nearby. Potentially also noteworthy here is the *Fulgencius* in Cambridge, Pembroke College, MS 230. This book, with a text of the stripe that Stockton had originally copied, appears as Corpus UC43.114, a college list of book donors, c. 1490. The donation is ascribed to Mr John Norwich, supposed to have been a Fellow, s. xiv² (Emden, *BRUC* 428). So there is contemporary evidence for both textual forms in Cambridge.

A couple of large fascicular books show extensive overlaps in contents with Queens' 10. However, their diverse and plentiful contents suggest that these may represent accidental affinities, patrons gathering

---

[164] See Lawler, *Jankyn's Book*, 2:55. For the information in the following paragraph I am grateful to Estelle Gittens at Trinity, who supplemented my on-site inspection with lovely images.

[165] Apparently a version like that in two manuscripts to be mentioned below, Bodley 571; and Worcester F.154. For the only effort at a map of the transmission, see N. F. Palmer, 'Bacchus und Venus: Mythographische Bilder in der Welt des späten Mittelalters. Mit einem Textanhang', *Literatur und Wandmalerei II: Konventionalität und Konversation*, ed. Eckart C. Lutz et al. (Tübingen, 2005), 189–235, at 228. Palmer's account is incomplete, not including Queens', for which I rely on images the librarian, Tim Eggington, generously allowed me to make.

wads of similar *predicabilia*, along with a wide range of other materials. Worcester Cathedral, MS F.154, from a monastic house prominently committed to sending students up to Oxford, probably reflects the same impulses as spawned these texts in the first place, and neither its copy of Map's *Dissuasio* nor its *Fulgencius* can have come from materials shared with Queens' 10. However, BL, MS Royal 7 C.i, although its monstrous 434 folios might be expected to throw up connections with just about anything, may be a different kettle of fish altogether. The manuscript is contemporary with (even, perhaps, a little older than) Queens' 10, and it is the only contemporary copy that shares with it a truncated version of Ridewall's *Fulgencius*, one that ends with the discussion of Perseus. The two certainly shared the same, or very similar, materials for this text. The book also has a clear provenance; it was made at Ramsey Abbey (Hunts, OSB).

So, we are engaged with another central East Midlands site, maybe 30 miles north of Cambridge. There's further evidence for relevant books in the vicinity. The library at Peterborough (OSB) was catalogued, s. xiv ex. It had two copies of 'Fulgentius', Corpus BP21.45a and 143i; given that this is the way the Pembroke inventory refers to its copy of Ridewall, one can't be sure whether the entries refer to the late antique text or to its fourteenth-century 'metaphorical' version. In a different direction, 30 miles to the east of Cambridge, there's abundant contemporary evidence for books relevant to Queens' 10 at Bury St Edmunds (OSB). The librarian Henry Kirkestede was active in the 1360s and 1370s. Although he had visited other libraries and had other sources, his *Catalogus* is always believed to reflect the abbey library; it includes a rich array of titles that also appear in Queens' 10.[166]

Finally, there is some rather distant confirmatory evidence. Berlin, Staatsbibliothek Preussicher Kulturbesitz, MS theol. lat. qu. 159 has a copy of Ridewall's text, apparently written in England a little later than Queens' MS 10. The text here again ends with Perseus, and it shares with Queens' 10 and one of Adam Stockton's two sources an idiosyncratic numbering of Ridewall's mythographies. Its owner was a

---

[166] Viz. K4.21 and K73, Alberic (ascribed to Neckam); K185.1, Fulgentius; K337.1 and 9, John of Wales's *Breviloquium*; K520.1, Ridewall's *Fulgencius*; K586.5, Bersuire; K606.2–3, Map + Trevet's commentary. A rather different pattern of circulation occurs in a sequence of surviving books that join only Ridewall and Bersuire: BodL, MS Bodley 571 (related to the Pembroke and Worcester manuscripts, and probably to Adam Stockton's original copy); CUL, MS Ii.1.20, from Norwich OSB; and Durham Cathedral, MS B.IV.38, from Durham.

theologian, Jakob von Soest, associated with Prague and Cologne, the former a site persistently, from s. xiv med., infiltrated by Oxonian texts. Moreover, Jakob was by trade a Dominican inquisitor.

No smoking gun, perhaps nothing that even veers toward certainty. But I'd conclude that the Queens' MS is very probably from a Dominican house and, although there are a number of East Midland candidates, the most proximate at Thetford and Northampton, most probably from that in Cambridge. There is, further, the probability that this manuscript has never moved very far from where it was made.

Indexes

Medieval authors and texts prominently mentioned
(with some emphasis on commonplace non-vernacular examples)

Ælfric of Eynsham, *Catholic Homilies* 38–39
  grammar 61
Æthelwold, Old English translation of Benedictine Rule 66–67
Alberic of London/Mythographus Vaticanus III, *Scintillarium poetarum* 137, 146
Ancrene Riwle 91 n.102
Arnulf of Orleans, *Interpretationes* [of Ovid] 139–40, 145
Augustine, *Enarrationes in Psalmos* 37
  In Johannem evangelium 111

Bersuire, Pierre ('Berchorius'), *Ovidius moralizatus* 139–40, 145
Bracciolini, Poggio, letters 114 and n.129
Butler, William, Oxford OFM 89

Chaucer, Geoffrey, *The Canterbury Tales* 35 n.44, 75, 84
Cicero, *Academica* 105
  De re publica 37
Clementinae 38
'Considerans' 14 and n.16
Constantine the African, *Pantegny* 38 n.48

Constitutiones Ottonis et Ottoboni 18 n.21
The Crafte of Lymnyng 2

de Turrecremata, John *De ecclesia* 105–06

Felton, John 24–25
Frontinus, *Strategemata* 144
Fulgentius, *Mithologiae* 140, 146

Gascoigne, Thomas, life of Jerome 89
Geoffrey of Burton 25
Giles of Rome, *De regimine principum* 54; see also Trevisa, John
Gower, John, *Confessio amantis* 76–77
Gratian, *Decretum* 60 n.67
Gregory the Great, *Moralia in Iob* 37
Grosseteste, Robert 14 and n.17, 24–25, 124

Higden, Ranulf, *Polychronicon* 20, 88
Hilton, Walter 109
Horae beate virginis Marie 18 and n.22, 55
Hugh Ripelin of Strasbourg/ps.-Aquinas, *Compendium theologie* 106

James of Varezzo, sermons for Lent 107
Jerome and Gennadius, bibliographies 38 n.48
ps.-John Chrysostom, *Opus imperfectum* 106

Langton, Stephen, *Interpretationes nominum hebraicorum* 58
Lombard, Peter, *Sententiae* 37, 55, 105
Love, Nicholas 19
Ludus Coventriae or *N-Town Plays* 97
Lyndwood, William, *Provinciale* 18

'The Macro Plays' 101–02
Macrobius, *In somnium Scipionis* 37
Malachy the Irishman, *De veneno* 112, 139, 144
Mandeville's Travels 17
Map, Walter, *Dissuasio Valerii* 86, 112, 136, 144

Office of the Dead 32, 107, 109

Peraldus, William (Guillaume Peyraut), sermons on the gospels 106
Piers Plowman 1, 4 n.6, 17, 19, 21, 36
The Prick of Conscience 36, 109–10

Priscian, *Institutiones grammaticae* 60
psalter 53, 55–58

Raymond de Penyaforte, *Summa de penitentia* 18
Registrum brevium 18
Ridewall, John, *Fulgencius metaforalis* 112, 133, 139, 144–45
Rolle, Richard 19, 76, 82, 83, 107, 108

Sallust, histories 97
Seneca sr/the elder, *Declamationes* or *Controversiae* 140, 144 and n.158
Sir Gawain and the Green Knight 20
Statutes of the Realm 13–14, 18, 72, 105

Trevisa, John 54, 88, 96 n.108

Waleys, John/John of Wales, *Breviloquium* 140, 143–44
William of Nottingham, commentary on Clement of Lanthony 105
William of Paull, *Summa summarum* 58
Worcestre, William, *Itineraries* 19
Wycliffite Bible 14, 113 and n.127, 130–31 and nn.153–54

Medieval institutional owners

Bobbio (OSB) 37
Buildwas (Salop, OCist) 73, 132
Burton-on-Trent (OSB) 25, 63
Bury St Edmunds (and librarian Henry Kirkestede) (OSB) 130, 149
Byland (NRY, OCist) 119
Canterbury: St Augustine's Abbey (OSB) 33, 138–39 and n.138
Corbie (OSB) 38 n.48
Crediton collegiate church, Devon 100

Durham Cathedral/Durham College, Oxford 24 n.29, 27 n.33, 37
Easby (NRY, OPraem) 27 n.33
Fountains (NRY, OCist) 22
Kirkstall (WRY, OCist) 27 n.33
London: St Bartholomew's, West Smithfield (OSA) 129
Luxueil (OSB) 37
Northampton (OClun) 20
Oxford Greyfriars (OFM) 14

Pershore (Worcs., OSB) 106
Peterborough (OSB) 149
Ramsey (Hunts., OSB) 149
Reading (OSB) 45 and n.54
Rievaulx (NRY, OCist) 123 n.146
Robertsbridge (Sussex, OCist) 121 n.141
Shrewsbury OFM 130–31
Southwick (Hants, OSA) 100–01, 118–19
Syon Abbey (Mids., OBrig) 85 n.99
Westminster Abbey (OSB) 100
Winchester Cathedral (OSB) 36

Medieval private owners and patrons

Berkeley, Sir Thomas IV/Berkeley Castle (Glos.) 55, 116
Chambron (Champernon), Henry OFM 132
Chaworth, Sir Thomas of Wiverton (Notts.) 16–17
Gascoigne, Thomas, chancellor of Oxford 124
Grandisson, John, bishop of Exeter 121 n.141
Humfrey, duke of Gloucester 114 n.129
Laugharne, Mr Richard 123–24
Morton, John, archbishop of Canterbury 115 n.130
Stotevyle, Thomas 124 n.146
Taylard family of Offord D'Arcy and Diddington (Hunts.) 128–29
Thomas of Woodstock, duke of Gloucester 129 and n.152
Thorlthorpe, Henry, vicar choral of York 123 n.145
von Soest, Jakob OP 149–50
Welles, the Lords 123 n.146
Whetenhall family of Norfolk 56

Medieval persons engaged in book production and trade

Capgrave, John, OESA of King's Lynn 72
Caxton, William 42
de Worde, Wynkyn 42 n.51
Dodesham, Stephen, OCart of Witham and Sheen 72
Dyg(g)on, John, 5th recluse of Sheen (OCart) 71, 89, 101 n.114, 109
Eadwine, monk of Canterbury Cathedral 60, 73
Ebesham, William 72, 108
Gybbe, William, of Wisbech 72
'the Hammond Scribe' 72
Kirkestede, Henry, *see* Medieval institutional owners index, Bury St Edmunds
Martell, John, Fellow of Oriel College 101 and n.114
Maynesford, John, Fellow of Merton College 120
Mere, Henry 72
Michel of Northgate 47, 67 n.75
Newton, Humphrey of Pownall (Chs.) 98 n.111, 100–01 n.113
Parkyn, Robert 7 n.10; *see also* Manuscripts cited index, Oxford, Bodleian Library, BodL, MS lat. th. d.15
'scribe delta' (London) 116
scribe of Harley 2253 71
Shirley, John 42 n.51, 70–72
Stockton, Adam, OESA of Cambridge 111–12, 148–49
Thornton, Robert of East Newton (NRY) 90, 97–98, 100 n.113, 124

'the tremulous hand of Worcester' 72–73 n.81

Werken, T. 72

Modern owners and collectors

Allen, Thomas 125
Bale, John 3, 6
Batman, Stephan 126
Brereton, Sir Richard of the Ley (Chs.) 123 n.145
Cobbes, James 101–02
Cotton, Sir Robert 45 n.52, 92–93 n.102, 119, 122, 125–26
Dee, John 119–20 n.138, 125
D'Ewes, Sir Simonds 125
Duke of Gloucester 114
Halliwell, James O. 57
Harley, Sir Robert 126

Hassoll, Ralph 131 and n.155
James, Richard 45 n.52
Kerdiff (or Cardiff), Thomas 130–32
Lambarde, William 126–27
Moore, John, bishop of Norwich 119
Parker, Matthew, archbishop of Canterbury 126
Savile, Henry, of Banke 125
Spelman, Sir Henry 126 n.147
Wall, William, prebendary of Chester 67 n.75
White, John, owner of Southwick (Hants, OSA) 100–01

Manuscripts cited
(ignores numerous passing references)

Aberystwyth, National Library of Wales, MS Peniarth 392D ('The Hengwrt *Canterbury Tales*') 35 n. 44
Alnwick Castle (Nhb.), MS 79 14 n.16
Berlin, Staatsbibliothek Preussicher Kulturbesitz, MS theol. lat. qu. 159 149–50

Cambridge College libraries
Corpus Christi College, generally 126
　MS 178 (II) 65–66, 68
　MS 210 19
Emmanuel College, MS 35 82, 90
Jesus College, generally 30, 85
　MS Q.A.14 (James 14) 37–38
　MS Q.A.15 (James 15) 37–38
　MS Q.B.12 (James 29) 37–38
　MS Q.B.17 (James 34) 123 n.146
　MS Q.B.18 (James 35) 83

　MS Q.D.3 (James 45) 27 n.33
　MS Q.G.7 (James 55) 27 n.33
　MS Q.G.13 (James 61) 92 n,103
　MS Q.G.15 (James 63) 114
　MS Q.G.26 (James 73) 31 n. 38
　MS Q.G.28 (James 75) 27 n.33
Pembroke College
　MS 36 21
　MS 142 21
　MS 230 148
Peterhouse, MS 11 105
Queen's College, MS 10 10, 79 n. 89, 91, 133–50
Sidney Sussex College, MS 85 45 n.53
Trinity College
　MS R.3.2 ('The Trinity Gower') 75, 106
　MS R.17.1 60; *see also* Medieval Persons index, Eadwine
Trinity Hall, generally 30

Indexes

Cambridge University Library
  MS Dd.1.17 17, 127 n.148
  MS Ff.1.6 97, 101 n.113
  MS Ii.1.15 47
  MS Ii.1.20 149 n.166
  MS Ii.1.30 25
  MS Ll.1.15 82

Canterbury Cathedral, MS Lit. A.8 52
Claremont CA, Hunnold Library 57
Coventry History Centre, MS BA/A/1/2/3 25
Dublin, Royal Irish Academy, MS 12 R 29 n.35, 49
Dublin, Trinity College
  MS 69 92 n.104
  MS 75 131 n.154
  MS 115 111–12, 148
Durham Cathedral, MS B.IV.38 149 n.166
Edinburgh, National Library of Scotland
  MS Advocates' 19.2.1 ('The Auchinleck MS') 32
  MS Advocates' 19.3.1 100 n.113
Edinburgh, William Zachs, 'The glossed Luke' 33–34, 77–78
Exeter Cathedral, MS 3501 ('The Exeter Book') 21
Hereford Cathedral, generally 29–30
  mappa mundi 33 n.41

London, British Library
  MS Additional 22283 ('The Simeon MS') 16
  MS Additional 28208 19
  MS Additional 33995 110
  MS Additional 49622 ('The Gorleston Psalter') 57
  MS Additional 63642 25
  MSS Cleopatra C.ix 44 n.52
  MS Cotton Augustus A.iv 16
  MS Cotton Nero A.x ('The Gawain MS') 55
  MS Cotton Titus D.xviii 92 n.102
  MS Cotton Vespasian A.ii 119
  MS Cotton Vespasian D.viii 97
  MS Cotton Vespasian E.iii 44 n.52, 63
  MS Cotton Vitellius A.xv ('The Beowulf MS') 21 n.25, 122
  MS Egeron 617+618 17, 129 n.152
  MS Harley 2253 71, 75 n.83
  MS Harley 2942 129
  MS Harley 7055 126 n.147
  MS Royal 6 E.iii 31
  MS Royal 7 C.i 108 n.123, 149
  MS Royal 17 C.viii 69–70, 79 n.88
  MS Sloane 2275 36, 76 and n.86, 92 n.103, 108 n.123
  MS Sloane 3489 98–99

Other London libraries
olim The Duke of Gloucester 114
Gray's Inn, generally 30 and nn.36–37
Lambeth Palace Library
  MS 330 54
  MS 487 111
olim Sotheby, sale of 25 April 1983, lot 91 57
University of London Library, MS S. L. V.88 ('The Ilchester *Piers Plowman*') 21

Los Angeles, UCLA Library
  MS Rouse 50 113 and n.128
  MS Rouse 52 1
  MS Rouse Doc/XIV/ANG/1 15, 129–30
Manchester, Chetham's Library, Gorton chest 30
New Haven, Yale UL, MS Osborn fa.54 ('The Heneage MS') 51 n.63
Nottingham UL, MS 250 ('The Wollaton Antiphonal') 17

Oxford, Bodleian Library
  MS Ashmole 61 14
  MS Ashmole 751 89
  MS Auct. E.inf.2 ('The Great Bible') 83
  MS Auct. D.1.3, etc. 130
  MS Barlow 22 31
  MS Bodley 2 121
  MS Bodley 43 106
  MS Bodley 52 108–09
  MS Bodley 61 (II) 110
  MS Bodley 132 121 n.141
  MS Bodley 571 148 n.165, 149 n.166
  MS Bodley 953 55
  MS Bodley Rolls 3 and 5 14 n.16
  MS Cherry 36 26
  MS Digby 233 54
  MS Don. d.85 56
  MS Douce 132 99
  MS Douce 137 99
  MS Dugdale 46 49
  MS Eng. poet. a.1 ('The Vernon MS') 16, 45 n.53
  MS Eng. poet. d.208 116 n.133
  MS Greaves 56 89
  MS Junius 1 ('The *Orrmulum*') 19, 36
  MS lat. th. d.15 83
  MS Oriental 62 83–84
  MS Rawlinson C.397 109
  MS Rawlinson C.894 78
  MS Rawlinson D.913 14
  MS Rawlinson poet. 175 109–11
  'Register of Benefactors' 29
  MS Tanner 194 78
  MS Tanner 201 118
  MS Tanner 221 78
  MS Tanner 224 78
  MS Tanner 337 18
  MS Tanner 450 18
  MS Wood empt. 18 89
  MS Wood empt. 19 85

Oxford College libraries
  Balliol College, MS 26 92 n.104
  Christ Church
    MS 91 85, 100
    MS 92 26, 47 n.65, 55, 97
    MS 98 55
    MS 99 100
    MS 104 115 n.130
    MS 111 92 n.102
    MS 152 84
    MS 339 26, 28 n.34, 29, 52, 62
    MS Allestree F.1.1 56, 82
    MS Allestree L.4.1 43, 82
    MS Allestree M.1.10 85
  Corpus Christi College
    MS 201 36
    MS 221 41
  Keble College, MS 49 ('The Regensburg lectionary', s. xiii$^{3/4}$) 55, 83
  Magdalen College, generally 30 n.38
    MS lat. 6 82, 100–01 and nn.112, 114
    MS lat. 9 94
    MS lat. 17 121
    MS lat. 24 31 and n.39
    MS lat. 43 85
    MS lat. 51 38 n.48
    MS lat. 57 (I) 124
    MS lat. 79 109
    MS lat. 93 89
    MS lat. 97 94
    MS lat. 98 108
    MS lat. 99 108
    MS lat. 100 31, 58
    MS lat. 113 55
    MS lat. 114 123–24
    MS lat. 127 83 and n.96
    MS lat. 134 58
    MS lat. 155 94
    MS lat. 162 44, 76
    MS lat. 174 121
    MS lat. 198 92 n.104

MS lat. 248 14 n.16
MS 776 23 n.27
pb Arch. B.II.4.1–7 (and MS LCE 2) 117 and n.135
Merton College, generally 21 and n.24, 32
  MS 68 78, 89, 108 and n.123
New College, MS 93 92 n.102
St John's College, generally 29
  MS 1 17, 45 and n.54, 111
  MS 2 105–06
  MS 11 45 nn. 53 and 54
  MS 14 94
  MS 15 103–04
  MS 16 103–04
  MS 23 71
  MS 26 60
  MS 39 20, 24 n.29, 32 n.39, 37
  MS 40 41
  MS 48 132
  MS 50 105–06
  MS 54 42
  MS 56 42
  MS 58 71
  MS 61 58
  MSS 62 119
  MS 64 41
  MS 69 42
  MS 74 105–06
  MS 75 97
  MS 78 54
  MS 80 41
  MS 84 97
  MS 94 104 n.118
  MS 95 92 n.103
  MS 96 106
  MS 97 41
  MS 98 108, 110
  MS 99 108, 110
  MS 102 106
  MS 113 110
  MS 126 99–100
  MS 127 76 and n.85
  MS 128 52
  MS 141 42

MS 147 42, 108
MS 152 60
MS 154 61
MS 178 100
MS 185 119
MS 203 45 n.53
MS 235, fragment 56 58
MS 257 71, 105
MS 266 42
MS 293 55

Paris, Bibliothèque nationale
  MS lat. 12161 38 n.48
  MS lat. 15700 76
Princeton UL
  MSS Garrett 66, 75, and 85–87 106–08, 128
Saffron Walden Town Hall, MS E.1104/3476 128–29
St Andrews UL 32
San Marino CA, Henry E. Huntington Library
  MS HM 132 20
  MS HM 501 131 n.154
  MS HM 30319 148
  MS EL 26 A 13 42 n.51
  MS EL 27 C 9 ('The Ellesmere Chaucer') 25
  MS HU 1051 47–48
Shrewsbury School, generally 21
  MS 13 31–32
Stoke-on-Trent, Potteries Museum and Art Gallery, K550 48 n.58
Vatican City, Bibliotheca Apostolica Vaticana, MS Vaticanus latinus 5757 37
Verona, Biblioteca capitolare, XL (*olim* 38) 37
Wellesley MA, Wellesley College, MS 8 119
Wolfenbüttel, Herzog-August Bibliothek, MS Guelf. 105 Noviss. 2° 29 n.35
Worcester Cathedral, MS F.154 148 n.65, 149

Scholars cited
(does not, as a rule, cite the editors of collaborative volumes, or of texts)

Abukhanfusa, Kerstin 24
Adams, J. N. 12 n.13
Alexander, J. J. G. 52, 55, 56
Allmand, C. T. 147 n.163
Andrist, Patrick 102–03 n.117
Avril, François 56

Babcock, Robert G. 24
Ball, R. M. 124
Barker-Benfield, Bruce 33, 64 n.73, 98 n.111, 110 n.138
Bataillon, Louis J. 86
Batlle, Columba M. 86
Beadle, Richard 8, 19, 102, 116 n.132, 124
Beit-Arie, Malachi 61 n.69
Bejszy, István P. 85
Bell, H. E. 117
Benskin, Michael 75–76
Berlioz, Jacques 85
Binski, Paul 56
Bischoff, Bernhard 68
Bishop, T. A. M. 7 n.10, 64–66, 68
Black, William H. 99
Blanchfield, Lynne S. 19 n.23
Blomefield, Francis 130
Bloomfield, Morton W. 85
Boffey, Julia 100 n.113
Bowers, Fredson 3
Bowman, Alan K. 12 n.13
Boyle, Leonard 9
Bradshaw, Henry 116 and n.132
Breay, Claire 56
Briquet, C.-M. 39
Brown, Carleton 86
Brown, T. Julian 35
Burrow, J. A. 14 n.18

Cappelli, A. 80
Carley, James P. 125

Cavanaugh, Susan H. 123, 129 n.152
Cheney, C. R. 5 n.8, 18 n.21, 41 n.50
Chetwynd-Stapylton, Henry E. 128 n.150
Christianson, C. Paul 115
Clément, J. M. 86
Coates, Alan 74 n.82
Colker, Marvin L. 111–12
Connolly, Margaret 72
Coulson, Frank 139
Cunningham, I. C. 97 n.111

de Hamel, Christopher 9, 52, 60, 62, 79, 85 n.99, 125
de la Mare, A. C. 14 n.16, 22
de Meyier, K. A. 136
Dean, Ruth J. 88
Dekker, Eligius 86
Denholm-Young, Noël 7 n.10
Dennison, Lynda 5 n.8
Derolez, Albert 68
Destrez, Jean 69
Dickens, A. G. 7 n.10
Doyle, A. I. 3 and n.4, 7, 50 n.62, 72, 73–74, 75, 78, 101 n.114, 106, 115
Doyle, Kathleen 17
Drage, Elaine M. 73
Duffy, Eamon 19 n.22
Dutschke, C. W. 136

Ehrle, Franz 37 n.46, 70
Elder, P. J. 133
Elliott, Kathleen O. 133
Emden, A. B. 120 and n.138

Fehrenbach, R. J. 122–23
Fink-Emera, G. 69
Foot, Mirjam M. 31
Foster, Joseph 130 n.139
Franzen, Christine 72 n.81

Gameson, Richard 6, 50 n.61, 52, 58 n.66, 62 n.70, 84 n.98, 130 n.153
Gaskell, Philip 38–39
Gibbons, Anne 33
Gibson, Strickland 24 n.30, 27 n.33
Gilissen, Léon 61, 77
Gillespie, Alexandra 2 n.3, 4 n.7
Gonzales, Anna Suárez 24
Greatrex, Joan 120 n.140
Gregoire, Reginald 86
Gregory, Gaspar R. 35 n.43
Griffiths, Jeremy ix n.1, 1–2, 71, 72, 74, 105
Gullick, Michael 73, 78–79, 94–95 n.107, 117
Gumbert, J. P. 77, 90, 94 n.106, 102–03 n.117

Hamel, Mary 123–24 n.146
Hamesse, Jacqueline 85
Hardman, Phillipa 100 n. 113
Harris, Kate 2–3, 101 n.113, 123
Harrison, Tony 13 n.15
Haselden, R. B. 15
Heawood, Edward 40
Hickes, George 126 n.147
Hicks, Michael A. 119 n.137
Hilka, Alfons 85
Hobson, G. D. 23 n.28
Holford, M. L. 14 n.16
Holtz, Louis 60
Horobin, Simon 126
Hudson, Anne 75 n.83, 89 n.101
Hunt, R. W. 5, 14 n.17, 57 n.65, 117–19, 125, 137
Huws, Daniel 68

Irigoin, Jean 42
Ivy, G. S. 9, 34

James, Montague R. 5 and n.8, 11, 15 n.19, 99, 117–19, 121, 133, 141
Jayne, Sears R. 122
Johnson, William A. 13 n.15

Johnston, Michael 75 n.83
Jones, Leslie W. 61
Jones, Michael 41 n.50

Kane, George 3
Keiser, George 112, 124
Ker, Neil R. 5, 14, 23 n.27, 24, 27, 38, 62, 84 n.97, 117–19, 120 and n.140, 122, 124, 125, 136
Kidd, Peter 57 n.65
Kirchner, Joachim 70
Kraebel, A. E. 112, 126
Kwakkel, Erik 36, 104 n.118

Leedham-Green, E. S. 116, 121–22, 122–23
Lehnhardt, Andreas 24
Lewis, R. E. 86
Liebaert, Paul 37 n.46, 70
Lieftinck, G. I. 7, 68, 76
Lindenbaum, Sheila 101 n.114
Lindsay, W. M. 81 n.92
Lowe, E. A. 37, 48 n.58, 81 n.92
Lucas, Peter J. 38, 72
Lunelli, Aldo 37 n. 47
Luxford, Julian 25, 98
Lyall, R. J. 40

Mabillon, Jean 6, 63–64
Macray, William D. 117 n.135, 125
Madan, F. 116
Mai, Angelo 37
Mandelbrote, Scott 24
Maniaci, Marilena 7
Marett-Crosby, Anthony 120 n.140
Marks, Richard 56
Martin, Charles T. 81 n.92
Martin, Henri-Jean 60
McFarlane, K. B. 19 n.23
McGann, Jerome J. 3
McIntosh, Angus 74
McKendrick, Scott 17, 56
McKenzie, D. F. 4
McKisack, May 127

Meale, Carol 123
Minnis, A. J. 145 n.161
Monroe, W. H. 14 n.16
Mooney, Linne R. 70 n.78, 72 and n.80, 74, 76
Moran, Jo Ann H. 101 n.114
Morgan, Nigel 56
Muzerelle, Denis 7
Mynors, R. A. B. 5 and n.8, 24 n.29, 72, 73, 117–19, 136

Nafde, Aditi 126
Netz, Reviel and William Noel 37
Newhauser, Richard 85
Nichols, Anne E. 56

Oldham, J. Basil 26
Olszowy-Schlanger, Judith 24, 84 n.97
Ormerod, George 127
Ostos Salcedo, Pilar 7
Overty, Joanne F. 127

Pächt, Otto 56
Page, R. I. 126
Palmer, Nigel F. 147 n.163, 148 n.165
Panayotova, Stella 52, 56
Parkes, M. B. 1, 5, 6 n.10, 10, 11 and n.12, 33 n.41, 46, 48 and nn.57–58, 64, 66, 68, 69 n.77, 70 n.79, 72, 75, 80 and n.91, 106, 115–16, 126, 136
Parry, Graham 127
Parsons, Peter 13 n.15
Pearsall, Derek 2 and n.2, 3 and n.4, 4 n.6
Pearson, David 115, 122, 123
Pelster, Franz 45
Pelzer, Auguste 81 n.92
Pfaff, Richard W. 5 n.8, 15 n.19
Piccard, Gerhard 40
Piper, Alan 7 n.10
Pollard, Graham 4 n.4, 9, 16, 23 n.28, 34 and n.42, 115, 121

Powicke, F. M. 5 n.8, 18 n.21, 21 n.24, 119
Pryor, Francis 8

Ramsey, Nigel 125
Rand, Kari A. 88
Revard, Carter 71, 75 n.83
Robbins, Rossell H. 86
Roberts, Colin H. 12
Roberts, Jane 71, 76 n.85
Roberts, R. J. 125
Robinson, Pamela R. 12, 69, 76 n.85, 99, 102, 114 n.130
Ross, Braxton 68 n.76
Rouse, Richard H. and Mary A. 1 and n.1, 14 n.18, 46 n.55, 102, 105 and n.119, 113 n.128, 129, 136
Roy, Bruno 139
Rückert, Peter 40
Rundle, David ix n.1, 24, 67 n.74, 74

Salcedo, Pilar Ostos 7
Salisbury, Matthew C. 11 n.12
Salter, Elizabeth 2, 4 n.6
Samaran, Charles 78
Scappaticcio, Maria C. 13 n.15
Scase, Wendy 101 n.114
Schrader, Charles F. 147 n.163
Schram, Wilbur L. 117
Schulz, H. C. 1
Sciacca, Christine 55
Scott, A. B. 146 n.161
Scott, Kathleen L. 54 and n.64, 77, 94 n.105
Scott-Fleming, Sonia 50 n.62
Scragg, Donald 8
Shailor, Barbara A. 9
Sharpe, Kevin 126
Sharpe, Richard 5, 25 n.31, 45 n.54, 80 n.89, 86, 117 n.136, 122 n.143, 125, 133, 139
Sheppard, Jennifer M. 73
Shonk, Timothy A. 1 n.62
Simpson, G. G. 68

Skeat, T. C. 12
Skeat, Walter W. 71
Skemer, Don C. 106 n.121, 128
Smalley, Beryl 93, 96 n.109
Solopova, Elizabeth 49 n.59, 113 n.127, 130 n.153
Spector, Stephen 97
Stevenson, Alan H. 38 n.49, 39
Stirnemann, Patricia D. 56
Storm van Leeuwen, Jan 26 n.32
Story, Joanna 56
Streeter, Burnett H. 29
Stubbs, Estelle 70 n.78, 76
Swanson, Jenny 140
Szirmai, J. A. 23
Szyller, Slawomir 85

Temple, Elźbieta 56
Thomas, J. David 12 n.13
Thompson, John J. 98 n.111, 100 n.113, 112
Thomson, Rodney M. 73 and n.81, 94, 102 n.116, 117, 121 n.142
Thomson, S. Harrison 70
Thorp, N. 56
Tite, Colin G. C. 125

van Dijk, S. J. P. 79
van Thiel, Helmut 70
Venn, John and J. A. 120 n.139
Vezin, Jean 9, 60

Wakelin, Daniel 2 n.3, 4 n.7, 84 n.98
Walters, H. B. 127
Walther, Hans 85
Wanley, Humfrey 126
Wansbrough, Henry 120 n.140
Warnicke, Retha M. 126–27
Watson, Andrew G. 1, 5, 30 n.37, 69, 101, 120 n.138, 125
Webber, Teresa 73, 121–22
Wenzel, Siegfried 80 n.90, 132
Wieck, Roger S. 18 n.22
Wilcox, Jonathan 38
Willoughby, James 5–6, 45, 101 n.114
Winger, Howard 115
Winstanley, D. A. 57 n.65
Woods, Marjorie C. 133 n.158
Wright, C[yril] E. 71, 125, 126

Youngs, Deborah 100–01 n.113

General topical index
(largely terms associated with medieval book production)

2° fo, *see* secundo folio

A (abgewandt) 38
abbreviations 80–81
above top line 62–63
agenda format, *see* holster book
alphabet 95–96
anglicana 66
arabesque initial 49–50
ascender 15, 48 and n.58, 64, 65

bands (for binding) 23
below top line 62–63
bifolium 25, 77–78

bindings 20–29
  signatures 91–93
blind stamping 26–27
  'in blind' 26, 61
boards (binding) 23, 26
booklets (or fascicles) 99–108
booklists 123–24
bosses 29
bounds 60–61

cancel (erroneous word or leaf) 82–83
caret 83–84
caroline minuscule 63–66

catchwords 89–92
cauciones 120–21
chain lines 39
chain-staples 29–30, 121
chained library 29–30, 121
champ 54
chemise 26
chiaroscuro 69 n.77
clasps 20, 27–28
codex 12
codicising 109–11
collation 97
colours and palette 49–50
columns 58; *see also* mise en page
common mark of abbreviation 64, 68, 81
composite manuscripts 99–102
conjoint (bifolium) 89–91
constat inscriptions 118–19
corner- and centrepieces 29
correction 81–84
coucher, *see* lectern-book
court hand 66
crayon 62, 63
cross-row, Christ-cross-row 96
cursive script, continental cursive 66
cuttings (excised decoration) 57–58

dated manuscripts 41–42, 68–70
decorative openings 49, 52
demivinet 52–54
descender 15, 65
dicta probatoria 45
diminuendo opening 49, 52
diplomatic 5 n.8, 63–64
the Dissolution 6, 74 n.82, 124–25
double columns 59
drawings, doodles 56–57
drypoint, ruling in blind 61
ductus 67–68

elecciones 120–21 and n.142
excised illustration 57–58
exemplar 79, 82

explicit 82
expunction, expunged 82

fascicles, *see* booklets
felt-side 38
filler 107
finding tabs 85
finishing 47–48
flesh-side 34–35
flourishing 50
flyleaf, binding leaf 25–26
foliation 43–45, 100 n.112
fore-edges 31
format (of page), *see* mise en page
frame 61
furniture (in binding) 27–29

girdle books, *see* pocket books
gleyre 54
glossed books 59–60
    gloss hand 59, 66
gothic bookhand 52, 64, 66
guides 47–48, 62

hair-side 34–35
hand 67–68
heading 48, 79
hierarchy of script 48–49
historiated initial 52
holster book (or agenda format) 19
humanistica 66

illumination 52–56
illustrative cycles 54–55
incipit 79–80, 85–86
inhabited initial 52
initials 49–51; *see also* arabesque; lombard
ink, ruling in 62
insular minuscule 48, 65–66
interlineation 83

labels (under horn) 22, 31–32
lead ruling 61–62

lectern-book 16–17
libraries 121–22
lines, number per page 15
lombard/lombardic initial 51–52
lower board (of a binding) 23, 27–28

majuscule scripts 65
membrane (or skin) 33–36
miniature 52
minim 65
minuscule scripts 65
mise en page 58–60
monastic book production 73–74
mould (paper) 38–39
mould-side 38

open-sheet copying 77–78
open signing 111 n.126
opening 45 n.53
ordinatio, see mise en page
over-sewing 90
ownership inscriptions, see constat inscriptions

palimpsest 36–38
paper 38–43, 97–99
papyrus 13
paraph, paragraphus 48, 49, 51
parchmener 34
pastedown 24–25
pins (of a binding) 27–28
plane/planing, binder's 32, 61, 82 n.3, 93
plummet 62
pocket books 17–18
pouncing 34
prices for books 116–17
pricking 60–61
proofreading 81–82
protogothic bookhand 66
point, punctus ('full stop') 75
prepared bound-book copying 78
provenance 113ff.

punctuation 75
punctus elevatus 75

quire/quaternus 23, 77–78, 89–91

reading books 19
recto 43
roll (or scroll) 12–14
Roman square capitals 52
rubbing (binding) 26–27
rubric, see heading
ruling 60–63
rustic capitals 49, 52, 65

schedula 14
scribes 63–69, 71–74
    monastic scribes 73–74
script 64–67
scroll, see roll
secretary script 66
secundo folio 45
shelfmarks 31, 122
signatures 89, 92–96
    and binding 91–93
    see also open signing
signe de renvoi 84
silk guards (or curtains) 55
sizes (of books) 15–19
    how to measure 15
skin, see membrane
skins, copying on open sheet 77–78
slant-bar 75
solidus 75 n.84
sors, see electiones
spelling in vernacular MSS 74–75
stab-binding 90
straps (of binding) 23, 27–28; see also clasps; pins

tablet, table 12
tabula 58, 88
tacket 95 n.106

textualis, textura, *see* gothic
    bookhand
transcription 70, 79–80
transposed words 84
turn-ins (of binding) 23–24

uncial 52
upper board (of binding) 23, 27–28
uterine vellum 36

va...cat 82–83
verso 43

vinet 52–54
virgule 75

watermarks 39–42
    sequencing of 97–99
whittawed skin 22, 23, 34
wire lines 39
writing area 15

x-height (or minim-height) 65

Z (zugewandt) 38

www.ingramcontent.com/pod-product-compliance
Lightning Source LLC
Chambersburg PA
CBHW071411300426
44114CB00016B/2261